TELLING THE TRUTH ABOUT ABORIGINAL HISTORY

Bain Attwood is a leading authority on Aboriginal history and the author of several books, including *The Making of the Aborigines, A Life Together, a Life Apart*, and *Rights for Aborigines*. He is also the editor of *In the Age of Mabo*, and the co-editor of *Telling Stories: Indigenous History and Memory in Australia and New Zealand* and *Frontier Conflict: The Australian Experience*.

Born in New Zealand in 1956, Bain received his MPhil from the University of Auckland and his PhD from La Trobe University. He has taught History at Monash University in Melbourne since 1985. He has held research fellowships in the History Program and the Centre for Cross-Cultural Research at the Australian National University, and is currently an associate professor at Monash University and an adjunct professor at the Australian National University.

The Making of the Aborigines was co-winner of the Australian Historical Association's W.K. Hancock Prize for 1988-89, and *Rights for Aborigines* was one of three short-listed books for the Ernest Scott Prize for the most distinguished contribution to the history of Australia or New Zealand in 2003.

Bain Attwood

TELLING THE
TRUTH ABOUT
ABORIGINAL
HISTORY

ALLEN&UNWIN

Allen & Unwin
83 Alexander Street
Crows Nest NSW 2065
Australia
Phone: (61 2) 8425 0100
Fax: (61 2) 9906 2218
Email: info@allenandunwin.com
Web: www.allenandunwin.com

National Library of Australia
Cataloguing-in-Publication entry:

Attwood, Bain.
    Telling the truth about Aboriginal history.

    Includes index.
    ISBN 1 74114 577 5.

    1. Aboriginal Australians - History. 2. Aboriginal
    Australians - Treatment. 3. Australia - History. 4.
    Australia - Historiography. 5. Australia - Race relations.
    I. Title.

994.0049915

Typeset in 11/15 pt Minion by Midland Typesetters, Maryborough, Vic.
Printed in Australia by Southwood Press, Sydney

10 9 8 7 6 5 4 3 2 1

● CONTENTS

List of illustrations   vi

Preface   vii

Introduction   1

Part I PRESENT

1 Nation   11

2 Democracy   36

3 Politics   60

Part II PAST

4 Genocide   87

5 War   106

6 Law   124

7 Culture   136

Part III FUTURE

8 History   157

9 Memory   170

10 Truth and recognition   184

Acknowledgments   197

Notes   198

Index   259

• ILLUSTRATIONS

1. 'Our rival storytellers', *Australian*, 27–28 September 2003   64
2. 'Meet Mr Right', *Age* and *Sydney Morning Herald Good Weekend Magazine*, 17 May 2003   70
3. 'Stand back!', *Weekend Australian Magazine*, 27–28 September 2003   73
4. Keith Windschuttle and Henry Reynolds, National Press Club, 19 April 2001   89
5. 'The History Wars', *Canberra Times*, 29 December 2002   100
6. Robert Manne and Keith Windschuttle, Melbourne Writers Festival, 27 August 2003   102

• PREFACE

From time to time, historical controversies occur in the public realm that demand the attention of academic historians and dictate that we set aside other writing. Late in 2003, I returned to Australia after spending much of the year travelling in Europe and working in New Zealand, France and England on a couple of research projects. I had a book to write. I had also agreed, though, to write an article on the so-called war over Aboriginal history, which had been fought throughout most of the previous year. I sat down to fulfil this obligation first. But I soon decided that the nature of the ongoing public conflict over Australia's Aboriginal past warranted my writing more than just an academic essay. It deserved an entire book. The other book would have to wait.

I had come to believe that the 'Aboriginal history war' could have serious consequences for both historical understanding and public life. I had also become convinced that it was the responsibility of an academic historian to respond when severe public criticisms are made of the scholarship done in their field of expertise. At the same time, it became more evident to me that the controversy discussed in this book reflects broader cultural changes of considerable significance for the nature of historical knowledge in the public sphere. This, too, is worthy of a professional historian's attention.

At stake in the most recent round of controversy over the truth about Aboriginal history—or rather historiography—in Australia have been matters of long-standing interest to me. I have worked in the field known as Aboriginal history for over twenty years as a researcher, writer, editor and teacher. I have also read, taught or written extensively about history and theory, memory, myth, oral history, identity and the uses and abuses of history. Here, I reflect on some of these vexed issues in the context of Aboriginal history.

I had several audiences in mind as I wrote this book: first, those inside and outside the historical profession who, in recent years, have followed a series of controversies about the past, history and memory, both here and overseas, and who are puzzled about the causes and significance of these; second, those members of the general public who are interested in understanding the ways that historians go about their work, the nature of the historical enterprise and the claims for historical truth that historians and others make; third, those who have been confused by the claims and counter-claims of the principal figures in the current dispute over Aboriginal history; fourth, those readers, including professional historians, who seek elucidation of the main historiographical matters at stake in the present imbroglio, or who want some clarification of the principal arguments; and fifth, historians and students of history who have a special interest in ongoing debates about history and theory, history and memory, and public history.

Bain Attwood
Monash University and the Australian National University
March 2005

•INTRODUCTION

In recent decades there has been mounting controversy over the past, particularly the pasts of nation states. Rarely has history been the subject of so much discussion. Conventionally, historical conflicts have been confined to small circles, chiefly those of academic historians. This is no longer the case. They have become important far beyond the community of professional historians. Furthermore, these controversies have been characterised by an unusual degree of intensity. At their heart has been a fundamental question: 'What is or ought to be the relationship between what happened in the past and how we interpret and present history in the present?' In many cases, the controversies about the nature of the past have concerned what has come to be called the public memory of nations—that is, the ways in which the national past is remembered, commemorated and celebrated. In short, these are debates about national identity.[1]

Australia has been no exception. Indeed, it may well be that settler societies like Australia, South Africa and Canada are now especially prone to such controversy.[2] In Australia, and in similar nation states, much of this controversy has concerned matters of race (such as immigration), but more particularly the historical relationship between the nation's non-aboriginal or settler peoples and aboriginal peoples. This is an especially difficult past to confront, all the more so in the Australian case because of the nature of national history-making in the past. In Australia, the last three or more decades have been punctuated by major debates over land rights, native title, a treaty, the removal of Aboriginal children (the stolen generations) and reconciliation. There has been a struggle over who controls this past, who can influence the interpretation of this past, and who can determine the historical truth about the nature of colonialism. The contestation over this terrain has deepened in the last decade or more, particularly since the return of the conservative Liberal–National Party Coalition government in 1996 and the growing influence of the new conservatives in public life.[3]

Recently, a new chapter in the long-running controversy over the historical relationship between settlers and Aboriginal people, or between the state and Aboriginal people (since the state looms especially large in Australia's history), has been added. This has been occasioned by the writings of Keith Windschuttle, especially *The Fabrication of Aboriginal History* (2002), the first in a projected series of volumes, and the support lent these by new conservative sympathisers.

Windschuttle has argued that the dominant historical interpretation of the treatment of Aboriginal people on the frontiers of white settlement in Australia amounts to a fabrication. He claims this is the result of work done by a generation of politically inspired academic historians. Their work is characterised by poor historical method and by lack of evidence, and they have invented stories, made up figures, suppressed evidence, falsely referenced sources and deceived their readers. In short, he has claimed that their picture of the country's colonial past has no basis in reality. Much of Windschuttle's criticism is not new, but his full-blooded assault on scholars in the field of Aboriginal history—not to mention the support it has received in some quarters—has drawn into question the credibility of academic historians and the integrity of intellectual life in Australia.

Windschuttle's work has aroused widespread controversy and attracted a considerable amount of media attention. Within weeks of the publication of *The Fabrication* in November 2002, it had been reviewed in several major newspapers, and its principal claims had been discussed in feature articles, reported in numerous news stories and debated in opinion pieces. In the early months of 2003, material about the book proliferated, mainly in broadsheet newspapers such as the *Australian*, though television and radio channels also devoted some time to it. *The Fabrication* also attracted the attention of the international media. A series of public debates took place, mostly in or near the country's largest cities (Melbourne and Sydney). At times, this resembled a travelling circus, yet most of these occasions attracted large audiences.[4] Nearly all the participants in the controversy were Anglo- or white Australians. By midyear, the author of a magazine profile of Windschuttle could observe that the controversy over Aboriginal history renewed by his work had turned this relatively unknown figure into a minor celebrity. By the year's end, almost a hundred articles and hundreds of letters to the editors of newspapers had been published about *The Fabrication*; a book of essays seeking to rebut it had been published; and a study of the 'history wars', which paid some attention to it, had been released. Much of the controversy was fiercely passionate in its conduct, some of it bad tempered and bitter, even vitriolic and savage. It was like a fast-breaking news story, not a story about history. It left many academic historians shell shocked, fearful, frustrated and angry. By any standards, the affair was an extraordinary one, and all the more so given that Windschuttle's book was primarily historiographical rather than historical.[5]

Windschuttle's work has become a lightning rod for a good deal of anguished debate, not only about the treatment of Aboriginal people on the Australian frontier, but also the nature of historical knowledge, truth and authority. In other words, it has raised issues that go far beyond his writings. Seldom does a historical controversy touch on fundamental questions about the nature of the historian's business. Can history be objective or is it always in some sense political? Is history a science or an art? Whose knowledge is history? For what purposes are histories told? To whom are historians responsible? How should professional historians react to claims of identity, whether they be national or racial? How should they respond to the claims of memory? How can the history of a traumatic event be told? How should we, particularly settler Australians, relate to this past today? What are the limits to the historical craft? Who decides which histories should have authority, and how can this be determined? If the answers to questions like these were once obvious, they have not been for some time now. Beyond these historical questions, there have of course been questions about the nation and national identity. What kind of nation is this? What does this controversy about the past reveal about the nation?

Among academic historians and other scholars, there seems to be a range of opinions about the controversy reignited by Windschuttle's work and/or how to respond to this, which could be glossed as follows: (1) The controversy is overblown. It concerns the nation, yet the 'debate' has not been conducted nationally. Rather, it has mostly been confined to the broadsheet newspapers, just one of the many forums for public culture that we now have, and one which fewer and fewer people read. Most people probably learn their history from movies, television and museums instead of history books and newspapers. Popular historical consciousness has moved beyond any history war. Historians should consider assigning this little skirmish to the past. (2) The controversy has undoubtedly been dramatic, but it is doubtful that its effects will be long lasting. As with the controversy over Helen Demidenko's novel, *The Hand that Signed the Paper* (1994), this will not prove to have the import feared by the principal critics of Windschuttle's *Fabrication*.[6] (3) By seeking to rebut Windschuttle's work, academic historians only draw more attention to it. By refusing to respond, we could diminish or even deprive it of the publicity it has attracted. More specifically, Windschuttle's work is a form of denialism. Academic historians should not engage with such work. Debating deniers in print, on radio and television, in debates, in schools or anywhere else, provides them with a forum, an audience and a legitimacy they would not otherwise have. (4) This 'history war' is a very white or Anglo-Australian one. These perspectives dominate, while those of other settlers and Aboriginal people have seldom been evident. The terms of the controversy are very narrow and have been determined by Windschuttle and accepted by his fellow positivist or realist academic historians, and this has made it very difficult for others to participate in public discussion. Whites participating in this dispute only serve to marginalise Aboriginal historians or Aboriginal history-making and make white concerns seem normative. (5) This is a quarrel among a particular generation of historians with ready access to the cultural and political pages of the major broadsheet newspapers. They are all middle-aged or older. They see themselves as occupying very opposing positions, but really they look very similar to outsiders. This squabble is tedious. It serves their own interests, especially when they seek to redeem their own honour or the reputation of others who have been maligned. (6) Windschuttle is not really a historian, but a journalist and a writer. His work does not contribute to historical discourse and so there is little if anything to be gained from an engagement with his work. (7) The so-called history wars have made it difficult to explore the more interesting terrain that lies between and away from the poles often presented by these. Any scholarly work presented in the public realm is so badly misrepresented by new conservative commentators that it makes serious intellectual discussion of it very difficult, and so one is best to retreat into the safe professional harbours offered by the academy. (8) Academic historians and academic history have not been well served by participating in this controversy. On the contrary, academic historians must learn how to participate in public controversies of this kind, even get lessons on how to do this better. Otherwise, it would be best not to take part at all. (9) Debates such as this distract academic historians from their real work, which is research, writing, teaching and supervision. In an age where the demands on academics have increased enormously, participating in this controversy is just one task too many. (10) Lastly, Windschuttle's historiography and history are seen as largely accurate and/or have provoked debate about history, and this is regarded as being for the good.[7]

My evidence here is largely anecdotal. It is difficult to be sure how many historians hold one or more of these opinions. It seems, though, that several of these opinions have many adherents, while a few have hardly any. In my view, many of these opinions, or at least the concerns that underlie them, are legitimate. Nevertheless, I have concluded that academic historians should take part in this historical controversy. (Here it should be noted that there are still very few academically trained Aboriginal historians in Australian universities. Where I discuss academic historians, I am referring primarily to white historians.)

Recently, Iain McCalman, a leading historian and the president of the Australian Academy of the Humanities at the time he wrote, asserted: 'We must face the brutal reality that it is the public and the government, rather than our own academic peers, whom we must persuade of our social and intellectual worth and who, directly or indirectly, pay for our research. Part of what is at stake in the History Wars is how we are able to assert and defend our territory as expert professionals'.[8]

It is largely in this spirit that another leading historian, Stuart Macintyre, wrote a book with Anna Clark titled *The History Wars*. In the wake of Windschuttle's *Fabrication*, he described past and present historical controversies in Australia, and explained how academic historians went about their professional work and how readers could tell good history from bad on scholarly grounds. Performing this task in a judicious and even-handed fashion, Macintyre did much to uphold the integrity of academic history.[9] Yet at some points he is rather partisan; for example, sometimes he gives the impression that only conservatives or new conservatives are responsible for the historiographical conflicts he discusses. There is also something rather dated about Macintyre's approach. Much of the argument in his book could have been made twenty or thirty years ago. There is little acknowledgment of how the terrain of history has changed during this time, and hence little engagement with the profound episte-mological and ethical issues that have been prompted by the popularisation and democratisation of history, the rise of memory and the emergence of subaltern histories (such as Aboriginal history). Macintyre appears to suggest that academic historians can simply go about their business as usual, and seems to imply that we can just assert our intellectual author-ity once again.

Many academic historians might agree with the almost exclusively professional criteria applied by Macintyre in his treatment of the Australian 'history wars'. I have had considerable sympathy for this position myself. However, it seems to me that, by adopting this approach, profes-sional historians miss much of the significance of the ongoing controversy over Aboriginal history in particular and history more generally. This concerns the relationship between professional history and other histori-cal discourses at work in the larger public arena or, to be more precise, the different ways in which professional history and these other historical discourses tend to relate the past and relate to that past. This controversy raises the question of whether or not academic historians can so neatly separate the professional sphere of history and the public sphere, and whether or not we should primarily define history in purely professional, objective (third-person) terms. Further reflection on the critical features of this controversy might contribute something to professional historians' understanding of the importance of *their* relationship to the past, and the implications of this for the ways *they* represent the past. Of particular significance here is the role historical work can play in a process in which fundamental aspects of the past are either acted out (repeated) or worked through in public arenas.[10]

In this book I am seeking to provide an account that not only makes sense of the ongoing controversy over Aboriginal history by tracing its underlying roots, but also responds critically to the claims new conservative or so-called revisionist authors have made about the frontier, and suggests approaches that Aboriginal history seems to demand of settler Australians as historians or/and citizens. In the first part of the book, I argue that the causes of the controversy have been long developing and reside in diverse circumstances which converged near the end of the last century. In the second part, I present an interpretation of Keith Windschuttle's work that primarily seeks to demonstrate its principal flaws, but also to account for these. (This does not pretend to be a comprehensive rebuttal of his work. That would require a very different book.) In the third part, I discuss the ways in which academic historians might tackle their research in the field of Aboriginal history (or at least frontier history), and the roles that historical research and historical discourse might play in the public sphere in relation to the place of that past in the present.

Finally, I will say a word or two about my position in relation to the subject matter of this book. I regard myself very much as an academic historian. It is a profession I have now pursued for more than twenty years. I spend most of my time researching, reading, writing and teaching, much of it on Aboriginal history. I consider academic history to be a force for good in the world and, in my opinion, the tradition of rational and courteous historical debate is potentially one of the main casualties of the 'history wars'. This said, I regard academic history as a limited good, and believe that this should be acknowledged more frequently than it is. I have also been dismayed by the deleterious impact of the conduct of the 'history wars' on the cause of justice for Aboriginal people and the project of reconciliation, and the implications of this for Australian democracy. I am both a settler Australian, by virtue of migrating here more than twenty years ago, and a Pakeha (white) New Zealander. This double consciousness—of being an insider (a settler) and an outsider (a migrant)— also informs my work.

Questions of nation and national identity are, of course, central to this historical dispute, so this is where we shall begin.

PART I

PRESENT

NATION

1

Over 30 years ago, an English historian forecast the death of the past. For a long time, J.H. Plumb argued, human beings had drawn on history in various ways, but in contemporary society this was no longer the case: 'The strength of the past in all aspects of life is far, far weaker'. He attributed this decline to modernity, which did not seem to need a sense of the past: 'Its intellectual and emotional orientation is towards change rather than conservation, towards exploitation and consumption. The new methods, new processes, new forms of living of scientific and industrial society have no sanction in the past and no roots in it'. In the years since, Plumb's prognosis has been proven both right and wrong. A sense of the past has continued to decline in one way, but it has grown in another. On the one hand, more of the past has become less and less present; on the other, images of the past have become increasingly pervasive in innumerable tangible forms, especially but not only in popular culture. The more the past itself recedes, the more it returns as representation, it seems. This contradictory mixture has characterised historical consciousness for several decades now.[1]

The growth in public interest in the past has occurred in many countries. As another English historian, Raphael Samuel, observed, 'history as a mass activity—or at any rate as a pastime—has possibly never had more followers than it does today'. The spectacle of the past, he pointed out, attracts the kind of attention that earlier epochs in modernity attached to the new and the future. Increasingly, film, radio, television and newspapers have demonstrated a predilection for covering historical subjects and monitoring historical debates; commemorations and memorials have

proliferated; museums, art galleries, archives and libraries have mounted
historical exhibitions; heritage houses have opened one after another; historical re-enactments, pilgrimages and tours have flourished; family histories
and genealogies have been avidly researched; historical authenticity in
musical performance has become fashionable; history books for the general
public have abounded; and autobiography and historical fiction have been
in great demand among publishers and readers.[2]

The present salience of history can be attributed to forces outside the
discipline, yet why has history acquired so much significance? This has
been the subject of considerable speculation, but little consensus of
opinion has emerged so far. Some commentators see it as the result of a
crisis of temporality caused by rapid changes in communication and information technology, mass media, and patterns of work and consumption.
This has provoked the desire for some kind of anchor in a world of increasing flux. Andreas Huyssen has written: 'Perhaps the fascination with the
past . . . is to be taken seriously as a way of slowing down the speed of
modernisation, as an attempt, however fragile and fraught with contradiction, to cast lifelines back toward the past and to counteract our culture's
undisputed tendency toward amnesia'. Huyssen has also suggested: 'The
faster we are pushed into a future that does not inspire confidence, the
more seductively a past world beckons in which life seemed simpler,
slower, better'. Other commentators have noted that memory has become
more and more central to personal and collective identity. Whatever the
reasons, history has become a growing preoccupation of the increasingly
important realm of the arts and the media—often referred to as the culture
industry. But it has also been intrinsic to debates about the nature of the
nation and national identity, which have once again become central to
politics in many states. In these various contexts, representations of the
past have become an object of desire; history (or memory) is now a commodity believed to be of immense economic, cultural and political value.
Securing the past in the present is seen as critical to securing the future.
Consequently, the ways in which the past is represented have become the
subject of contestation and thus controversy. This has been nowhere more
evident than in settler societies such as Australia, particularly in reference
to matters of race, and especially in regard to the past concerning aboriginal peoples.[3]

Narratives and nations

Narratives (or stories) in general, and historical narratives in particular, are basic to nations. It is narratives that largely provide a nation's people with a sense of nationality—a sense that they belong together to the community called the nation. This community, Benedict Anderson has explained, is an *imagined* community: 'the members of even the smallest nation will never know most of their fellow-members, meet them, or even hear of them, yet in the minds of each lives the image of their communion'. A nation's peoples come to know their nation through the telling, hearing and seeing of stories about it. These stories, but especially historical ones, are the primary reason why nations have come to command 'profound emotional legitimacy', Anderson suggests.[4]

Historical narratives are critical to nations because nations are neither ancient nor eternal, but historically novel; they are invented where they once did not exist. The primary role of history has been to lend moral legitimacy to a revolutionary phenomenon. This task is very difficult, if not impossible, to achieve without the telling of highly coloured stories, in which most of the time (or past) of the place the nation has occupied is forgotten. 'Forgetting, I would even go so far as to say historical error', the French writer Ernest Renan once famously observed, 'is a crucial factor in the creation of a nation'. A failure and a fabrication of memory, in other words, lies at the heart of the nation state. Historians in recent decades have concurred. English historian Eric Hobsbawm, for example, has argued that national histories comprise 'anachronism, omission, decontextualisation and, in extreme cases, lies'.[5]

The discipline of history has long had a close relationship with nation states, particularly in liberal democracies. Its rise more or less coincided with the rise of nation states. Indeed, were this not so, history would never have enjoyed the prestige it has had. Its practitioners have long played a central role in persuading citizens that they should pay greater allegiance to the nation rather than to their religion, race, class, neighbourhood, and so on. Historians have performed this pedagogical task largely by telling powerful stories about the nation. These stories are best called myths, since this characterises their function, which is one of providing a simple charter for the nation's present and future rather than seeking to understand the past in all its messiness.

The role of historical narratives and historians has been especially important to settler societies such as the United States, Canada, South Africa, Australia and New Zealand. All nation states have had to undergo a transition from *de facto* coercive power to *de jure* authority, but this seems particularly to be the case for settler nations, perhaps because the violence upon which they are founded is relatively recent. Furthermore, there can be little doubt that history has had a privileged intellectual position in public life in Australia, and that many practitioners of history continue to enjoy considerable authority. (In part, this is because story-telling is very important to any culture and because historical writing has continued to be relatively accessible.) Were this not the case, there would have been no 'history war' of the kind that has occurred in Australia.[6]

A settling history for a settler nation

National historical narratives can be regarded as a means of organising a sense of time and space. This has been particularly evident in modernity, but no more so than in settler societies since they are modern societies *par excellence*. At the heart of modernity has been a vision of progress, in which there is a constant movement that continuously breaks with the past, particularly that of local places (as compared with metropolitan ones).

In order to sanction the new nation, the task of national histories has been one of creating a historical relationship in time and space between various peoples and events. In the Australian case, the national history told of the British or white colonisation of the country in the following way. This story began in a particular time in place, which was the point at which there was a British presence, thus privileging time more than space, as history has long tended to do. In doing this, it displaced the (ab)original people and their relationship to the country.

This history then proceeded to tell a story of progress, which had several major strands. It told a heroic tale of the British as the discoverers, explorers and pioneers of the country, of how these white men came to settle a strange country and transform it by their science and technology, capital and labour, thus creating a civilisation out of a wilderness. It celebrated the founding of a political order based on the rule of law and parliamentary democracy. It rejoiced in the founding of a nation of people bound together by ideals of Britishness and mateship. It marked the blooding of the nation in wars fought on foreign shores and celebrated its taking a place in the world as a British nation.

This was not only a story of success, though. This myth also featured the courage, hardship, suffering and battles of white men and sometimes women. Indeed, these are the subject matter of Australia's most famous white stories. The convicts were expelled from their native land; the pioneers struggled on the land; the people fought the hierarchical order of the Old World to found a new egalitarian one; young men died in war. Many of these stories were memorialised not only in story books but also in monuments and commemorations throughout the settler nation. Loss, grief and sacrifice—a narrative in which British Australians were rendered as victims—became as critical to Australian national identity as the story of triumphant progress.[7]

In this settler history-making, the primary subjects were the British and their white Australian descendants. They were the agents who made the nation what it had become. Aborigines were depicted as all the British Australians were not. The British were a civilised race; the Aborigines a savage one. The British were a populous people; the Aborigines were few. The British settled the land and created wealth; the Aborigines wandered over it and created nothing. The British had law; the Aborigines had none. And so on. Above all else, the right to the country and to rule its peoples was based on a *historicist* representation of Aborigines and Aboriginality. This was common to the way in which Europe imagined itself as modern by inventing a primitive other. It made itself thus through the making of this other. But this was especially marked in the Australian case. This theory of history held that Aboriginal people had no place in the modern and progressive nation because it deemed that they were an ancient and even regressive people. Indeed, they were commonly regarded as a dying race. This outcome was seen as natural. This was the course of history. It might be considered a tragedy, but the British were not responsible for it. They had settled a sparsely peopled land with little if any resistance from its occupants. There was some settler violence, but most of it was committed by lesser beings such as convicts. Government had treated Aboriginal people in accordance with the highest principles of British law and justice. They had sought to alleviate their suffering and to save them by offering the gifts of civilisation and Christianity. But the Aborigines just faded away. They were savages who killed one another, and they had no resistance to disease. They could not adapt to the ways of the white man. In short, they were a doomed race. More than this, though, Aborigines were not considered to be the proper subjects of history. As an ancient people, they belonged to the discipline of anthropology, not history.

There can be few better examples of the way in which the settler historical narrative forged a relationship between their people and Aboriginal people in reference to time and place of this country than a school primer written by Walter Murdoch and published in 1917, the introduction of which states:

> When people talk about 'the history of Australia' they mean the history of the white people who have lived in Australia. There is a good reason why we should not stretch the term to make it include . . . the dark-skinned wandering tribes who hurled boomerangs and ate snakes in their native land for long ages before the arrival of the first intruders from Europe . . . for they have nothing that can be called a history. They have dim legends, and queer fairy tales, and deep-rooted customs which have come down from long, long ago; but they have no history, as we use the word. When the white man came among them, he found them living just as their fathers and grandfathers and remote ancestors had lived before them . . . Change and progress are the stuff of which history is made: these blacks knew no change and made no progress, as far as we can tell. Men of science [i.e. anthropologists] may peer at them . . . but the historian is not concerned with them. He is concerned with Australia only as the dwelling-place of white men and women, settlers from overseas. It is his business to tell us how these white folk found the land, how they settled in it, how they explored it, and how they gradually made it the Australia we know to-day.

By 1959, little had changed. A leading Australian historian, John La Nauze, observed in a survey of the settler historiography of the preceding 40 years: 'unlike the Maori, the American Indian or the South African Bantu, the Australian Aboriginal is noticed in our history only in a melancholy anthropological footnote'. He did not regard this as a problem.[8]

A new Australian history

A decade later, an eminent Australian anthropologist, W.E.H. Stanner, presented the prestigious Australian Broadcasting Commission's Boyer Lectures. In the course of these, he coined a phrase to describe the nation's settler history-making: 'the great Australian silence'. This was not a complete silence on all matters Aboriginal, Stanner pointed out; instead, it was 'the story of the things we were unconsciously resolved not to discuss with them or treat with them about; the story, in short, of the unacknowledged relations between two racial groups within a single field of life'. Stanner rejected the possibility that such inattention could be attributed to absentmindedness; rather, it was 'a structural matter, a view from a window which has been carefully placed to exclude a whole quadrant of the landscape'. It might have 'begun as a simple forgetting', he conceded, but it had 'turned under habit and over time into something like a cult of forgetfulness practised on a national scale. We have been able for so long to disremember the aborigines', Stanner concluded, 'that we are now hard put to keep them in mind when we most want to do so'. This silence had descended in the twentieth century, especially in the middle decades as history became increasingly professionalised.[9]

The great Australian silence had not only been a historical silence, but a silencing as well. Settler history-making had reigned over 'the other side of a story'. 'The telling of it', Stanner commented, 'would have to be a world—perhaps I should say an underworld—away from the conventional histories of the coming and development of British civilisation'. At the time he gave his lectures, Stanner knew the situation he described was changing: 'something very remarkable has happened', he wrote; 'the fact that the aborigines having been "out" of history for a century and a half are now coming back "into" history with a vengeance'. In this return of the suppressed, Stanner had two things in mind: Aboriginal people were making history as political subjects demanding their rights; and they were becoming subjects of history since they were telling their stories, and archaeologists, anthropologists and historians had begun to pay more attention to the Aboriginal past. Stanner did not think 'the great Australian silence' would survive this history-making.[10]

Over the next twenty years, a large body of historical work was produced by and about Aboriginal people. In professional circles, much of this occurred in the context of the rise of social history, which sought to tell the stories of peoples previously 'hidden from history'—the working class, women, migrants, aboriginal peoples, and so on—and was particularly attuned to their *experience*. It was also a radical or critical history. It brought into question the monumental settler history, particularly its fiction of a unitary nation and an egalitarian society and its grand narrative of progress. Professional studies of the Aboriginal past were undertaken by many hands across a broad range of disciplines. The most important practitioners were not always historians, but scholars working in anthropology, archaeology and linguistics. They increasingly challenged the manner in which their own disciplines had treated the Aboriginal past as something other than history. With historians, they created a multidisciplinary field that came to be called 'Aboriginal history' (which will be discussed at length in Chapter 2), and over time they helped to forge a new *national* history (though in many ways this differed little from the story some *colonial* historians had told about the frontier in the nineteenth century).

What was the nature of this scholarly historical narrative? This new national history might be characterised as an Aboriginal turn—a turn to an Aboriginal historical perspective of Australia. It began by changing the country's chronology. This historical narrative did not begin in 1770 (with the voyaging of Captain James Cook) or 1788 (with British colonisation), but tens of thousands of years earlier. As a result, the archaeologist and historian D.J. Mulvaney suggested, 'the two centuries since Captain Cook's arrival dwindle into insignificance', because they are 'no more than 0.5 per cent of the human story of Australia'. By altering the country's historical chronology, Aboriginal people became principal actors. As Mulvaney pointed out in *A Prehistory of Australia* (1969), the first 'discoverers, explorers and colonists' of the country were Aboriginal, not British. Aboriginal people were further represented as subjects of history in their own country by the work of anthropologists and archaeologists, who demonstrated that they were historical agents with a deep sense of kinship, religiosity and law and a very close relationship to the land, and who argued that they had shaped much of the landscape (by firing the land).[11] Historians also showed that Aboriginal people had fought to retain possession of this land and their culture in the wake of British colonisation.[12]

This research sundered the relationship the settler history-making had sought to naturalise between the British and Australia in the country's time and space. Most importantly, the turn to Aboriginal history revealed the revolutionary nature of the nation. Once it was acknowledged that Aborigines were here prior to the British and in place, the British were rendered out of place, so their colonisation of the country could be seen more clearly as an act of *invasion* rather than *settlement*. The moral legitimacy of British possession of the land was further brought into question by highlighting the means by which this was achieved: wars against the Aboriginal people, a denial of their rights to land as the indigenous peoples, and white exploitation, extermination and exclusion of them. Quite clearly, the new Australian history was a story of colonialism that shed a very critical light upon the ideals of British justice, humanitarianism and egalitarianism that lay at the heart of the Australian national identity constructed by earlier myth-makers. In focusing on Aboriginal loss, the new history also memorialised *their* suffering and questioned the status of victim previously monopolised by whites. The Aboriginal turn brought into focus the burden of the Aboriginal past for the Australian present. This critical history challenged the ideal so central to modernity: the sense of the present continuously moving away from the past.

The new Australian history had profound implications for the way in which its settler peoples envisaged the nation. As Henry Reynolds, one of those historians who answered Stanner's call for historical work, observed in 1988, the white nation's bicentennial year: 'It is not just a matter of attaching Aboriginal history to the back left-hand corner of the old homestead, or of even glassing in the back verandah. The changes will ultimately have to be far more radical—a new floor perhaps, even new foundations. In this reconstruction many familiar, comfortable old rooms will be changed beyond recognition'. In making these comments, Reynolds was responding to the unsettlement the new history was causing many settler Australians, but particularly conservatives associated with the traditional legends of white pioneering.[13]

Aboriginality, Aboriginal rights and Australian national identity

The scholarly turn to Aboriginal history came to have a major impact beyond the circles in which it was first produced and consumed. Indeed, the significance of this new Australian history would have been limited had the past signified by Aboriginal people and Aboriginality not assumed a central position in contemporary considerations of Aboriginal rights, Australian nationhood and Australian national identity. This can best be understood in the context of two interdependent factors in the post-1945 world: the international recognition of human rights, including indigenous rights; and Australia's need to redefine its national identity. Without this nexus, it is unlikely that Aboriginal history would have become so significant. After all, Aboriginal people comprise less than 2 per cent of the Australian population.

At the end of the Second World War, the Nazi destruction of European Jewry and other minorities, and the ongoing challenge to imperial rule posed by colonised peoples in Asia and Africa, provoked worldwide interest in human rights among many of the people and governments of First World countries. In particular, this prompted a major intellectual and political movement, which has been called anti-racism. In settler states such as Australia, New Zealand and Canada, this took the form of demands for the assimilation of indigenous peoples into the nation and the granting of equal rights. In Australia, it culminated in a referendum for constitutional change in 1967 in which settler Australia treated the question of Aboriginal rights as though it were a matter of whether or not Aborigines should become citizens of the settler nation.[14] However, indigenous rights—by which is meant rights that only aboriginal peoples can claim—became an increasingly significant demand among Aboriginal people in Australia,[15] as they did among indigenous peoples in other settler societies. These comprised rights to the lands of which aboriginal peoples had been dispossessed, but also cultural and political rights such as self-determination. These indigenous rights are peculiarly historical because they are grounded in a particular past: an indigenous past which precedes the settler nation. They call up and call upon historical narratives such as Aboriginal history, rather than the traditional history of the settler nation.

The demand for citizenship rights could be accommodated relatively easily by liberal democratic nation states, since it was a call for equality and inclusion within the nation. To a limited degree, such states have also been able to meet demands for different rights for indigenous peoples where these have called for special treatment to address disadvantage. But demands for *indigenous* rights and sovereignty have proven to be much more difficult for such states to accept since they are based on a claim for permanent rather than temporary historical difference, and for group rather than individual rights. The calls for land rights, but more especially the recognition of sovereignty (in the form of a treaty or forms of self-government) and indigenous law, pushes liberal democracies to their intellectual limits. In the Australian case, the conservative parties, such as the Liberal Party, have had more difficulty than socialist and social democratic parties, such as the Australian Labor Party. As Judith Brett has noted, liberalism is a form of political thinking that anticipates and celebrates a historical trajectory in which people are drawn away from their traditional, group-based identities and communities and become individuals bearing certain rights and obligations and having the right to choose and determine their circumstances. In this view, group-based identities such as Aboriginality, and rights such as indigenous rights, are relegated to a premodern past. As Brett has claimed, this way of imagining modernity has had a special charge in *Australian* liberalism. It has set its face resolutely to the future and the benefits of progress, especially material ones. According to Brett: 'Transported to a new country, a country without history as far as the colonisers were concerned, liberalism's arguments for the rights of the future became the country's commonsense and flourished unchallenged for the first 180 years of European settlement'.[16]

At the same time as Australia had to grapple with demands for rights for Aboriginal people in the post-Second World War era, it was confronted by the need to redefine its national identity. This became particularly evident in the 1960s, when Britain declared that its economic relationship with Europe was more important than any commitment to a worldwide community of British peoples, and announced its military withdrawal from Southeast Asia. Government in Australia realised that its racial policies and practices were attracting increasing criticism from post-colonial nation states in Africa and Asia and that it was necessary to do business with these governments; at the same time, it recognised that significant changes in the demographic make-up of Australia, which were the result of a considerable number of non-British migrants arriving in the postwar boom, had rendered the ideal of a British nation less viable; and it realised that the policy of assimilation did not meet the nation's ongoing need to attract and retain non-British migrants. In these new circumstances, the way in which Australia had primarily defined itself as a nation had to be reconsidered. In particular, its white and British race ideal no longer seemed appropriate or useful. Australia needed to find another way of imagining itself. This task was made more urgent because global forces such as American popular culture continued to cross national boundaries and undermine the distinctiveness of national cultures. In order to forge another national identity, a new historical narrative was required, especially one that would grapple with Australia's racial past.[17]

It was by no means clear what this 'new Australian nationalism' would comprise, as James Curran has pointed out. Australian political leaders, at any rate, had considerable difficulty in defining what was distinctively Australian: 'If the need for nationalism in Australian political culture was strong, the question was now what or which myth could fulfil the same emotional and cultural needs as Britishness'. (Arguably, the answer to this question has not been found and might never be.) In the early 1970s, following the election of the Whitlam Labor government, a policy of multiculturalism was adopted. This was a means of addressing racism at home and countering perceptions of Australia as a racially prejudiced British and white country in an Asian-Pacific sea, but it was also a new way of defining Australia. Australia was increasingly cast as a culturally diverse nation and its history figured as the outcome of the voyaging here of its many peoples, including Aborigines (which most Aboriginals rejected, since it diminished their status as indigenous people). In this, the British were represented as part of a rich mosaic. However, this formulation of Australianness has never served its purpose very satisfactorily since multi-culturalism cannot provide the distinctiveness a national identity requires, and the country's British history cannot readily be treated as just one among many since its institutions have continued to dominate the nation's political culture.[18]

At the same time multiculturalism was invoked in the search for a new national identity, so too was Aboriginality. In some respects it was much better suited to make good the serious deficits that now seemed evident in Australia's national identity, because it could easily be represented as distinctive. This was largely because it was deemed to have particular historical properties. Most of these had been part of the way Europe had imagined its modernity and indigenous people's antiquity (as we noted earlier), but they were revalued in these postwar years. In the Australian case, at any rate, this historical temporality depended upon its bearers always being in another place. 'Real Aborigines' and 'real Aboriginal culture' were only to be found in 'remote Australia', especially 'the Centre' (Central Australia) and 'the Territory' (the Northern Territory).

Aboriginality was valued primarily on the grounds of its apparent ancientness. Australian nationalists had traditionally sought to compensate for their nation's short history by celebrating its ancient British heritage, and its flora and fauna. Now they sought to secure such a past by celebrating Aboriginal culture. Tens of thousands of years were added to human time in Australia during these years as a result of archaeological research, which gave rise to the concept of a deep past or deep time for Australia. At the same time, appreciation of 'traditional Aboriginal culture' continued to be nurtured by the work of Australian anthropology. The celebration of a rich precolonial Aboriginal past was nowhere more apparent than in *Triumph of the Nomads* (1975), a book by Geoffrey Blainey, one of Australia's most famous historians, which popularised the archaeological and anthropological research of many scholars.

The significance of this Aboriginal past in the context of the nation and nationalism became all the greater because Whitlamite nationalists championed the ideal of a national heritage and advocated the incorporation of deep time into the national culture. As a result, Aboriginality became central to the concept of a national estate. In large part this was formulated around calls to conserve the Aboriginal past by preserving particular places (or 'heritage sites') that were deemed to embody this. National parks were recreated as Aboriginal, most notably Kakadu and Uluru (in the Northern Territory), and promoted for World Heritage listing. This has not only served the interests of nationalism, but also some forms of capital as well. The tourist industry had long recognised the appeal of places that could be presented as both natural and old, but in parks such as Kakadu the ancient Aboriginal past now became a much more valuable commodity. This appropriation of Aboriginality occurred alongside a burgeoning interest in Aboriginal art, which was nurtured by the promotion of the arts in Australia in the wake of the new nationalism. This was apparent in a booming art market and the eagerness of major galleries to host large exhibitions. Significantly, both Aboriginal art and sites became a major way in which the Australian nation sought to present itself to the world, and both were deemed to symbolise an ancient Aboriginal relationship to the land.[19]

Traditional Aboriginal culture also came to be valued by nationalists for reasons other than its antiquity. In Australia, as elsewhere, many non-Aboriginal people were also drawn to indigenous cultures in a context in which the changes wrought by modernity were questioned and aboriginal cultures were deemed to possess the qualities of primordiality and primitiveness that could offset or address these problems. For example, Aborigines were cast once more as exemplars of the original people of the world. They were deemed to have access to old religious and philosophical truths, and so to be able to restore other peoples to the sacred order they had lost as a result of modernisation. More particularly, it was held by some that the Aborigines could redeem settler Australians. As the first peoples of the land, they could understand the country in ways that later waves of peoples could not, and so they could help settler Australians to know this place and thus feel at home in it.[20] Similarly, traditional Aboriginal people were once again portrayed as noble savages—a people living in harmony with nature. Their culture was increasingly regarded as a model of how other Australians could alter their relationship with the natural world. Many championed traditional Aboriginal culture as a source of knowledge for reversing the environmental damage caused by 200 years of white settlement.[21] Many also came to believe that Aboriginality could make good the problem of unprecedented and unrelenting historical change. Figured as unchanging, even timeless, Aboriginal culture was seen to provide the modern world with a much needed sense of permanence as well as a sense of enduring succession.[22]

Just as Aboriginality was celebrated as the bearer of these qualities of 'the past', attention was drawn to another dimension the past often carries: precedence. As the historical geographer David Lowenthal has remarked, precedence tends to be valued because it can demonstrate a heritage or a lineage that predates others. In a colonial context this is, of course, inherently problematic for the nation state. Precedence draws attention to the first people's claims upon a country. The more Australia drew upon Aboriginality to articulate its national identity, the more it could be required to address Aboriginal rights. The problems of Australian national identity and Aboriginal rights became increasingly intertwined. In one way or another, the historical work of archaeology and anthropology, and the popular discourses they influenced, had above all else represented Aboriginal people or culture as connected to the land of Australia, while a political campaign for Aboriginal land rights and the new Australian history had drawn attention to the dispossession and destruction of Aboriginal people and culture.[23]

Many settler Australians came to believe that Australia faced a critical moral problem because its historical foundations were mired in the crimes committed against its first peoples. They saw this as an original sin, a problem of guilt or a shameful past, which had to be atoned for the sake of the nation. Until this occurred, Australia would continue to be diminished in its own eyes as well as those of other nations. This was regarded, in other words, as a crisis for the whole culture—a moment of instability as the country's colonial legacy came to haunt settler Australian identity.[24]

By the time of Australia's bicentenary in 1988, Aboriginal culture and history had gained enormous prestige as a result of their representation in several national discourses. This gave them considerable moral authority. This discursive power was apparent in a slogan that emerged at the time: 'White Australia has a black history'. Many settler Australians now wanted to learn about this past, and they wanted this past as their history. Aboriginal history had become central to their narrative of the nation.[25]

Managing historical difference

From the late 1960s, federal governments in Australia became increasingly involved in Aboriginal affairs in Australia. In large part they did so in order to address the increasing problem of what can be called Aboriginal people's historical difference. There was a mounting acceptance that the Aboriginal minority had a different historical relationship to Australia because they were the nation's first peoples, and because they had been disadvantaged by colonial dispossession and racial discrimination. The main issue for government, though, was how to manage this difference.

The upsurge in Aboriginal demands for indigenous rights as well as sovereignty, growing criticism of the racial dimensions of the policy of assimilation, a mounting realisation of the huge cost of implementing that program, a genuine concern to address the chronic disadvantage of Aboriginal people, and an ongoing apprehension about international criticism of Australia's treatment of Aboriginal people prompted governments—first the conservative Coalition (the Liberal Party and the Country or National Party), then a social democratic party (the Australian Labor Party)—to consider a change in the direction of their Aboriginal policies. As a result they abandoned assimilation as a goal and adopted self-determination. In doing so, they accepted the permanent presence in Australia of the Aboriginal communities that their predecessors had long sought to undermine, even destroy, and instead they tried to nurture these as a locus of Aboriginality. Under this new dispensation, Aborigines were recognised by successive governments, both Labor and Coalition, as a people (though not as a nation), and were granted special rights to some parcels of land (but not compensation) on the grounds that they were culturally different and had suffered historically because of racial discrimination. Governments sought to nurture Aboriginality by creating new forums for political representation, establishing new forms of bureaucracy, and funding Aboriginal cultural producers in the areas of art, theatre, dance, music, literature, history, and so forth. In doing this, they championed Aboriginality as a central part of what they saw as the nation's culture.[26]

Federal governments in the 1970s and 1980s had only partial success in managing the problem of Aboriginal historical difference, however. During this period, Aboriginal leaders continued to seek recognition of indigenous rights and sovereignty and the return of more land, which rested on their status as the first peoples, and they increasingly presented these demands in international forums. Furthermore, relations between Aboriginal leaders and government deteriorated when the Hawke Labor government reneged on a commitment to introduce national land rights legislation in the face of a campaign on behalf of capital interests in the mining industry, and abandoned its offer of a treaty or a compact. (Unlike in other areas of British settlement, such as Canada, New Zealand and the United States, no treaties were ever negotiated by governments in the Australian colonies in the eighteenth and nineteenth centuries.) In this context, the government proposed in the early 1990s a formal process of national reconciliation between Aborigines and other Australians. In keeping with what had been a more or less bipartisan approach to the problem of Australia's Aboriginal history for much of the preceding two decades, the other major parliamentary parties supported this.

Keating's history

History—already important to the articulation of national identity in Australia—came to occupy an even more significant place in the 1990s as historical narratives of the nation were exploited in an unprecedented manner by the leaders of the two major political parties. As a result of the steady decline of the left—most notably after the fall of communism in the late 1980s—the main political parties in liberal democracies such as Australia increasingly espoused very similar economic and social policies. Consequently, they found it necessary to distinguish themselves from one another on other grounds. To do so, these parties turned to the realm of culture and history, which had become increasingly important for the reasons discussed earlier. In this process, political leaders now played a greater role as shapers of national opinion than they had once done.[27]

In the Australian case, Paul Keating and John Howard spoke of Australian history more than any of their predecessors. Keating was previously renowned or reviled for the neo-liberal economic reforms he had championed during the Hawke Labor government (1983–91). Partly to offset this, he sought to advance a 'big picture' for Australia and to position the Australian Labor Party as the standard bearer of a distinctive Australian nationalism. He advocated a deeper Australian embrace of its Asia-Pacific 'destiny', called for an Australian republic to replace Australia's constitutional ties with the British monarchy, and embraced the cause of reconciliation between Aboriginal and non-Aboriginal Australians. In a series of historical speeches, he connected these causes to critical forces and events in the nation's past, interpreting them in the light of the new Australian history and an earlier radical nationalist history. At the same time as he gave voice to 'aggressive Australianism', he attacked the conservatives as disloyal Anglo-Australians, derided their slavish devotion to Britain and the British Empire, and blamed them for delaying the development of a distinctive Australian identity. He singled out the most important conservative prime minister in the postwar era, Robert Menzies

(1949–66), as the arch villain in perpetuating this oppressive legacy. In contrast to Gough Whitlam, Malcolm Fraser and Bob Hawke, Paul Keating drew distinctions between what was 'Australian' and what was 'British'. For Keating, James Curran has noted, 'Britishness [w]as an unfaithful representation of Australia's "true" self'.[28]

In embracing the story which the new Australian history told of the country's Aboriginal past, Keating deployed a politics of sentiment. He spoke the language of shame (but not guilt) as he called upon settler Australians to tackle the burden of this history and so redeem the white settler nation. In one of his most famous historical speeches, delivered in Redfern Park in Sydney to mark the International Year of the World's Indigenous People, Keating asserted: 'It begins, I think, with an act of recognition. Recognition that it was we who did the dispossessing. We took the traditional lands and smashed the traditional way of life. We brought the diseases. The alcohol. We committed the murders. We took the children from their mothers. We practised discrimination and exclusion. It was our ignorance and our prejudice. And our failure to imagine these things being done to us'. For Keating, acknowledging and redressing this past was a matter of truth for the nation. It was a test of whether Australia really was a democracy—'that we are what we should be—truly the land of the fair go and the better chance'—and it was test of 'how well we know the land we live in [and how] well we know our history'. More than any other Australian prime minister, Keating joined the fate of Aboriginal people to the future of the nation: 'we cannot give indigenous Australians up without giving up many of our own most deeply held values, much of our identity—and our own humanity'.[29]

During his prime ministership, Keating melded together two causes: native title and the republic. The former stood for an acknowledgment that Aboriginal people had been the original owners of the land (and so worked like some colonial treaties); the latter stood for Australia's independence from Britain. He saw these as a means of creating a new foundational history that could address the very historical problems—the British dispossession of the Aboriginal owners of the country and Australia's Britishness—that undermined Australia's legitimacy as a nation, especially one located in the Asia-Pacific region. In the case of native title, Keating construed the High Court of Australia's 1992 *Mabo* judgment as a historic decision since he regarded it as a matter of historical truth: 'The Court's decision rejected a lie and acknowledged a truth. The lie was *terra nullius*—the convenient fiction that Australia had been a land of no one. The truth was native title'. As such, it could be the foundation of a 'new relationship between indigenous and non-Aboriginal Australians'. In the case of the republic, he saw the deep past of Aboriginal culture providing Australia with the ancient history that the British heritage had previously lent the nation.[30]

By embracing Aboriginal history in this manner, Keating's government created the impression of a nation that had confronted its own regime of racially discriminatory practices and brought this colonial past to an end. In reality, it had done no such thing. The approach adopted by his government was more a matter of rewriting the history of the nation than it was a means of redressing the consequences of the past it represented for Aboriginal people. Furthermore, none of the moves his government made were radical ones in respect of their economic and social impact on settler Australians. In no fundamental sense did they change Australia's economic and social structures or the way the country was governed. In this sense, very few, if any, settler Australians were disempowered.[31]

The turn to the Aboriginal past in the historical narrative of the nation, however, *did* have revolutionary consequences for settler Australia's culture and identity, as we have observed, and Keating's championing of the new Australian history served to highlight these. In the political realm, the new Australian history increasingly provoked arguments about remembering, forgetting, responsibility, guilt, shame, atonement, apology and compensation, which had formerly characterised countries such as Germany. As David Carter has remarked, this confrontation with Australia's colonial past has been profoundly unsettling for settler Australians because they have not been accustomed 'to thinking of [their] history as being as . . . contentious, morally compromised or volatile, as dangerous, as, say, Japanese or South African history'.[32]

Unsettled settlers

The new Australian history was unsettling for several reasons. Since most people know their country and understand their place in it through narratives such as a national history, a dramatic change in such stories can make what has long seemed familiar unfamiliar, thus undermining a sense of home or belonging. In times of rapid change, histories can be especially important psychologically, providing people with a sense of order and composure. The story of Australia's colonial past that many settler Australians now encountered was confronting because it threatened to deprive them of a familiar and comforting map of the past.[33]

Most of all, though, the new Australian history unsettled because it drew into question the moral basis of British colonisation in the past and so the Australian nation in the present. The significance of this emotionally cannot be gainsaid. In large part, nations are deeply cherished ideals because of their moral status. This, Gyanendra Pandey has observed, is what gives them their greater or lesser appeal and hence their staying power. In the eyes of some—particularly conservatives—the new national story, by drawing attention to settler racism and the dispossession and destruction of the original rightful owners of the country, threatened to strip the nation of its moral legitimacy and draw into question whether it was worthy of anyone's love and loyalty. They were accustomed to seeing their forebears in positive, not negative terms, playing roles that were a matter of celebration, not reproach. It seemed inconceivable to them that they could feel pride *and* shame in respect of their beloved nation's past.[34]

The new Australian history also unsettled many settler Australians because it seemed to weaken the nation's connection with its British past, which had been *the* traditional history, and which had been regarded by them as the principal source of the nation's moral and legal order. The fears of conservatives were all the greater because they had long emphasised the importance of a sense of communion between past and present. Now Aboriginality was deemed to provide this in the form of its deep past. They feared, in other words, that the Aboriginal past would displace the British past as Australia's history. As so often in nation states, these fears fastened upon changes that were mooted for its key symbols, such as the Australian flag.

Many settler Australians were also unsettled by the way in which the new Australian history changed their position in relation to the status of victimhood. They were used to seeing their forebears as victims, not oppressors, as sufferers, not perpetrators. The new Australian history placed their forebears in a past in which they were responsible for heinous deeds. Most importantly, it called for mourning in respect of another people's historical experience.

In the mid-1980s, in the context of the plans for Australia's bicentenary, conservative spokespeople began to mount an attack on the new Australian history. This was influenced by the assault new conservatives had launched on critical history in Britain and the United States, but the historian Geoffrey Blainey also lent it intellectual legitimacy. Their writings had several themes: there was an elite or new class comprising a very small group of historians on the left who were seeking to dictate how Australians saw the past and the future of Australia by telling a story which amounted to a falsification of *our* history; these historians had a deep sense of grievance about Australia's past treatment of minorities and were blackening the national history by telling Australia's history in the bleakest terms as a story of destruction and persecution; they were trying to instil a sense of shame among their fellow Australians; their rewriting of the nation's history was undermining Australia because it rejected national unity and told instead of the country's diverse cultures and origins; historians were failing to assert the worth and authority of the nation's Western traditions. In particular, these critics refused to accept that Australia was established on the basis of dispossessing and destroying another people. Instead, they asserted pride in what the old history of Australia had narrated: the achievements of economic development, political freedom and social harmony.[35]

These conservatives also sought to retell the old colonialist account of the frontier, particularly during the debate ignited by the High Court's *Mabo* decision. In doing so, they largely repeated some of the themes in Blainey's earlier historical writings. They claimed: British possession of the land was legitimate and legal; the displacement and dispossession of Aboriginal people was bound to have occurred sooner or later because the course of history has depended on the overthrow of the ancient by the modern; cultures are not equal, and some will prosper while others will decline; claims of genocide and widespread massacres were nonsense; the rule of law was upheld; Aborigines were only able to mount local resistance; by far the most important cause of Aboriginal death and decline was disease; vengeance killings exacted a far greater toll than any depredations by Europeans; and humanitarian endeavour was heroic.[36]

The prospect of native title especially stirred conservative fears, largely because it was informed by a history that overturned the way in which conservatives had long imagined the space and time of *their* nation. Blainey and other conservative spokespersons attacked the court's decision as ahistorical, complaining that it was revolutionary and that it overturned ancient legal doctrines. They claimed that the enactment of native title would threaten the nation's progress because it would pass land into the hands of Aboriginal owners whose culture was archaic rather than modern. And they alleged that it would further Aboriginal separatism to such a degree that Australian sovereignty would be undermined and the nation dismembered.[37]

The conservative account of Australia's past and future circulated widely during the debate over native title, and helped to limit its scope. However, the conservatives did not prosper politically. Rather, Keating's take on Australia's history and its historical destiny seemed to appeal to many voters. History, quite unquestionably, represented political capital. In 1993 the Australian Labor Party was returned to office. It marked the fifth successive defeat for the Liberal–National Party Coalition. The conservatives were prompted to take up an opposing position on Australia's history in a more strategic fashion.

Howard's history

John Howard, soon to resume the leadership of the Liberals, led the way. In large part, he returned to a theme in a policy document released in 1988. He had claimed then that confidence in the country's past had been undermined by 'professional purveyors of guilt', who had assaulted 'Australia's heritage', told Australians 'they should apologise for pride in their culture, traditions, institutions and history', and taught them 'to be ashamed of their past'. As a result, 'hope and confidence in the future were transformed into concern and despair'.[38]

Howard now circulated his opinions on the matter in the pages of the conservative magazine *Quadrant*. He claimed that Keating was using Australian history as a 'political weapon' so effectively that he was entrenching Labor 'as the only true product of Australia's political soil' and marginalising the 'conservative side of Australian politics'. He urged his party to take up history as a political tool and go into battle: 'Australia's national identity and debate about what it is to be an Australian will continue as important issues throughout the nineties'. Howard reiterated objections to Keating's position that he and old and new conservative spokespersons had been putting for a decade: 'Much of his rhetoric about building a so-called new Australia is built on a denigration of our past and its achievements. We are continually told that Australia's history is a litany of intolerance, bigotry and narrow-mindedness . . . So much of Paul Keating's rhetoric on the national identity is the rhetoric of apology and shame . . . In these circumstances, Liberals should become the party of the Australian achievement. There is latent sentiment in the community that legitimate expressions of pride about the past have been stifled'.[39]

Howard's determination to fight a war over Australia's history had been bolstered by Blainey the previous year. He had not only criticised the new Australian history once more, but also (in a lecture later published in *Quadrant*) provided its detractors with a tool by coining the phrase 'black armband history'. As historian Mark McKenna has noted, the wearing of black armbands (and red headbands) had become a symbol of mourning and protest among Aboriginal people and their sympathisers regarding the dispossession and destruction of Aboriginal people and culture. The attack on black armband history reflected an inability or at least an unwillingness to mourn this history. It was also informed by the creed of Australian liberalism discussed above as well as Howard's own identification with the old Australian history—especially an affection for its British heritage—and his unfamiliarity and unease with Aboriginal history and culture.[40]

At the heart of the Liberal Party's campaign in the 1996 election were the matters of race, history and national identity. The party sought to articulate a sense of grievance, particularly among the so-called battlers, by claiming that the agenda of the Keating government was dominated by 'special' or 'sectional' interest groups such as Aborigines and by 'elites' who championed their rights at the expense of the national interest. This was encapsulated in the Liberal Party's slogan: 'For all of us'. It was dog whistle politics. Howard incorporated the telling of Australia's history into this appeal. He wanted 'to see [Australians] comfortable and relaxed about their history'; he insisted that it was very important they did not spend their lives 'apologising for the past'.[41]

Once in office, Howard and his party launched an assault on ATSIC (the Aboriginal and Torres Strait Islander Commission), which in their eyes was the symbol of the policy of Aboriginal self-determination. Over the next few years the Howard government made clear both its support for a return to a policy of assimilation and its opposition to indigenous rights, especially native title and land rights. It also undermined the cause of reconciliation. Reconciliation had appealed to those settler Australians who have been called 'the sorry people'.[42] They mourned the loss of their ideal nation and they sought to redeem it by supporting means to redress the historical condition of Aboriginal people. Howard's move appealed to those who might be called 'the angry people' (as did Pauline Hanson's One Nation Party). They were depressed by the loss of their imaginary nation and sought to retrieve it by rejecting 'black armband' history. Howard's approach offered the opportunity to once more escape the burdensome Aboriginal past.

This political direction entailed an assault on Aboriginal history. In the early months of his government, Howard emphasised his vision of Australia's history in a series of speeches that echoed the rhetoric American new conservatives had used in the culture wars they had launched in order to address their fears about whether the United States was a righteous and innocent nation. Howard claimed that there had been a systematic attempt 'to rewrite Australian history in the service of a partisan political cause', 'stifle voices of dissent' by establishing 'a form of historical correctness as a particular offshoot of political correctness' and 'demean, pillory and tear down many great people of Australia's past'. Blainey's coinage came in handy. Howard asserted: 'This "black armband view" of our past reflects a belief that most Australian history since 1788 has been little more than a disgraceful history of imperialism, exploitation, racism, sexism and other forms of discrimination. I take a different view. I believe that the balance sheet of our history is one of heroic achievement and that we have achieved much more as a nation of which we can be proud than of which we should be ashamed'. He called for the return of this history, a dose of patriotic therapy to bolster the self-esteem of anxious and vulnerable settler Australians.[43]

In the course of the next several years, Howard's supporters launched highly politicised attacks on many aspects of the new Australian history, and on the principal figures and institutions they held responsible for this narrative—none more so than Aboriginal history and its practitioners.

DEMOCRACY

· 2

Since the end of the Second World War, enormous changes have occurred in the content of historical narratives of nations such as Australia, but there has also been a tremendous shift in terms of who has produced histories, and the forms and forums in which they have done so. Traditionally, national histories were largely a creation of middle- and upper-class men. They sought to tell the history of the nation as though it could be comprised by a single storyline (though, in fact, different narratives *were* produced). It was a heroic or monumental history, which celebrated the making of a unitary nation, mostly by virtue of the deeds of their fellow middle- and upper-class men. This was largely a political history, mostly told in one literary form or another and done primarily by researching written sources. It presented its knowledge as scientific, and therefore as value-free, neutral and objective. Most importantly, it claimed this knowledge as an absolute and universal truth; that is, it laid claim to not just being true in particular circumstances but to being true everywhere and always. It was a form of intellectual absolutism.[1]

From the 1950s, however, histories have increasingly been produced by and about those whose story had been 'hidden from history'. Historians such as Eric Hobsbawm and E.P. Thompson helped create 'history from below', or 'social history'. It was a *critical* history since it condemned a good deal of what happened in the past, but also sought to recapture those moments that demonstrated the possibility of a better way of life or to recover other, more satisfactory, directions that might have been taken. By representing pasts previously absent from the story history had told, this work also offered a much more complex picture of the past. By pointing out what the previously dominant narrative of the nation had excluded, it also demonstrated that this history had always been intensely subjective and political in its construction. This new historical work continued to be presented in writing but it increasingly took oral and visual forms, and it was based on historical sources that were not only written, but also oral, visual and material. During this time, history has become more and more popular socially and has become the subject of popular culture in many forms and forums.[2]

Together, these changes have amounted to what can be called the democratisation of history. As a result, the nature of history as a form of knowledge and the ways it is transmitted have been transformed in many respects, and history has become the subject of great contestation and struggle. The intellectual absolutism of scientific history has been over-thrown as many have interrogated historical narratives by asking questions like: Whose history is this? Who is telling this story? Whose interests are served by it? What kind of truth does this history tell? This has been apparent in a number of historical fields in Australia, but none more so than the one that came to be referred to as Aboriginal history.

Critical history

This history, like any history-making, has been shaped by the present as well as by the past. Traces of the past, if they exist at all, exist in the present. In telling histories, we always approach these traces by starting out from the present and so our histories are necessarily informed by this. When academic historians belatedly turned their critical attention to Australia's Aboriginal past in the mid-1960s, one of their purposes was political, as it had been for the historians whose narratives they now challenged.

Settler Australian historians began their study of colonialism at a time when the cause of indigenous people and other such oppressed peoples (such as African Americans) had started to have a considerable political impact and governments were trying to respond to their needs and demands. The most important figure was a liberal historian and public administrator, Charles Rowley, who had assumed the task of overseeing a large project on Aboriginal people in contemporary Australia sponsored by the Social Science Research Council of Australia. Rowley was convinced that the key to Aboriginal affairs was inherently historical: government policy and practice had operated in a vacuum, but it was impossible to understand the Aboriginal predicament unless its historical dimensions were grasped. A thorough knowledge of the history of relations between Aborigines and settlers, and particularly between Aborigines and government, could alter the way in which settler Australians saw 'the Aboriginal problem'. It could also lead to a more humane and just approach, and create a demand for reform, which would result in a fairer society. This pedagogical project has been described by another liberal historian, Henry Reynolds, in these terms: 'Much critical, revisionist history . . . is written in hope and expectation of reform, crafted in the confidence that carefully marshalled, clearly expressed argument can persuade significant numbers of [settler] Australians to change their minds and redirect their sympathies. Beyond that confidence in individuals is a firm belief in the capacity of Australian democracy to respond to new ideas which in time can reshape politics and recast institutions, laws and customs'.[3] (Critics of 'black armband history' overlook these premises.)

Most of the other historians who began to work in the field shared Rowley's project (as I observed many years ago).[4] In some cases, they were drawn into the field by their own contemporary encounters with the colonial past; in others, they were compelled by their own involvement in political causes that included Aborigines, and a commitment to doing 'history from below'.[5] In undertaking this work, though, these historians remained committed to the scientific ideal of objectivity, which had characterised history as a professional venture since its rise in the nineteenth century. Historical objectivity, as the American historian Peter Novick points out, has rested upon a series of assumptions, which include 'a commitment to the reality of the past, and to truth as correspondence to that reality; a sharp separation between knower and known, between fact and value, and, above all, between history and fiction'. (He might have added a sharp separation between conceptual work and findings.) Novick continues: 'Historical facts are seen as prior to and independent of interpretation: the value of an interpretation is judged by how well it accounts for the facts; if contradicted by the facts, it must be abandoned. Truth is one, not perspectival. Whatever patterns exist in history are "found", not "made"'.[6]

This first wave of historians—among whom Rowley, Reynolds, Bob Reece, Raymond Evans, Lyndall Ryan and Michael Christie were the most prominent—argued that what they called the frontier had set down the basic pattern of relationships between Aborigines and settlers, and that this history continued to affect Aboriginal people. In studies primarily of New South Wales, Victoria, Tasmania and Queensland, they assaulted earlier accounts of the British colonisation of the country. They created the following picture. Colonisation was not a matter of settlement but an invasion. Its frontiers were characterised by considerable conflict, particularly over land, which amounted to a war. The settlers dispossessed Aborigines of their land and appropriated their sources of food and water. Aborigines fought a war of resistance by launching attacks on the settlers and their property. Settlers wreaked violence on Aborigines, some of which was premeditated and fuelled by racism, some the result of the brutalising conditions of the frontier. The conflict was sporadic but the cost was high: perhaps 20 000 Aborigines and 2000 settlers died. The Aboriginal population drastically declined, but this was largely the result of smallpox, measles, influenza, venereal diseases, respiratory diseases (such as tuberculosis), malnutrition and alcohol abuse. Aborigines were forced to come into white settlements, where they largely became helpless and hopeless fringe-dwellers because their labour was not required in most areas. For a time, humanitarians sought to uphold the rights of Aborigines as British subjects, though not their rights to land, but their impact in the colonies was limited: there was an inherent conflict between colonising another people's country and respecting their rights; government favoured colonial development and so was vulnerable to settler pressure; and government found it difficult to protect Aborigines on a far-flung frontier. The state sometimes played an active role in dispossessing Aborigines by providing military and para-military units, including native police forces.[7]

In forging this story of the frontier, much of which had previously been articulated by Aboriginal spokespersons, and journalists, novelists, political campaigners and academics in disciplines other than history,[8] these historians adopted an approach that was conventional in nearly every respect. They worked within the disciplinary confines of history; their sources were the literary ones upon which historians had long relied; and they ultimately laid claim to the truth of their interpretations on empirical grounds. For example, Henry Reynolds asserted in his first major book: 'It is based on extensive [historical] research among a vast array of historical records'.[9]

Historical revision

By the end of the 1970s, this first wave of historical scholarship had become the subject of serious criticism. In an overview of the field, Bob Reece pointed out the dangers in recent works revealing the bloody nature of Australia's frontier: 'recitation of this inglorious side of our history may become fashionable and self-serving. If there has been a "cult of forgetfulness" towards Aborigines in the past, then surely there is a "cult of anti-racism" among Australian intellectuals'. This 'anti-racism and its "conscience history" have serious limitations', he warned. 'Recitation of iniquity upon iniquity comes closer to polemics than to history and there is a danger of over-simplification'. In 1982 Reece criticised 'the whole genre of what might be called "massacre history" as it is pursued by white historians and activists'. In 1987 he complained that Reynolds and other historians had been so eager 'to document the bloodiness of the process of colonisation' that they had paid insufficient attention to 'documenting and highlighting that other major characteristic of Aboriginal–European interaction: accommodation'. He claimed that Reynolds' 'dispossession–resistance "model" or interpretation of Aboriginal–European interaction' had become 'a powerful academic orthodoxy'.[10]

Others echoed Reece's criticisms. In 1985, a leading anthropologist and historian in the field, Diane Barwick, chastised historians for their tendency to 'commemorate examples of confrontation with more eagerness than they describe the processes of accommodation'; in 1989, D.J. Mulvaney criticised those historians who emphasised 'the thread of [Aboriginal] resistance', and argued that '[t]hey also should acknowledge that there were communities . . . which chose a very different response'; in the same year, I was critical of the tendency of historians to disregard contact experiences their approach failed to explain; and in 1994, Richard Broome, the author of the most widely read general history of relations between Aborigines and settlers, pointed out that there was 'a popular (but not universal) conception that Australian frontiers were violent places where whites slaughtered Aborigines indiscriminately'.[11]

By the mid-1980s, another school of interpretation had clearly emerged in the academic historiography. Several historians challenged the emphasis on conflict, settler violence and Aboriginal resistance by pointing out relationships of cohesion or cooperation between settlers and Aborigines. Reece argued that, in the Swan River district in the 1830s and 1840s (now Perth), Aborigines did not necessarily see settlers as inimical to their interests; he said they were willing to share their resources with them and treated the newcomers as a means of strengthening their position in reference to Aborigines they considered to be their traditional enemies. In a similar fashion, Beverley Nance and Marie Fels contended that the violence in the Port Phillip District (now Victoria) in the 1830s and 1840s was mainly perpetrated by settlers, that Aborigines killed relatively few whites, and that most of their attacks on white property should not be characterised as resistance. Nance also argued that retributive Aboriginal attacks upon one another outweighed those against whites and played a significant role in Aboriginal depopulation. Reynolds' model of the frontier was questioned further by Ann McGrath, who suggested in a study of the Northern Territory that the frontier should not be seen as a rigid boundary, since Aborigines moved backwards and forwards across it so that they effectively lived on both sides. In work on the Western District of Victoria, Jan Critchett added to this picture of the frontier by insisting that Aborigines and settlers lived side by side on the frontier: '[It] was represented by the [Aboriginal] woman who lived nearby and was shared by her Aboriginal partner with a European or Europeans. It was the group living down beside the creek or river, it was the "boy" used as guide for exploring parties or for doing jobs now and then'. Mulvaney performed much the same function by drawing attention to a series of intimate cross-cultural encounters across Australia. Reynolds himself played a role in rendering the frontier a more complex historical phenomenon in his book *With the White People*, which largely focused on Aboriginal labour in northern Australia. The primary role of disease in the decline of the Aboriginal population tended to be neglected by historians who had become specialists in the field, but it was the subject of research conducted by other scholars, such as Noel Butlin and (later) Judy Campbell.[12]

Historians also focused attention on humanitarianism, particularly during the critical decades of the 1830s and 1840s (when large-scale

pastoral expansion first occurred). Henry Reynolds sought to demonstrate that key figures in the British Colonial Office adopted an approach
primarily determined by moral and legal imperatives and that this led them
to recognise Aboriginal rights to land. However, many scholars, including
D.J. Mulvaney, A.G.L. Shaw and myself, were not persuaded by this
argument, and Bob Reece and S.G. Foster had already reached a different
conclusion.[13]

By the early 1990s, it was evident that the usual process of academic
historical argument and revision, which tends to carry professional rewards
for those who challenge dominant schools of interpretation, had occurred.
Reviewing these recent studies in 1991, Peter Read remarked: 'the previously fairly tight homogeneity between non-Aboriginal writers of
Aboriginal history has widened, and is likely to widen further'. Much of
this interpretive work, moreover, lent itself to conservative perspectives
and moderated the account of the frontier produced by the earlier, radical
wave. A new consensus had emerged in the academic historiography:
much confrontation and conflict had occurred between Aborigines and
settlers, but a fair amount of sharing and accommodation had also taken
place.[14] (It should be noted, moreover, that most of the work now being
done is concentrated on the later, post-frontier phases of colonialism.)[15]

Aboriginal history

After academic historians began to devote attention to the study of colonialism in Australia, the most significant development was the emergence
of 'Aboriginal history' as a field of historical discourse. 'Aboriginal history',
it can be argued, emerged in the mid-1970s among a group of anthropologists, archaeologists and historians associated with the Australian
National University and the Australian Institute of Aboriginal Studies
(later renamed the Australian Institute of Aboriginal and Torres Strait
Islander Studies). They began a scholarly journal, which they called
Aboriginal History. The most important figure was the Canadian-born and
trained scholar Diane Barwick.[16]

For these scholars, the term 'Aboriginal history' did not simply refer to
a subject—a past which included Aboriginal people—however basic this
was to their project. More importantly, it signalled a realisation, indeed, a

conviction, that the task of representing this past entailed ways of practising history that departed from those historians had traditionally used.
'Aboriginal history', in other words, was not just a past whereby Aborigines
were added and stirred without history changing significantly. These
scholars were aware that 'Aborigines' and 'history' had long been seen as
a contradiction in terms: Aborigines belonged to antiquity and were the
object of anthropology; history belonged to modernity and non-Aboriginal
peoples were its subject. In giving the name *Aboriginal History* to their
project, they signalled that this was to be a different kind of history. It would
necessarily challenge many of the conventions of the discipline.

Aboriginal history has come to have several characteristics. It can be
defined as a matter of historical perspective; that is, it is an attempt to see
the past from the position or point of view of Aboriginal people. Henry
Reynolds' *The Other Side of the Frontier*, first published in 1981, is
commonly regarded as the best academic example of this. It was the first
work of its kind in Australia. (Such work had long been done by historians in Africa, the Americas, New Zealand and the Pacific.) Whereas the
previous historical work had been overwhelmingly Eurocentric in its
approach, Reynolds sought to understand the frontier from the perspective of the traditional landowners. As a result of this shift, Reynolds'
interpretation differed in significant ways from earlier accounts. He
contended that Aboriginal people often perceived the British newcomers
as returned kinsmen, and so tried to include the newcomers in their
kinship system and teach them its ethic of reciprocity; and he argued that
the Aboriginal landowners were angered less by the British trespass on their
land than by the intruders asserting an exclusive proprietorial right to it.[17]

In focusing on Aboriginal perspectives, Reynolds also treated
Aboriginal people as the primary subjects or agents of his historical
inquiry, rather than as mere objects. They became important not simply
because of what was done *to* them by the colonisers. This research
prompted other academic historians to investigate how Aboriginal people
saw themselves and others on the frontiers of settlement. For example,
Marie Fels considered what it might have meant to be a member of the
native police force in the Port Phillip District by endeavouring to reconstruct how Aboriginal policemen tried to make sense of the colonial order
and forge a place for themselves and their people in it. In projects like this,

historians drew into question the assumption that Aboriginal people comprised one common group rather than a large number of local ones. In turn, they realised that relations between and among groups of Aboriginal people continued to be very important to them, often much more so than their relations with settlers. Research of this nature moved Aborigines and Aboriginality to the centre of historical inquiry.[18]

In order to do this work, historians had to expand their horizons in another respect. Many began to use sources other than the written ones they had traditionally relied upon. This included interviewing people about the northern frontiers of settlement ('oral history'), but also using the historical remains exploited by archaeologists, such as Aboriginal middens and rock art, and the sources used by linguists, such as word lists. The work of historians became more cross-disciplinary in the sense that they drew upon the knowledge of other disciplines. This was especially so where they used a picture of Aboriginal culture at the point of their first contacts with Europeans and other intruders in order to understand Aboriginal responses to non-Aboriginal intruders. Reynolds' account of the Aboriginal response to settlers in *The Other Side of the Frontier*, for example, owed much to recent anthropological studies of the nature of Aboriginal groups and boundaries. At the same time as historians drew upon other disciplinary approaches in their work, more practitioners of these other disciplines became interested in historical questions and doing historical work. This is apparent in the range of disciplines represented by contributors to the journal *Aboriginal History*.

The emergence of Aboriginal history as a historical field occurred at a time when there was a renaissance of Aboriginal culture in Australia. Fundamental to this was an assertion of Aboriginal people's status as the original or indigenous peoples of the land, but also an assertion that they were a people who had been oppressed in the past. Both assumptions were, of course, inherently historical in nature: they referred to history as the past, but also required history as a narrative of that past. As such, they provoked a need and a demand for history. Aboriginal people became the authors of their own history. This, more than any other change in the making of Aboriginal history, revealed that historical work involves power and that much history tends to be someone's history—a story told by someone from a particular point of view.

It soon became evident that the history made by Aboriginal people differed in many respects from that of non-Aboriginal scholars. In Aboriginal history-making, the past has been regarded as part of the present and the future of Aboriginal people, rather than a time that has passed. In other words, the very temporal categories—past and present—that lie at the heart of academic history are drawn into question. History was seen by Aboriginal people as critical to their identity as Aborigines: for acquiring, ascribing and asserting a sense of Aboriginality of some kind or another. For some Aboriginal people, the past has been seen as the source of a real Aboriginality, often considered to be that of traditional or classical Aboriginal culture; for others, it has been treated as a resource for learning more immediately who you are because of where you come from and who your people are.

As a result, much Aboriginal history-making has been both personal and parochial. Aboriginal people have told their own histories and those of their own families and kin, and they have done so for their own people. As one group of Aboriginal historians asserted in the early 1980s: 'Aboriginal historians are writing history for Aboriginal people . . . for our families and children . . . [Our] responsibility to family, kin and community is keenly felt'. Most Aboriginal histories have been concerned to assert or affirm a sense of both survival and continuity, challenging the narratives of destruction and discontinuity found in settler histories. In the words of one Aboriginal historian, James Miller: 'the story of the survival of their people as a culturally significant minority in Australian society in the face of enormous oppression is a story of triumph'.[19]

Consequently, a question of authorship and authority—of who could, would and should do Aboriginal history—became a critical one. There has been competition and contestation over the control of the story about the Aboriginal past. This is all the more so because the vast majority of settler Australians only know Aboriginal people through narratives or discourses that purport to represent them. The anthropologist Marcia Langton has observed: 'The most dense relationship is not between actual people, but between white Australians and the symbols created by their predecessors. Australians do not know and relate to Aboriginal people. They relate to stories told by former colonists'. Some Aboriginal people have sought to curb the dominance of academic histories by claiming the right of custodianship, even ownership, of the Aboriginal past on the grounds that *they* are the guardians of Aboriginal history. More commonly, Aboriginal spokespersons have argued that the problem lies not in the fact that their past has continued to be represented by settler historians, but in how they do this and what authority they claim for their knowledge. In this context, many have advocated collaboration between non-Aboriginal scholars and Aboriginal people in the hope that Aboriginal histories will reach a non-Aboriginal audience.[20]

Aboriginal history-making grew enormously in the last three decades of the twentieth century as the currency of the past increased. Indeed, by the mid-1980s the linguist Peter Sutton could observe that an 'Aboriginal history movement' was 'sweeping the whole of urban and rural Australia'. This occurred in several ways: many Aboriginal people recorded their life histories and/or stories handed down in the oral tradition with anthropologists, linguists and literary critics; others recorded their memories in oral history interviews with academic historians and journalists; many wrote, painted, danced, photographed, filmed and sang their own and/or their people's stories; some curated historical exhibitions in galleries, museums, libraries and archives, or founded Aboriginal keeping places (or museums); groups joined with lawyers, anthropologists, linguists and historians in preparing historical claims for land tribunals; individuals worked with lawyers and historians to seek redress from the courts for personal injury; communities worked alongside archaeologists to excavate, preserve or rebury Aboriginal remains; young and old recreated genealogies as they sought to find lost relatives and restore broken families; and Aboriginal intellectuals scoured non-Aboriginal representations of the Aboriginal past to help articulate and promote their sense of Aboriginality.[21]

In much of this history-making, Aboriginal people have presented accounts of the past in forms that have differed markedly from those traditionally used by academic historians, but which mirror those sometimes used by settler Australians. Consequently, their histories have presented a profound challenge to the truth claims that the discipline of history has conventionally made. Aboriginal histories depart from the conventions of historical objectivity or realism primarily because they mostly take the form of life histories, family history, oral history, myth or legend. Nearly all these contradict an academic insistence on distance, or even a disjunction between knower and known, since a strong connection between these is the prerequisite for this Aboriginal history-making. More fundamentally, perhaps, Aboriginal histories do not depend on a correspondence between historical reality and historical facts in making a claim for historical truth; they have different approaches to verifying stories. As Peter Sutton has observed: 'In a number of ways, traditional Aboriginal approaches to myth and remembered events, and the newer Aboriginal understandings of history, resemble each other. Neither is heavily committed to the canons of empiricism. Both are heavily constitutive of identity, and charged with strong feelings . . . Both focus on identities and events without giving central importance to generalisations about processes or external forces . . . Both are linked to competition for economic and political benefits'. This, of course, is true of myths told by any people.[22]

A consideration of Aboriginal narratives known as Captain Cook stories illustrates some of the differences between Aboriginal histories and objectivist or realist academic histories. One such story—or rather, its gloss—reads:

> Captain Cook, thinking about acquiring more land, sailed from London to Sydney, where he admired the country, and landed bullocks and men with firearms. A massacre of local Aborigines followed. Cook then made his way to Darwin, where he behaved in much the same way. He sent armed horsemen to hunt down Aborigines in the Victoria River country. Cook was responsible for founding the cities of Sydney and Darwin, and he gave orders to Gilruth [an administrator of the Northern Territory in the early twentieth century], the police, and the managers of the cattle stations on how to treat Aborigines.

Quite clearly, stories such as this one bear little relationship to those accounts academic historians have traditionally regarded as history. Here, for example, we are told of Cook being in places and times he never was. It might be concluded that these histories lack historical authenticity because what they narrate is sharply at odds with what actually happened, and so are no use whatsoever in helping us answer conventional historical questions such as who did what, where and when.[23]

Yet, once we read these histories in another way—for example, as myth—professional historians are readily able to accept them as the bearers of historical truth. Captain Cook stories do not purport to treat Cook as a historical personage, but rather as a mythic character who symbolises British colonisation by encompassing a large set of people, processes, events and the like. As such, they do not seek to provide an account of relations between particular peoples in a particular place at a particular time. Instead, they tell of the general relationship between two peoples: the British colonisers and the Aboriginal landowners. Cook is chosen for these stories not because of his role in the past, but because of the place he has been given in settler histories. In those myths he is valorised as the discoverer of this country and the founder of white settlement; in the Aboriginal myths he is castigated as the archetypal coloniser who dispossesses the Aboriginal people of their land and imposes an immoral and unjust law on them. It is significant, as anthropologist Kenneth Maddock pointed out, that in most Captain Cook stories, '[r]elations between Aboriginal and alien are treated as a medium for transferring property, yet anything like balanced exchange is missing': gift and theft never occur in the same story; gifts are rarely accepted; thefts are never foiled; Aborigines never give to aliens and rarely steal from them. As such, it can be argued that these narratives faithfully render the nature of frontier relations and so can be called true histories.[24]

Public history

In response to a changing cultural and political environment, many non-Aboriginal scholars in the field of Aboriginal studies altered the way they did their work. Professional bodies guiding the practice of anthropologists and archaeologists formulated rules for the conduct of their research, which included codes of ethics. Many scholars undertook research projects that involved consultation, cooperation and collaboration with Aboriginal people. Others remained apprehensive of radical Aboriginal demands and were reluctant to cede any degree of control that might limit their access to information and their freedom to interpret it.

Increasingly, many non-Aboriginal practitioners of Aboriginal history, like others doing the new social history, did their work in places other than just archives and libraries. They did fieldwork, not unlike anthropologists, archaeologists and linguists. They went to the places they were studying; they surveyed sites; they observed, talked and listened to people; and they worked, travelled and ate with them. They also asked questions of themselves in relation to the subjects of their research. As a result, the relationship between past and present in their work underwent a major change. The ideal of historical distance, so fundamental to the way history has been practised conventionally, was drawn into question.

Most importantly, there was an increasing recognition among scholars that their knowledge was shaped by their own premises, which were largely a result of their own backgrounds, not the least of which were the disciplines in which they worked. Non-Aboriginal writers increasingly acknowledged that their knowledge was interpretive in nature, and thus a partial truth rather than an absolute or universal one. As a result, it was possible to envisage Aboriginal history as a field of dialogue, a place of speaking as well as listening, in which historians, archaeologists, anthropologists, linguists, and so forth—Aboriginal and non-Aboriginal people—could all participate by exchanging their histories and ways of doing history.

Yet, among historians, the growth in Aboriginal history-making, as well as the rise of a body of work often called postcolonialism, encouraged many to move away from the forms of Aboriginal history I have been describing. (It should be noted that the intellectual work labelled as postmodernism had very little impact on historians in the field of Aboriginal history. Instead, different ways of conceiving and practising history were provoked simply by doing 'history from below' and reflecting upon its implications.) From the late 1980s, historians began to pay more attention to their own people's 'white' history. Originally the focus here was upon questions of representation, particularly on the ways in which Aboriginal people and culture had been depicted in colonial discourses such as anthropology, and the ways in which these forms of knowledge empowered colonisers, not least by playing a role in governing Aboriginal people. But historians soon turned to consider the ways in which settler Australians tried to handle the presence of Aboriginal past, both precolonial and colonial, as they sought to forge a sense of place for themselves and their peoples in a land that was old but was still novel to them. In this work, historians began to concentrate not so much on history as the past as on the histories that have been produced.[25]

The rise of Aboriginal history, like history more generally, meant that the Aboriginal past increasingly attracted the practitioners of other disciplines. This is not just a matter of more anthropologists, linguists and archaeologists entering the field, but also those in disciplines such as geography, literary studies, philosophy, legal studies, gender studies, political science and cultural studies, which had previously had little (if any) interest in the subject. These scholars enriched an understanding of the Aboriginal past by provoking new questions, providing different perspectives and fresh insights, introducing novel methods of research, and suggesting new conceptual tools and other narrative forms. It also meant that Aboriginal history was increasingly produced by scholars who had never been trained in history and who had a rather different conception of historical knowledge to that of academic historians.

The developments in the field of Aboriginal history I have been describing have intersected with one of the most significant changes to have occurred in history-making more generally in the last two or so decades—the rise of memory or memorial discourse, in which the influence of the past and the present upon the production of historical accounts tilts towards the present rather than the past or, at least, the connections between past and present. As the British historian Jay Winter has remarked, memory has become 'the historical signature of our generation'. This has had a good deal to do with the attention that democratic history has paid to *experience*. Dipesh Chakrabarty has noted: 'The more we attend to experience in our historiography the more history gets entangled with memory'. In many quarters, memory has come to be associated with testimony, and this has become a critically important way in which we relate to the events of our time. This is most evident when it is associated with trauma, a phenomenon that has also acquired enormous significance in recent years. In much contemporary culture, people who have witnessed a traumatic event, or can claim a relationship to one, have been given a particular kind of legitimacy. Winter has observed: 'The person who suffered knows about a mystery—the mystery of evil and the miracle of survival—and we who listen may thereby enter the mystery and share the miracle'. Together, trauma, memory and testimony privilege those who ostensibly tell it how it was, especially where they are regarded as victims rather than perpetrators or bystanders. These narratives might best be described as 'affective histories' (to use a term coined by Homi Bhabha). They, rather than the contemporary historical record, are deemed by many to be the authentic voice of the past or the authoritative bearers of the truth about history.[26]

Memory or memorial discourse, it must be emphasised, has become powerful not only in small academic circles but in popular culture and politics. This is evident in the enormous popularity of (auto)biography, memoir and life stories, television shows that rely on individual testimony, and historical films and radio programs which feature one or two talking heads. It is also apparent in much-publicised controversies regarding the authenticity of traumatic memories (such as 'recovered memory syndrome') and authorship of books that allegedly draw on these (such as the cases concerning Binjamin Wilkomirski, Helen Demidenko and Norma Khouri).[27] Memory has also taken centre stage in public inquiries, commissions and trials about the past in recent decades, where much of their considerable impact can be attributed to the distinctive kind of storytelling they call forth—namely, memory in the form of personal testimony. In Australia, the best-known example of this is the Australian Human Rights and Equal Opportunity Commission's inquiry into the separation of Aboriginal children from their families, in which the testimony of Aboriginal people was featured both in the hearings and the report. This bore some similarity to the proceedings of the South African Truth and Reconciliation Commission. The power of memory presumably owes something to the crisis of representation in contemporary society in which many have become deeply suspicious of stories translated by the media, which have expanded their technological forms from newspapers, television, radio and records to video/DVD, compact discs, the internet and so on, and which have become more important than ever in shaping public discourse.

The growing popularity of Aboriginal history, which was discussed in the last chapter, drew it increasingly into the public sphere where it became a public history—a history which is produced and consumed, used and abused in an array of public contexts. Over the last three decades or so, Aboriginal history has been done in a large range of forms and forums, most of it by those who are not trained in academic history—for example, autobiographies and life stories such as Margaret Tucker's *If Everyone Cared*, Bruce Shaw's *My Country of the Pelican Dreaming: The Life of an Australian Aborigine of the Gadjerong, Grant Ngabidj*, Judith Wright's *The Cry for the Dead*, Ruby Langford's *Don't Take Your Love to Town*, Peter Coppin's *Kangkushot: The Life of Nyamal Lawman, Peter Coppin*, Daryl Tonkin and Carolyn Landon's *Jackson Track*, and Myles Lalor's *Wherever I Go*; memoirs such as Colin Macleod's *Patrol in the Dreamtime*; biographies and biographical studies such as Pat Jacobs' *Mister Neville*, Peter Read's *Charles Perkins*, Jackie Huggins' *Auntie Rita*, Don Baker's *The Civilised Surveyor: Thomas Mitchell and the Australian Aborigines*, Barry Hill's *Broken Song: T.G.H. Strehlow and Aboriginal Possession* and Isabel Flick and Heather Goodall's *Isabel Flick: The Many Lives of an Extraordinary Aboriginal Woman*; family histories such as Phillip Pepper's *You Are What You Make Yourself to Be*, Sally Morgan's *My Place* and Margaret Somerville's *Ingelba and the Five Black Matriarchs*; guides to doing Aboriginal history such as Diane Smith and Boronia Halstead's *Lookin For Your Mob: A Guide to Tracing Aboriginal Family Trees*; oral histories such as Bill Rosser's *Dreamtime Nightmares*, Luise Hercus and Peter Sutton's *This is What Happened*, Peter and Jay Read's *Long Time, Olden Time* and Stuart Rintoul's *The Wailing*; local histories such as Don Watson's *Caledonia Australis*, Cassandra Pybus' *Community of Thieves*, Pamela Lukin Watson's *Frontier Lands and Pioneer Legends: How Pastoralists Gained Karuwali Lands*, Ian Crawford's *We Won the Victory: Aborigines and Outsiders on the North-West Coast of Kimberley* and Mark McKenna's *Looking for Blackfellas' Point*; popular or populist histories such as Bruce Elder's *Blood on the Wattle* and Al Grassby and Marji Hill's *Six Australian Battlefields*; collections of papers such as Neil Gunson's *Australian Reminiscences and Papers of L.E. Threlkeld*, N.J.B. Plomley's *Weep in Silence: A History of the Flinders Island Aboriginal Settlement* and John Mulvaney, Howard Morphy and Alison Petch's *From the Frontier: Outback Letters to Baldwin Spencer*; archaeological works such as Josephine Flood's *The Riches of Ancient Australia: A Journey into Prehistory* and D.J. Mulvaney and Johan Kamminga's *Prehistory of Australia*; essays such as Peter Read's *The Stolen Generations*, Tim Rowse's *After Mabo: Interpreting Indigenous Traditions* and Robert Manne's *In Denial*; lectures such as Bernard Smith's

The Spectre of Truganini, Henry Reynolds' *The Breaking of the Great Australian Silence* and Inga Clendinnen's *True Stories*; collections of essays such as Murray Goot and Tim Rowse's *Make a Better Offer: The Politics of Mabo* and Michelle Grattan's *Reconciliation*; juridical histories such as Henry Reynolds' *The Law of the Land* and other work conceived for the courts and other legal tribunals, which includes innumerable land claim books; court cases such as *Mabo, Wik* and *Hindmarsh Island* (over land), *Gunner and Cubillo v the Commonwealth* (over the removal of children); public inquiries such as the Human Rights and Equal Opportunity Commission's investigation into the removal of Aboriginal children; the historical programs of the Council for Aboriginal Reconciliation; novels such as Thomas Keneally's *The Chant of Jimmie Blacksmith*, David Malouf's *Remembering Babylon* and Kim Scott's *Benang*; plays such as Jack Davis' *First Born* trilogy, Jimmy Chi's *Corrugation Road* and Rodney Hall's *A Return to the Brink*; history paintings and sculptures by artists such as Gordon Bennett, Robert Campbell Jnr, Fiona Foley, Gordon Hookey and H.J. Wedge; art histories such as Peter Sutton's *Dreamings*; photography by Leah King-Smith among others; music by No Fixed Address, Yothu Yindi, Kev Carmody, Ruby Hunter and Archie Roach; New Age books such as Robert Lawlor's *Voices of the First Day: Awakening in the Aboriginal Dreamtime*; temporary and permanent exhibitions such as *Power of the Land: Masterpieces of Aboriginal Art, Koorie, Between Two Worlds: The Commonwealth Government and the Removal of Aboriginal Children of Part Descent in the Northern Territory* and *Bunjilaka*; feature films such as *Blackfellas* and *Rabbit Proof Fence*; television drama series such as *Heartland*; documentary films such as *Lousy Little Sixpence, Frontier* and *Freedom Ride*; and countless feature articles, profiles, background stories and documentaries by journalists in radio, television and newspapers.

Needless to say, perhaps, there has been a large demand for much of this history-making, mostly among settler Australians. Had there not been, much of it would never have been produced. As we saw in the previous chapter, the increasing significance of Aboriginal history for Australian culture eventually led to it being appropriated as political capital by mainstream parties. At the same time, it has also played an important role in the rise of a new phenomenon: 'the public intellectual'. This figure, as David Carter has explained, is usually regarded as 'an "independent thinker": not an academic or not "just" an academic; not a specialist or expert, or not "just" a specialist'; but as someone 'prepared to range over questions of general cultural significance, always addressing their moral dimension'. In recent years, Carter has argued, public intellectuals have assumed a greater and greater presence in public forums, particularly in the media, by trading in ideas, ethics and conscience in reference to the most controversial questions of the day. Many of these have been closely connected to questions of place and race in the nation, especially in relation to Aboriginal matters such as land rights and native title, child removal, an apology, and reconciliation, but also the republic, multiculturalism, refugees and asylum-seekers. Among the writers Carter has in mind are Inga Clendinnen, Peter Craven, Robert Dessaix, Tim Flannery, Morag Fraser, Raimond Gaita, Helen Garner, David Malouf, Robert Manne, Drusilla Modjeska, Peter Read, Henry Reynolds, Andrew Riemer and Imre Salusinszky. Many of these public intellectuals have interpreted the controversies regarding these matters as moments of moral crisis for the nation. As a result of the rise of the public intellectual, Carter suggests, new kinds of public comportment, new forms of historical or moral authority and new modes of writing have come into being, which have often had considerable success.[28]

For the most part, these public intellectuals do not work as professional historians, most have no background in the field of Aboriginal history, and nearly all have rejected (as 'postmodernism') the democratic implications for intellectual work which have been thrown up, for example, by much of the Aboriginal history-making in recent decades. Their rise to prominence, Carter observes, 'has less to do with expertise than with the (real or apparent) embodiment of certain kinds of ethical or aesthetic qualities'. The mode they have favoured for their discourse has not been the scholarly historical monograph, but rather the essay, the memoir and (auto)biography (though more often than not there has been a merging of these genres), as well as writings in the mainstream press. Many of these, Gillian Whitlock has argued, have been provoked by Aboriginal history-making; in her terms, black testimony has triggered white memoir. In their work, many public intellectuals have fashioned an authorial presence in such a way as to connect their own personal histories to public issues of history and politics, and have thereby claimed an authoritative role for themselves as moral guides or arbiters for the nation. As Carter remarks, the public intellectual has come to be seen as 'a romantic hero, summoning the nation's conscience, bearing witness for us all and embodying the full burden of culture'. Robert Manne is probably the best-known example of this figure. A professor of political science, he has become a political commentator who has increasingly (re)turned to Australian history, and history as a discipline, in order to address questions about the nation. Many of these figures have offered a good deal, Carter points out, but they are a limited good. Their abundance has resulted in both a narrowing and a containment of public debate. Carter notes: 'The very gravitas, the weight of moral authority, evoked by Manne [and others] seems to silence other voices, other pleasures, other politics'. 'It's time', he suggests, 'to recall the virtues of historical work that is not about ethical performance or personal intensity'.[29]

Authority

The democratisation of history in recent decades has meant that many different historical narratives now jostle for acceptance in the public realm. The fact that history is enjoying such a boom has meant that these struggles over historical authority have become vitally important. In the case of Aboriginal history, this has been especially so because, as we have noted, not only have different stories been told by different people but they have told them in different forms and in different forums, and this history has become central to the definition of national identity. Stories that were once not regarded as history, such as myths, testimonies and films, are now frequently called histories; story-tellers who have never been called historians before, such as Aboriginal informants, museum curators and political scientists, now have this status or have it thrust upon them. All these history-makers claim their stories are true, of course, but the procedures they adopt to determine and demonstrate the truthfulness of their narratives vary enormously. As Dipesh Chakrabarty would argue, such a situation has given rise to '"relativist" talk about historical facts, divergent perspectives, multiple narratives'.[30]

This can be illustrated by a consideration of the various ways in which the conflict of the frontier has been represented. The works of research and synthesis that were originally done by academic historians specialising in Aboriginal history (and which have continued to be done), sought to reconstruct a picture of the frontier on a large canvas, such as the country, a colony, or a large part of a colony. To do this, historians mostly relied upon a range of written sources; they seldom drew on Aboriginal oral sources (even though they had often done some oral history) or upon settler myths (though they had often read these). Their accounts tended to works of exposition and analysis more than of narrative, and for the most part they used the language of the contemporary sources to describe settler violence. So, for example, Henry Reynolds has written a series of books based almost entirely on the contemporary and near-contemporary white record. In these he has sought to demonstrate the incidence of frontier conflict across Australia in the nineteenth and twentieth centuries and to explain why this violence occurred. He has argued that the conflict amounted to war and was widespread, but also contends that this was sporadic inasmuch as it was scattered and uneven, and so is best referred to as 'frontier skirmishing'. He has paid very little attention to white atrocities and has echoed contemporaries by referring to the worse examples of settler violence as 'punitive expeditions'. Reynolds has seldom referred to massacres unless he has been considering large-scale killings that have long been described in these terms (such as the Coniston massacre) or quoting contemporary treatments of violence. In the book where he most considers punitive expeditions, *This Whispering in Our Hearts*, he does so because he is focusing on humanitarians who, he points out, 'had a particular horror of the punitive expedition which, by its nature, was bloody, indiscriminate, disproportionate'. Other academic historians made a little more reference to massacres in their consideration of frontier conflict, but they also referred to ones in which Aborigines were the perpetrators (such as the Hornet Bank massacre). Like Reynolds, though, they did not contend that settler violence was dominated by such atrocities.[31]

This treatment of frontier conflict can be contrasted with that found in Aboriginal histories. These have almost all been very local in their focus, and they have tended to be based on Aboriginal people's own oral traditions and/or populist white writings, rather than the contemporary historical record. These Aboriginal histories do not seek to emulate the empirical studies of academic historians described earlier. Instead, they are narratives that more often than not assume the form of myth. They tend to render the past in terms of an event or events like massacres which, their tellers hold, are symbolic of the nature of frontier relations. An example of this is Mary Coe's *Windradyne: A Wiradjuri Koorie*. This is not only true for Aboriginal histories, though. Often local white settler traditions also relate the frontier past in terms of massacres, as David Roberts and Mark McKenna have pointed out.[32]

As Aboriginal history was democratised and became popular among the producers and consumers of books on the subject, accounts that represented frontier violence in dramatic terms of white massacres of Aborigines became more common, particularly among the authors of *narrative* histories, which had started to enjoy a revival as a form of historical writing. So, for example, at a time when academic historians had begun to shift their focus away from conflict and on to a broad range of relations on the frontier, a journalist, Roger Milliss, wrote a mammoth narrative history, *Waterloo Creek*, on the so-called Australia Day massacre of 1838, which was published as a trade hardback by a mainstream publisher in the early 1990s. In a similar fashion, a missionary teacher turned historian, Neville Green, told a local story, *The Forrest River Massacres*, which was framed by an oral tradition Aboriginal people in the East Kimberleys had related to Green in the 1960s, and this was published by a non-academic press that has made a name for publishing some fine historical works about Western Australia. As well as work of this nature, there have been much more populist works by journalists such as Bruce Elder's *Blood on the Wattle: Massacres and the Maltreatment of Australian Aborigines since 1788* and Phillip Knightley's *Australia: Biography of a Nation*, none of which was based on serious historical research by the authors. In other forms of history such as documentary films, which also tend to favour narrative and use a small number of examples to illustrate their points, there has also been a greater focus on events, such as massacres, rather than processes and structures, which are revealed in the small-scale incidents of violence typifying conflict between Aborigines and settlers. The television series *Frontier* is a case in point, despite an academic historian (Henry Reynolds) being engaged as one of its historical consultants.[33]

As Aboriginal history became the subject of other disciplines, so frontier conflict came to be portrayed in starker terms than academic historians had been representing it in their scholarly studies. For example, a political scientist, Rodney Smith, has mistakenly characterised frontier conflict in a textbook, *Australian Political Culture*, in terms of 'massacres' such as Forrest River. In part, this is because he has drawn on a small and narrow range of historical works, which includes a local narrative history of a massacre (Green's *Forrest River Massacres*); in part it is because he has misunderstood the historical framework of another (Reynolds' *This Whispering in Our Hearts*). Yet, even where historical research has been conducted, authors trained in disciplines other than history—for example, anthropologists and linguists—have used research methods that have mostly comprised a focus on the local rather than the regional or the national and the collection of oral testimony rather than archival data, and this has tended to lead to greater emphasis on particular events deemed to be symbolic, such as massacres, rather than the general pattern of frontier conflict.[34]

Truth

As histories of the Aboriginal past have increased, not only in number but in the range of their authors and the forms in which the past is represented, there has been a greater demand for historical truth. In an age of rapid change, it seems that many have turned to the past or history in the hope that it can somehow be a source of stability and certainty. At the same time, though, contemporary forms of technology—nearly all computer based, such as the World Wide Web—have become readily available and have served to democratise the production of knowledge, including history. They have provided a means of simulating the world in powerful ways, which has made it more and more difficult to distinguish between reality and appearance.

The democratisation of history has made it difficult to agree on what historical truth comprises. Are there not many truths, which differ according to the subjectivity of the author, their political beliefs, and so on? As the English historian Richard Evans has noted, questions like these have preoccupied historians for a long time, but in recent years 'they have become, if anything, more urgent and more perplexing than ever before'. This is especially true of Aboriginal history, since it has become a complex historical field in which history is being represented by different kinds of authors, for different purposes, in different forms and for different audiences. This, of course, has posed the question of how these different histories and their truths can be handled or negotiated, which ultimately entails a larger question about the nature of democracy in a nation state such as Australia.[35]

POLITICS

•• 3

During the 1990s, critical histories in Australia increasingly came under attack. By the middle of the decade, the account of the Aboriginal past presented in these had been cast as the principal example of a so-called politically correct history. At the turn of the century, Aboriginal history was subjected to a full-scale 'history war'.

The politicising of Aboriginal history

Unlike historical controversies such as the German historians' dispute (*Historikerstreit*) in the mid-1980s and the Goldhagen affair in the mid-1990s in Europe and elsewhere, in which academics played the leading roles, but like the *Enola Gay* imbroglio in the United States in the mid-1990s,[1] the historical controversy over Aboriginal history has been dominated by public intellectuals, few of whom have any contemporary relationship with the universities.[2] More particularly, it has largely been created by the work of a loosely connected group of public intellectuals who have been called 'Howard intellectuals', since they have promoted and backed Prime Minister John Howard and his Liberal–National Party government.[3] (By contrast, those such as Robert Manne might be called 'Keating intellectuals'.) In the war on Aboriginal history and/or culture, the principal figures across the 1990s and into the 2000s have been Geoffrey Blainey, Ron Brunton, Peter Coleman, Michael Duffy, P.P. McGuinness, Christopher Pearson, Roger Sandall and Keith Windschuttle. Minor roles have been played by Piers Ackerman, Janet Albrechtsen, Andrew Bolt, Frank Devine, Miranda Devine, Gerard Henderson, Peter Ryan, Paul

Sheehan and Angela Shanahan. They have presented more or less the same basic line. There are no doubt differences between these figures, but during the controversy renewed by Keith Windschuttle's book, *The Fabrication of Aboriginal History*, they seldom made these a matter of public knowledge.[4]

Nearly all these public intellectuals have worked in the print media as columnists, reviewers and editors. Indeed, they have come to have considerable power there. Many have been employed by Rupert Murdoch's News Limited newspapers, most of which have been broadsheets rather than tabloids, but some have also been engaged by the Fairfax press (which publishes the Melbourne *Age* and the *Sydney Morning Herald*). They now considerably outnumber alternative political voices in these forums. Nearly all have been connected to the conservative or new conservative journals of opinion, *Quadrant* and/or *The New Criterion*. Some have been associated with neo-conservative organisations in the United States and Australia, such as the American Enterprise Institute and the Institute of Public Affairs. Several, such as the former Liberal Party politician and *Quadrant* editor Peter Coleman, have long-standing conservative connections; a few, such as the current editor of *Quadrant*, P.P. McGuinness, were once radicals at the opposite end of the political spectrum. A small number have been very closely connected to the Howard government. The columnist Christopher Pearson, for example, was one of Howard's speechwriters when the Coalition first won government and was later appointed to the board of the National Museum of Australia.[5] Most can be regarded as part of a growing class of people whose work, by and large, is simply that of politics.[6]

Over many years now, the broadsheet newspaper the *Australian* has played a particularly important role in controversies over Australian culture and history—and not always from the aggressively new conservative stance it has adopted in the controversy over Aboriginal history. (For example, it once broadly supported the agenda of reconciliation, including native title, backed the cause of the republic and broke the refugee children overboard affair.) There are probably several reasons for this, only some of which are specific to the *Australian*. Over many decades, the broadsheet newspapers have faced severe competition from other forms of media, and their circulation has fallen considerably. In the struggle for market share, these newspapers have had to look for ways of enhancing their appeal. The *Australian* has sponsored certain kinds of debates and the figures to organise these, and has sought to create itself as an alternative source of knowledge to the universities. In keeping with its name, the *Australian* has always cast itself as a national newspaper, not only by seeking to report nationally but also by trying to articulate matters it has regarded as important for the nation and national identity. In doing this, it presumably sees itself as meeting the needs of its readership, two-thirds of whom are university educated. It devotes more space than any other Australian newspaper to controversies that might appeal to this audience. In performing this task, it has relied less upon its journalists reporting news and more on its columnists (who have primarily been or have become Howard intellectuals in recent years) to fuel these controversies, which its journalists then cover.[7]

For the most part, the assault unleashed by the Howard intellectuals on Aboriginal history has not been the result of any real degree of familiarity with this broad discursive field. Instead it has been determined largely by a political theory. In other words, their assault has been determined by a political stance. Since the principal charge they have levelled against the field of Aboriginal history is a claim about *its* political nature, this is rather ironic. The Howard intellectuals have adopted and adapted a theory promulgated by new conservatives in the United States. They tell a story that goes as follows. An unrepresentative cosmopolitan and university-educated elite have had a vested interest in advancing particular values, interests and policies in the public realm. They have favoured 'special interests', such as environmentalism, feminism, indigeneity, multiculturalism and other 'minority' causes. These are actually fashions. Their promoters regard themselves as morally superior, yet their causes have no authentic ethical dimension and no real public value. Most derive from overseas trends and international organisations related to 'human rights'. This elite originated in the 1960s among the left in universities, where they have since entrenched themselves. There they have corrupted knowledge and learning by championing theory (postmodernism) and politics (Marxism), betrayed Western civilisation and its canon, and created a regime of 'political correctness' that has censored freedom of thought and expression. Beyond the university, this elite has betrayed the interests of 'ordinary people', subverted the principle of equal rights for citizens, threatened the sovereignty and unity of the nation, and restricted freedom of speech by promoting the interests of 'special groups' rather than 'the mainstream'. The influence of this elite largely explains the major cultural changes that have occurred in Western societies since the 1960s. Its damaging, even destructive, impact must be curtailed for the sake of ordinary people and the nation (whose interests this new conservative elite claims to represent).[8]

In Australia, the Howard government and its intellectuals have probably emphasised some parts of this American story more than their American counterparts. Most importantly, they seem to have highlighted 'historical correctness' in their attack on 'political correctness'. Here, Howard's adoption of the term 'black armband history' has played an important role. This made it seem a greater problem than Geoffrey Blainey suggested when he coined the term. Similarly, they have accused scholars in the academy of playing a much greater role in public life than that conceived by American new conservatives.[9]

Howard's intellectuals have conducted their assault on this so-called academic elite by adopting the strategies of American new conservatives. Left-wing critics Guy Rundle and Paul Gillen have suggested that these public intellectuals have had little, if any, respect for the rules of civility that have traditionally governed much public discourse in Australia. Their style is often aggressive and confrontational, as they declaim and denounce with enormous gusto. They tend to assert rather than argue a case and they distort rather than clarify the matters at stake. They frequently treat their opponents as enemies rather than as adversaries—indeed, they demonise them, making malicious attacks on the reputations of their opponents. They often make allegations that are unwarranted, including some that are outrageously misleading. They repeatedly take words out of context and manipulate them to stoke indignation and provoke outrage. And they have little genuine interest in discussing the subjects on which they comment, let alone engaging in measured debate about them.[10]

In keeping with their political theory, the assault that the Howard intellectuals launched on Aboriginal history focused on the work of a particular generation of academic historians. (This will be discussed further below.) They also tended to represent the controversy over Australia's

Aboriginal past in terms of a gladiatorial contest between white historians, mostly between Keith Windschuttle and Henry Reynolds or Windschuttle and Robert Manne. (Many public meetings repeated this formula.) This strategy was anticipated by the manner in which two earlier historical controversies over Australian history had been cast by these new conservative intellectuals: as combats between two of Australia's best known historians, Geoffrey Blainey and Manning Clark, or Blainey versus the rest.[11] More particularly, some of these writers had previously mounted a vicious attack on Clark's reputation. As a result of the general approach these public intellectuals adopted in their war on history, they drew attention away from history as the past, making it appear as though it is merely a matter of representation.[12]

The Howard intellectuals have largely undertaken their work in the print media, which is peculiarly well suited to their rhetorical style. As Catharine Lumby has remarked, 'conflict is accorded an extremely high value in the news hierarchy'. For news worldwide, it is the third most supported criterion; in Australia, it is the first. As anyone who reads a daily

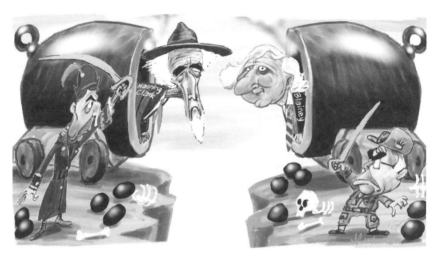

In the 1990s, both the Keating and Howard governments increasingly deployed history and historians as political weapons in their struggle over national culture. In September 2003, this cartoon illustrated a column in the *Australian*, in which one of its senior editors cast historical conflict in terms of 'rival story-tellers'. (Peter Nicholson, *Australian*, <www.nicholsoncartons.com.au>)

newspaper knows, 'the media tend to map political and cultural debates in oppositional terms'. In the war these public intellectuals launched on Aboriginal history, they repeatedly cast the matter in black and white terms and rarely captured the complexity that, as we have seen (in Chapter 2), characterises the interpretive work done in the field professionally.[13]

At the same time, the democratisation of history has created conditions ripe for the Howard intellectuals. The decline of the traditional hierarchies of expertise and knowledge means anyone and everyone can 'do' history or comment on historiographical matters. Likewise, these intellectuals have been the beneficiaries of a world in which it is increasingly difficult to distinguish between reality and appearances.

Keith Windschuttle

In 2000, the cause of the Howard intellectuals acquired a new ally in their culture and history war: Keith Windschuttle. Windschuttle was born in a suburb of Sydney in 1942 and raised there by his parents, who might be described as working class or lower middle class. At seventeen years of age he began work as a copy boy for a daily newspaper, the *Daily Telegraph*. He soon became a cadet journalist and worked as a reporter for six years on several Sydney newspapers and magazines. In 1965, Windschuttle enrolled as a full-time arts student at the University of Sydney. During this time, he was a Marxist. He became involved in the New Left, particularly in its opposition to the Vietnam War, preached violent overthrow of society and campaigned against American imperialism. He also edited the student union's newspaper and founded a radical magazine. He majored in history and obtained the rare distinction of a first class honours degree. Subsequently, he won a scholarship to do a PhD and was appointed to a short-term contract tutorship in the School of History at the University of New South Wales. During his time as a graduate student, Windschuttle received some further training as a historian by attending seminars in historical method at the University of Sydney. However, he never completed his thesis, which was to be a study of the making of the Australian working class, emulating the Marxist historian E.P. Thompson's great work. The thesis was the only component of a PhD degree in history in the Australian university system, so Windschuttle never earned a doctorate in the subject.

Some time later, though, he attained an MA in Political Science from Macquarie University (apparently for a study of unemployment).[14] From the mid-1970s, Windschuttle worked at a succession of institutions of tertiary education—the New South Wales Institute of Technology, the University of Wollongong, the University of New South Wales and Macleay College (which his wife established)—where he taught several different subject areas, including history, media studies, sociology, social policy and journalism. However, he never worked in a university department or school of history again. During these years, he wrote prolifically on what he has called 'issues in Australian society'. Some of this work had a historical dimension, but Windschuttle did not style himself as a historian. Nor was he a part of the historical profession or party to its work during a time when considerable changes were occurring in the way historians went about their work as researchers and writers. In the course of the 1980s, he became a social democrat before being attracted by the new conservatism.[15] In 1992 he resigned from the University of New South Wales. Around this time, he returned to the discipline of history—or at least to historiography—writing a swingeing attack on postmodernism, *The Killing of History*, first published in 1994 by Macleay Press, which Windschuttle himself runs.[16]

Between 2000 and 2002, Windschuttle published a series of articles and a book in which he assailed Aboriginal history. He argued that there had been an orthodox school of academic historians and that they had been responsible over the past 30 years for creating a story about widespread mass killings on the Australian frontier. Their work had been determined by a common intellectual framework, which governed the assumptions they made, the questions they asked, the research they undertook, the arguments they presented and the manner in which they interpreted their sources. In particular, according to Windschuttle, the work of this school has been defined by the approach of one historian: Henry Reynolds. These historians hardly ever criticise one another's work, but collude instead. This orthodoxy has functioned as a moral regulator, which has 'prevented thought, proscribed research and impeded the development of a more convincing interpretation'. Most importantly, this 'Reynolds generation' has had overt political objectives—indeed, a political agenda. They are left-wing historians of the 1960s and their historiography reflects what Windschuttle calls the academic politics of the period since this era. They have produced 'a version of Australian history designed to serve highly politicised ends'. Some, such as Reynolds, have become prominent activists and have been very successful in shaping government policy. They and/or others of the same persuasion have also played politics in the universities. They have ensured that historical dissenters are not employed as Australian historians in Australian universities and/or that these historians have remained quiet or abandoned the subject of Aboriginal history, made it difficult for recalcitrant authors to get their work published, and forced those such as Geoffrey Blainey out of the academy. As a result of the politicisation of academic history, the historians in the field of Aboriginal history have abandoned the critical standards of historical methodology and so ruined history. Most of their scholarship is 'very poorly founded, other parts are seriously mistaken, and a good deal of it is outright fabrication'. They only use sources that support their argument and omit, suppress or falsify the rest, and they make little critical assessment of the reliability of those sources they use as evidence. This amounts to academic deception and corruption. Consequently, their history of the Australian frontier does not rest on a body of historical evidence but is merely a fiction or a fabrication that has little basis in reality.[17]

In large part, there was nothing original in Windschuttle's assault. Its central claim about a politicised history repeated what conservative public intellectuals had been claiming for almost twenty years. What was new was his charge of fabrication.[18]

A history warrior

Windschuttle and his work have been peculiarly well suited for the war on Aboriginal history that the Howard intellectuals conceived. This is so for several reasons, which will be considered here at some length. (In the second part of the book, his specific arguments about the historiography and history of colonialism in Australia will be tested.) First, and perhaps most importantly, Windschuttle is genuinely concerned about truth. Unless this fact is accepted, it is difficult to understand his work or project. In respect of the conflict over Aboriginal history in which he has become involved, Windschuttle has asserted: 'I am trying to find the truth of the matter . . . My self is really irrelevant in this'. A consideration of Windschuttle's work over 30 or more years suggests that one of his ongoing preoccupations—in fact, probably the major one—has been truth. This is evident in the titles of three of his books: *Fixing the News: Critical Perspectives on the Australian Media* (1981), of which he was a co-editor; *The Killing of History: How a Discipline is Being Murdered by Literary Critics and Social Theorists* (1994); and *The Fabrication of Aboriginal History* (2002). The content of these, as well as other books he has authored, suggests that Windschuttle actually has a zealous commitment to truth and, moreover, that this is closely related to the matter of representation. Significantly, most of his work is informed by a conviction that truth is being endangered. Indeed, his concern for truth has long been informed by a perception that it has fallen into the hands of a powerful elite of which he is not a part.[19] In *Fixing the News*, the truth is manufactured by a monopoly-owned mass media in Australia that presents 'a distorted view of reality';[20] in *The Killing of History*, historical truth is being undermined by postmodern theory ('Paris Labels and Designer Concepts'), peddled by Michel Foucault, Jacques Lacan, Jacques Derrida, Michel de Certeau, Giles Deleuze, Jean-François Lyotard, Marshall Sahlins and Hayden White among others, and by academic historians, such as Simon Schama, Greg Dening and Inga Clendinnen, who have fallen under its pernicious influence; in *The Fabrication*, as we have noted, there is a 'ruling intellectual environment' that has controlled work and distorted the story.[21] The perception informing this work, it can be argued, is at odds with the actual situation. In most of these books, it can be argued, Windschuttle is engaged in a tremendous battle for truth against chimerical forces that he appears to have largely imagined. As the foregoing information might suggest, truth is not just a major concern in Windschuttle's work, it amounts to a cause. It has to be upheld at all costs, otherwise all is lost. In *The Killing of History*, he fears that historical knowledge will fall into an abyss: all 'postmodernists' reject aspects of the scientific method based on observation and inductive argument, and most deny 'the ability of human beings to gain any direct contact with or access to reality' and that 'we can know anything with certainty', and so the search for historical truth is threatened with extinction; in *The Fabrication* he frets: 'If the factual details are not taken seriously, then people can invent any atrocity and believe anything they like. Truth becomes a lost cause'.[22]

Windschuttle's role in the recent historical controversy not only owes much to his passion for truth, but also his conception of it. Even though it is significant in his work, truth for Windschuttle is not a complex or complicated affair. Truth is black and white; there are no greys. Consequently, seeking truth is not a matter of making fine distinctions. In keeping with this, Windschuttle tends to reduce historical truth to a matter of facts. In reference to *The Killing of History*, an American historian, Margaret Jacobs, has remarked that Windschuttle has a tendency to assume that 'history is about the search for truth *tout court*', while in regard to his work in Aboriginal history Australian historian Tom Griffiths has suggested that Windschuttle's argument that much frontier violence has been fabricated is 'partly a campaign for a simpler empiricism'. Windschuttle's approach to truth is informed by, and informs, a practice of reading that is often naïve. He has repeatedly taken what authors say at face value. On occasions when he has belatedly realised that their truth claims are a matter of interpretation and perspective rather than fact, he apparently feels he has been misled, even duped, and he has lashed out at the authors, rather than reflecting upon a reader's responsibility to read critically.[23]

Windschuttle's simple conception of truth is paralleled by an equally simple understanding of reality. Indeed, one is probably a consequence of the other. He seems to assume that reality is going to disappear unless we all believe very hard in it. In his work, Windschuttle seldom grapples with the messy reality of the world—past or present—but tends to caricature it instead. Reviewers of both *The Killing of History* and *The Fabrication* have been struck by this. In reference to the former, Jacobs referred to Windschuttle's 'simplemindedness', and Graeme Davison commented upon his 'simplified view of the historiographical landscape' and his refusal to consider 'shades of difference between or within works'; with regard to the latter, Inga Clendinnen observed that Windschuttle 'detests ambiguity' and projects 'an artificial simplicity on to the world of the past', and Alan Atkinson commented that he 'almost deliberately argues against the complexity of human nature, its mix of cruelty and kindness, beauty and evil'.[24]

The simple conception of reality and truth that Windschuttle promotes has enormous appeal in the modern democratic world of multiple and

MAY 17, 2003   THE SYDNEY MORNING HERALD MAGAZINE

GOODWEEKEND

Meet Mr Right
Combative historian Keith Windschuttle claims the left is
all wrong about white settlement, black massacres and their role in our past.
You got a problem with that?

by Jane Cadzow

PLUS: Bringing a classic to the screen ● Tattoo parlours go lifestyle ● World's best press photos

A history of blacks and whites, or histories in black and white? In the autumn of 2003 Keith Windschuttle posed with the family dogs, Bobby and Teddy, for a profile in the weekend magazine of two of the country's leading newspapers. Another caption read: 'There are few shades of grey in Keith Windschuttle's life'. (Sahlan Hayes/Fairfax Publications)

competing discourses and images. It meets a utopian demand for a stable reality that includes stable histories. Yet, in a contradictory manner, the central dynamic of books such as *The Killing of History* and *The Fabrication* consists of its author imagining an enormous threat to truth or reality by exaggerating any challenge that has been presented to it, and then attacking this spectre in order to settle down the danger that he unwittingly created in the first place. This tumultuous movement seems to lie at their very heart.

Simple conceptions of reality and truth often tend to lead to conflict for the self and a society. They constitute such a fragile bedrock for being in the world that they are inevitably unsettled. When the little stability they offer someone is threatened, the usual reaction is one of aggression. This is evident in Windschuttle's *Killing of History*. The American historian Dominick LaCapra has suggested that the basic purpose of Windschuttle's attacks on other historians, philosophers of history, literary critics, and so forth in this book seems to have been a ritualistic one of 'shoring up an embattled faith, exorcising one's own anxieties, and making convenient scapegoats of those who challenge one's point of view'. He has described Windschuttle's book as a 'reductive and indiscriminate survey' in which its author makes 'sweeping indictments of the current critical scene'. LaCapra also points out that in Windschuttle's broadside he has a tendency to construct an invading 'other'. This lends itself to fighting a war. So, too, does another tendency several critics have discerned in Windschuttle's *Killing of History*. LaCapra notes that Windschuttle amalgamates very different and at times mutually inconsistent approaches into one; Daniel Gordon remarks that Windschuttle lumps many thinkers together to such an extent that he polarises the debate and reduces the ability of readers to imagine the middle ground; and Jacobs observes that Windschuttle's approach contributed to a demonology conjured up by the culture wars in the United States. In *The Killing of History*, then, it is apparent that Windschuttle adopts a scapegoating mechanism that generates binary oppositions by projecting doubts about truth, as well as attendant anxiety regarding this, onto others. It is a means of trying to regain some 'original' security that others have ruined or made 'us' lose.[25]

The costs of such an approach intellectually are considerable, it should go without saying. Several reviewers of *The Killing of History* remarked upon this. LaCapra pointed out that Windschuttle's representation of the work of others lacks critical discrimination and that he has bowdlerised the complex figures he lambasts. Gordon was similarly troubled by such misrepresentation. At one point in his discussion he comments: 'Reading Windschuttle, I was troubled by the thought that not all his readers would know first-hand the thinkers to whom he refers and hence could not decide for themselves if his descriptions were accurate'; at another: 'Windschuttle is reading [Michel] Foucault as many of his opponents do but in a way that is simply unjust'. Significantly, Gordon pointed out that 'Windschuttle exaggerates the degree to which contemporary theorists deny the possibility of attaining truths about the past'. Another American scholar, Bradford DeLong, who has no sympathy for 'postmodernism', reported that reading Windschuttle's book made him feel like Tonto in the joke: '*Lone Ranger*: "Indians behind us, indians in front of us, indians to the right of us, indians to the left of us. I guess we're surrounded, old buddy". *Tonto*: "What do you mean 'we', white man?"' He also confessed that 'much of Windschuttle's book made me feel embarrassed for Windschuttle':

> Some of it is that Windschuttle's argument has all the precision of an exploding medieval bombard: his list of 'enemies of history' extends from Perry Anderson (who from beneath his Marxist blinders has always tried as hard as he can to tell the history as it really happened) and Terry Eagleton (who hates post-modernists with a passion) to David Hume (!) and Jürgen Habermas (?) to Thomas Kuhn (huh?) and Quentin Skinner to Jacques Derrida and Michel Foucault (OK, he has a point there) to Francis Fukuyama (whose claim that history has 'ended' is intelligible only to a card-carrying Hegelian idealist; for the rest of us what 'we' knew as history goes on in spite of the 'end of history') and Simon Schama.[26]

These weaknesses, however, are unimportant when one is fighting a history war. Indeed, they amount to strengths in this context.[27]

Despite the flaws in Windschuttle's approach to the work of an intellectual, he and other Howard intellectuals made claims for his authority as a writer by referring to his academic training. Windschuttle's training as a historian is not inconsiderable, however limited it might seem to a younger generation of academic historians.[28] Windschuttle and his backers also referred to his earlier work, in particular *The Killing of History*, claiming it as a work of history and asserting that it was an acclaimed study.

Likewise, they claimed that Windschuttle had standing as a historian by alleging that he had published widely on historiography and history in both popular and academic journals and by alleging he was one of Australia's foremost historians.[29] (On one occasion, Windschuttle used the law to defend his 'credit, profession, occupation and reputation' as a professional historian.)[30] In reality, *The Killing of History* is a work of historiography, not history, and it has been more or less damned by leading historiographers in Australia and the United States;[31] it was quite untrue to claim that Windschuttle has published widely on historiography and history in both popular *and* academic journals; and it was obviously false to allege that Windschuttle was one of Australia's leading historians, given his slight record of publication in the field.[32]

Windschuttle's supporters not only presented him as a historical insider in the sense of someone who was a historian and so knew the discipline of history; they also represented him as an outsider by claiming that he was a dissenter courageous enough to attack the prevailing academic 'orthodoxy' that they themselves have constructed. Likewise, Windschuttle was cast as a lone battler and ranger, and as an amateur historian taking

One of the cartoons Peter Nicholson created during the 'history war' of 2002–03 suggested that the bitterly fought struggle for authority between white historians threatened to displace the Aboriginal subjects of the very history they were fighting over. (Peter Nicholson, *Australian*, <www.nicholsoncartoons.com.au>)

on donnish university historians. This ploy has a special appeal in a culture that has championed a myth of egalitarianism: it makes it seem that history is a discipline that is easy to master, which is comforting, and that it is easy for any historical writer to tackle and vanquish a superior foe, which is pleasurable.[33] (Windschuttle's offer to correct any factual mistakes in his work on his website bolsters his appeal as a historian of the people as well as adding to the appearance of being a scholar committed to historical truth.)[34]

Windschuttle was also well suited for the role of conducting a war on Aboriginal history because of his familiarity and acceptance of many of the tenets of American new conservatism, which he helped import into Australia. In its fundamental approach, *The Killing of History: How a Discipline is Being Murdered by Literary Critics and Social Theorists* follows one of the new conservatism's classic texts: Allan Bloom's *The Closing of the American Mind: How Higher Education has Failed Democracy and Impoverished the Souls of Today's Youth*. In his book, Windschuttle repeats the claims made by Bloom and others by arguing that Western civilisation and its canon are under threat from a small academic elite who subscribe to postmodernism and postcolonialism. More specifically, he casts history as one of the triumphs of Western civilisation. Europeans had a history and were the subjects of it because they were always making it, whereas indigenous peoples had no sense of history and were merely the objects of it because they never made it. Further, history was a superior form of knowledge because it had become scientific, whereas the stories of indigenous peoples only amounted to myth. For Windschuttle, there can be only one history—this European objective one—and not a multiplicity of histories. He rejects approaches such as oral history and memory, which place indigenous historical perspectives on an equal footing with Western ones. They amount to cultural relativism and are fatal to the discipline of history. He also rejects the insights of scholars such as Marshall Sahlins, Greg Dening, Inga Clendinnen and Anne Salmond, who have done histories that are cross-cultural in their subject matter and method. In other words, he makes it clear he has no sympathy for the democratic changes that have characterised Aboriginal history as a field. In *The Killing of History*, he also damns historical critics who have taken the high moral ground and adopted a politically correct stance against their own countries by attacking colonialism. His attack on straw figures, which we have observed, emulates the new conservative strategy,[35] while his style (which will be discussed later) also resembles theirs.[36]

In the wake of the publication of *The Killing of History*, Windschuttle became connected to American new conservatives. His book was re-published by The Free Press, known to be a bastion of American new conservatism (since it has published titles such as Bloom's *The Closing of the American Mind* and Richard Herrnstein and Charles Murray's *The Bell Curve: Intelligence and Class Structure in American Life*). Subsequently, he was invited to give seminars and contribute articles and essays by organ-isations and journals associated with new conservatism and/or the attack on postmodernism, such as the History Society and *The New Criterion*. In time, Windschuttle was welcomed by Australian new conservatives, most importantly those at *Quadrant*, which has published many of his writings on Aboriginal history. Connections of this kind were invaluable when Windschuttle published *The Fabrication*: the editor of *The New Criterion*, Roger Kimball, endorsed the book ('Keith Windschuttle's first volume on the fabrication of Aboriginal history is a scholarly masterpiece. It is destined to become an historical classic') and commissioned a review of it by Geoffrey Blainey ('his book will ultimately be recognised as one of the most important and devastating written on Australian history in recent decades'). P.P. McGuinness also published in *Quadrant* a speech given to launch *The Fabrication* and long articles by Windschuttle and others responding to the critics of the book.[37]

The work of the critic

Keith Windschuttle was also well positioned for the task of attacking Aboriginal history because he has a penchant for the work of the critic—at least as he conceives this role. This might always have been the case, but in recent years he has become an adherent of a political and cultural tra-dition of libertarianism in Sydney, which is often connected with the philosopher John Anderson (though Windschuttle also connects this to the philosopher David Stove). Windschuttle calls this the 'Sydney Line' and has named his own website after it. Anderson was Professor of Philosophy at Windschuttle's alma mater, the University of Sydney, between 1927 and

1958. As his biographer Brian Kennedy has noted, Anderson dedicated his life's work to the task of inculcating 'the spirit of criticism' and encouraging 'the questioning of received opinions and traditions', and assumed a public role as a controversialist, stirrer and gadfly. Indeed, Kennedy emphasises that Anderson had a 'passion to oppose' and an inclination to 'the labour of the negative'. Windschuttle largely defines the 'Sydney Line' in terms of what it opposes, while there can be no doubt that his intellect is also poised for conflict. Anderson's biographer draws our attention to his subject's ambivalence about authority, his authoritarian streak and his lack of sympathy with humanitarian sentiment, as well as his loss of wider sympathies for humankind, his antagonism to religion, his dismissal of mystery and his thwarted romanticism. He also points to Anderson's zeal, extremism and intransigence in debate, his subsequent lack of common sense, decency and tenderness, and his inclination to go out of his way to be intellectually offensive, as well as his delight in disputation for its own sake, his tendency to develop arguments by criticising opposing views and to castigate his enemies rather than vindicate his most characteristic positions, and his denunciatory style of criticism. Further reference is made to his status as an outsider and his warrior characteristics, his weary pessimism (which could readily give way to despair) and his lack of an alternative vision for the future. Some might surmise there is a good deal that is Andersonian about the work of Windschuttle.[38]

Windschuttle's training as a journalist, polemicist and a propagandist has stood him in good stead for the task he has assumed in the war on Aboriginal history. As a journalist, he learned the art of clear writing as well as how to win a reader's attention by a striking storyline, an arresting turn of phrase or a sensational headline. As a polemicist, he knows how to render complex matters simple, create oppositions and deploy hyperbole. As a former activist, who worked by means of propaganda, he understands the value of spectacular attacks on symbolic targets such as particular events and particular people. Nearly all of Windschuttle's work as an academic also prepared him for the role he has played. He seldom wrote for academic peer-reviewed journals, but instead penned articles for political and popular magazines, such as *Australian Society*. The body of work Windschuttle produced as an academic was intensely political. Indeed, this was its *raison d'être*.

Windschuttle's personal style also equipped him well for the role of a warrior in the campaign the Howard intellectuals launched against Aboriginal history. This campaign has been aggressive, vitriolic and denunciatory, and these features also characterised Windschuttle's *Killing of History*, as several reviewers observed. For example, Graeme Davison remarked upon the gladiatorial manner in which Windschuttle conducted debate and Stuart Macintyre pointed out that Windschuttle disposed of theory by rejection instead of rebuttal. In *The Fabrication* Windschuttle repeatedly attacks professional historians in the same excessive manner. He alleges that they invent and falsify stories, falsely reference sources, make up figures, omit, suppress or falsify evidence, and dress up conclusions. He claims they are guilty of sleights of hand, sloppy and misleading work, pure speculation, fabrication, embellishment, wilful omissions, complete misrepresentation, sheer invention and manipulation of sources, and that they fudge their work and deceive their readers. He alleges that they have little interest in exploring the truth, are desperate to shore up their arguments, cannot be bothered to think issues through and have abandoned any critical standard. He maintains that they build their careers from the same shoddy materials, and are arrogant, patronising and lazy. In debates and interviews, Windschuttle has damned historians or their work as grotesque, pathetic and absurd, and accused them of corruption, malpractice and betrayal. In his own words, his style is one of 'take-no-prisoners' and 'no-holds-barred'. As Martin Krygier and Robert van Krieken have observed, Windschuttle pursues his work as a historical critic 'with such a heavy hand that it threatens to turn into, or at least invite, self-parody'. Dominick LaCapra discerned a similar contradiction in *The Killing of History*: 'Windschuttle argues for rationality, detachment [and] objectivity . . . but he does so in a vitriolic style . . . suited to the narrowest form of party-political agitation, if not to a bloody crusade. Moreover, his own approach is affected by the tendencies he condemns'.[39]

Windschuttle and (identity) politics

Keith Windschuttle also seems to have been drawn to the role of a history warrior because he regards himself as one of those who have been adversely affected by the political, social and cultural changes of the last two or three decades. He apparently identifies with those victims he has called 'dead white males'. He holds the 'politically correct' responsible for such changes, accusing the left of abandoning 'the cause of the workers to take up the cause of the Aborigines'. He objects to Aborigines, women, gays, blacks and migrants portraying themselves as oppressed and appropriating the powerful status of a victim, and he blames 'identity politics' for this. He also resents the academy of which he was once a member. He seems to attribute his failure to complete his PhD to the left's influence there: 'hapless postgraduate students like myself . . . tacked fruitlessly in search of local examples of working class heroes who could emulate those found in Britain by Edward Thompson and Eric Hobsbawm'. He has gone so far as to imply that this amounted to a form of oppression that deserves 'the postcolonial term Eurocentrism—or, more accurately, Anglocentrism'.[40]

Above all else, perhaps, Windschuttle bemoans the loss of an ideal of the nation he has belatedly come to embrace as a patriot. Significantly, Windschuttle has characterised this controversy as a debate about 'the character of the nation and, ultimately, the calibre of the civilisation Britain brought to these shores in 1788'. He sees it as a matter of mortal combat. 'This is very serious stuff', he told the journalist Jane Cadzow. 'It's about life and death . . . It's about the foundation of Australia—whether it was a legitimate foundation or whether it was just an imperialist invasion in which they rode roughshod over the Aborigines'. Krygier and van Krieken have suggested that this is the 'subtext that provides the motivation, rationale, the indefatigable energy and the spine of the larger work'.[41]

In a public debate in 2003, Windschuttle told the audience:

> Let me tell you what my intention was. The *last* thing I wanted to do was to write three volumes about Aboriginal history. I mean you'd have to be crazy to want to do it [Laughter from the audience]. Well, really, I mean it's such a huge burden of research. It's going to take years to do it . . . Whether it's worth it or not is now becoming very dubious in my mind. But I set out to write one book . . . with one chapter on Tasmania . . . The reason I ended up writing a volume on Tasmania is that I found so much of the academic story about what happened in Tasmania is corrupt . . . When I discovered they hadn't been telling the truth about this I felt duped. I felt personally affronted . . . Now I've saddled myself with this

huge task . . . It's not something I set out to do . . . If I could go back and change things I probably would never have done it had I realised what I got into.

This (as well as other evidence considered later) suggests that Windschuttle was largely drawn into the field of Aboriginal history for highly subjective reasons. One gets little sense that he has a genuine interest in, or commitment to, expanding our understanding of the colonial past as an end in itself.[42]

The last factor that makes Windschuttle an ideal warrior in this war on Aboriginal history lies in the fact that he is, somehow or other, complicit in the very phenomenon he attacks. At times, Windschuttle seems to acknowledge this, only to claim that this is a matter of the past and so is no longer present. Upon the publication of *The Fabrication*, Windschuttle asserted: 'I was a true believer in the Aboriginal story for 30 years . . . I taught a totally orthodox line'. A few months later he reported: 'I used to tell students that the record of the British in Australia was worse than the Spaniards in America'. At this time he also reflected: 'I suppose what I've been doing for the past decade is trying to undo some of the damage that people like me caused, to show how badly the left got it wrong'. In making these confessions, Windschuttle claims a personal authenticity for his work in keeping with the mode of presentation found in the work of public intellectuals (discussed earlier): I was once one of those politically correct historians in the 1960s and 1970s but I was duped; I have now done my own research, I have repented and I am now here to tell the truth. Yet Windschuttle was *not* one of the historians of Aboriginal history, as we have seen, and this story of violence was not the one they told, as we will see, but the one *he* apparently told his students. (I, for one, have never read any Australian academic historian who has compared the British colonisation of this country to the record of the Spanish in the Americas.) In other words, the politically correct history of settler violence is really a construction or invention of Windschuttle's, not that of the scholars who have worked in this field. Windschuttle's confessional play-acting disguises this. Most importantly, in my opinion, his writings suggest that he has a relationship to his subject-matter that he unconsciously disowns by projecting it onto others (as we shall see in Part II of this book).[43] Indeed, projection seems to provide his work with a direction and a dynamic it would not otherwise have.[44]

As we have observed, much of Windschuttle's intellectual orientation, working experience, mindset, and political training, affiliations and resources made him well suited and/or positioned for participating in a 'history war'—especially one largely fought in the media. He had a zealous commitment to the cause of truth; simple conceptions of truth and reality, and a hostility to those who threaten these; a feeling of certitude and a tendency to be dogmatic; a penchant for the work of the critic; an aggressive style; experience as a journalist; training as a polemicist and a propagandist; connections to new conservatism in the United States and Australia; capital (in the form of Macleay Press); and a familiar but fraught relationship to the academy and the left. As I have suggested, though, nearly all these characteristics mean that he was ill-equipped for the work of a scholarly historian, especially in the field that Aboriginal history has become. Most importantly, perhaps, we have seen here the degree to which the basic arguments he made against Aboriginal history were ones that he had previously made against other forms of knowledge and authority. This does not necessarily mean that his claims are wrong, but it might suggest that these reflect the nature of *his* concerns rather than the actual work of the academic historians he has attacked.

It should be emphasised that Windschuttle began to work on Aboriginal history because its subject matter had become important culturally and politically. It is unlikely he would have entered the field otherwise. Similarly, it is doubtful that his work would have received any serious attention had this historical controversy been conducted in the academy alone. The nature of its impact, moreover, has been the result of the fact that this dispute has largely been played out in a public domain dominated by the mass media. The apparent truthfulness of his writings depends upon a public arena dominated by mass media in which surfaces are readily confused for substance and appearances are often mistaken for reality. Windschuttle's work has all the trappings of academic history—he has done work in the archives; he develops and evidences his arguments as historians do; he provides footnotes—and he and his supporters have made much of this. However, a thorough consideration of Windschuttle's work reveals that it merely *resembles* scholarly history. It looks like history, but in the public media few can tell that it is actually very poor history.

Politics and Aboriginal history

The impact of Windschuttle's work has rested to a large degree on the charge the Howard intellectuals have made regarding 'political correctness'. The success of this claim owes much to the rise of public intellectuals in the Australian media, which was discussed in Chapter 2. In this realm, the Howard intellectuals' misrepresentation of Aboriginal history as merely the work of a small number of highly political academic historians was effective because this claim *seemed* to be true. Henry Reynolds, the only historian in the field of Aboriginal history who has come to have a really high public profile, had increasingly addressed the moral, legal and political dimensions of Australia's Aboriginal history in his work; he had increasingly presented it as though it amounted to a series of stark moral and/or political choices; he had made it clear that he had a strong political commitment to changing the present; and many had come to assume that his work has had legal and political outcomes.[45] The apparent truthfulness of the new conservative allegation that Aboriginal history was dominated by a politically correct approach was furthered when leading public intellectual Robert Manne, whose work is seen in many quarters to move towards judgement rather than understanding, commissioned a book that was represented as *the* response to Windschuttle's *Fabrication*.[46]

In other words, the new conservative attack on Aboriginal history worked because it was *plausible* in the very realm in which this controversy was conducted. It had a germ of truth. In the world of the media, this was enough for the claim about the politicisation of Aboriginal history to perform its highly political work successfully. It did not matter that the allegation Windschuttle and other Howard intellectuals had levelled depended on badly flawed assumptions and assertions rather than soundly based arguments. The weaknesses in Windschuttle's work as a historiographer and a historian will be considered in the second part of this book; here, I will discuss the case he and his supporters have made about politics and Aboriginal history.

Windschuttle, it will be recalled, has claimed that Aboriginal history has been dominated by the baby-boomer generation of academic historians who have a political agenda defined by the left of the 1960s. This picture has several flaws. First, it overlooks the fact that academic historians in this field span four or more generations now, beginning with Charles Rowley and John Mulvaney, born in 1906 and 1925 respectively. Second, the work these historians first conducted on the frontier did influence other academic historians enormously, but it was later subjected to a good deal of criticism and revision, as we observed in Chapter 2.[47] Third, the research of many of these baby boomers, such as Henry Reynolds, has itself changed over the course of many years and has considerable range in terms of its approach and argument. Fourth, few of the historians in the field of Aboriginal history were of the left of the 1960s[48]—Reynolds, for example, was never on the left. (Windschuttle *was*, as we have noted, but he projects this onto the historians of Aboriginal history.) In short, Windschuttle's orthodoxy is a straw person, which serves his purpose of attacking the work of the academy and demonising its historians. This, of course, is common in revisionist projects of this kind. Prior to *The Fabrication of Aboriginal History*, Windschuttle had done the same in *The Killing of History*, as we observed earlier. Such imprecision distinguishes the work of polemicists and propagandists, not scholars.

There is little evidence that politics has had the degree of influence on the field Windschuttle claims it has. It is telling that he evidences little of his argument regarding this (and sometimes provides American examples instead).[49] It is also striking that he does not try to demonstrate in any systematic way how the interpretive work of historians on the colonial era might have been determined by a particular political goal,[50] though such a case *can* be made for some of the research of Reynolds.[51] Windschuttle's account of the influence of politics relies heavily on a sketchy reference to Reynolds' work.[52] However, Reynolds is atypical of the academic historians in the field in several respects, not least in the public profile he enjoys. Windschuttle has also ignored the fact that Reynolds' work has been criticised consistently by academic historians, anthropologists and other scholars, mainly on the grounds of its moral and political dimensions, at the same time as Reynolds has increasingly commanded respect among readers beyond the university, largely for those very qualities.[53]

In making his claim about the influence of politics on Aboriginal history Windschuttle has conflated the work of academic historians with other history-makers. In particular, he has confused the work of journalists, who ply the trade he once practised, with that of academic historians.

More importantly, Windschuttle has exaggerated the influence of academic historians on other history-makers. Indeed, this is absolutely critical to his case against Aboriginal history, despite the fact that he does not even try to demonstrate this. In reality, the case Windschuttle has primarily made against Aboriginal history rests on the fallacy that the rich field of Aboriginal history (described in Chapter 2) is the creature of academic historians. In other words, at the very centre of Windschuttle's argument against Aboriginal history lies an erroneous assumption.

The claim Windschuttle and the other Howard intellectuals have made against politics in Aboriginal history also depends on several broader assumptions and inferences, which we will now consider since these are questionable. First, they seem to assume that present and past can be separated from one another in historical work. This is naïve. As E.H. Carr argued some time ago now, 'we can view the past, and achieve our under-standing of the past only through the eyes of the present'. Second, they fail to realise that the democratisation of history has not so much politicised history-making as exposed the reality that political viewpoints have long pervaded much normal historical practice. Instead, they turn this insight (which comes from democratic history) against Aboriginal history. Third, they seem to assume that political engagement and objective historical scholarship are necessarily in conflict. As such, they infer that a scholar's work can be dismissed simply because of his or her politics. Yet, as the American historian Charles Maier has argued, the assumption that you can separate absolutely scholarship from politics is untenable because this is impossible to achieve. (He also suggests that, even if it were, this would not always have valuable outcomes.) Other historians agree: Richard Evans has argued that it is unrealistic to demand that historians keep their politics out of their historical work; and Peter Novick has contended that schools of historical interpretation are never politically neutral since views of the past are tied in innumerable ways to visions of the present and future.[54]

It makes more sense to assume that subjective factors such as politics play some role in the work of historians and seek to determine at what point these might have influenced their research to such a degree that they have rendered their work untrustworthy. This would require detailed case-by-case attention to the work of historians. Windschuttle has not done this.

His case is crude: he claims that politics has not merely influenced the work of historians, but has instead determined (or largely determined) it; he argues that it has not only determined the subjects they have chosen and the questions they have posed, but also the research they have carried out and the interpretation they have made of historical sources; and he tends to imply that it has corrupted all their work rather than merely parts of it. Windschuttle also assumes that the role of politics in Aboriginal history is exceptional, even aberrant, just as he assumes that there was once a golden age of history in which history was free of politics. There is something very romantic, even utopian, about these assumptions.

Finally, it is difficult to take the pronouncements of Windschuttle and his allies regarding politics in Aboriginal history seriously when their own work is so political. While Windschuttle has damned other historians for being political in their research, he has made very little effort to curb the enormous influence that politics of one kind or another has had on his own writing over many, many years. Instead, he and the other Howard intellectuals maintain the conceit that everyone else is highly political, but they are not. As a result, their readers have been misled.

PART II

• • •

PAST

GENOCIDE

4

In the beginning of Keith Windschuttle's *Fabrication of Aboriginal History* is *that* word and that word is 'genocide'. It frames his book and is critical to its rhetorical work. Its dustjacket reads: 'Tasmania, or Van Diemen's Land as it was originally known, is widely regarded today as the worst example of relations between Aborigines and colonists in Australian history. Historians claim the Tasmanian Aborigines were subject to "a conscious policy of genocide" . . . Keith Windschuttle concludes that, despite its infamous reputation, Van Diemen's Land was host to nothing that resembled genocide or any attempt at it'. Windschuttle advances this same argument in the text. Why did he choose to frame his book in this manner?[1]

In the culture war American new conservatives had launched a decade or so earlier, Rush Limbaugh claimed many American historians had argued that the history of the United States was strewn with examples of genocide. Presumably, Windschuttle knew a similar claim—that Australian historians had treated the frontier in this country as an example of genocide—would have considerable public impact.[2] However, this is not a satisfactory explanation for the symbolic centrality of 'genocide' to Windschuttle's book. Some deeper factors are evidently at work.[3]

Windschuttle's 'genocide thesis'

In April 2001, Keith Windschuttle appeared in an ABC (Australian Broadcasting Corporation) television debate with Henry Reynolds. He spoke about why he had entered the field of Aboriginal history:

I got started in this business when I read [Phillip Knightley's] *The Biography of a Nation* where he said that what the Australian settlers did in the nineteenth century had been done by no other civilised society until the Nazis attacked the Jews in the middle of the twentieth century . . . I knew that was simply absurd. Henry [Reynolds] doesn't compare the Australian settlers in the nineteenth century to the Nazis but he leads other commentators up to the edge of that conclusion. They jump off and we've got the most anachronistic, inaccurate [work] . . . that really distorts the nature of history for all people.

Windschuttle's project is to redeem the character of the nation by correcting such histories. A few months earlier, Windschuttle had spoken to a journalist for the *Australian*, who wrote: 'The Reynolds version, and the body of thinking associated with it, lead, believes Windschuttle, to a history of Australia that portrays frontier pastoralists as murderous, indeed genocidal, a "bunch of Nazis" . . . [H]e says[:] "At the moment the Nazi conclusion is the logical comparison to draw—the Reynolds picture has been shaping our thought about this country for the past 20 years"'. In other words, academic historians are to blame for the kind of attack the journalist Phillip Knightley made on the nation. Windschuttle returns to the matter of genocide in his introduction to *The Fabrication*, where he also asserts: 'The colonial authorities wanted to civilise and modernise the Aborigines, not exterminate them. Their intentions were not to foster violence towards the Aborigines'.[4]

Windschuttle's reaction to 'genocide' owes much to the fact that he has come to his take on Aboriginal history largely through popular historical discourses. It derives from the way the term has been used in these rather than in any academic writings, though in both the concept has been shaken loose of its legal moorings, where it is primarily concerned with the matter of intent or intentions.[5] Significantly, 'genocide' has become, above all else, a marker or register of excess. Particularly in popular usage, it tends to carry two meanings, though these are often so intertwined that they cannot always be disentangled from one another. On the one hand, 'genocide' is a symbol of mass *killing*. In this case, the focus of those using the term is obviously upon actions and the intent of the perpetrators of these actions. It is used to draw attention to the killers. On the other hand,

The democratic politics of history in the age of new conservatism? In April 2001, several months after he had published a few articles in a conservative magazine, Keith Windschuttle (standing) was invited by the National Press Club to debate the leading academic historian in the field of Aboriginal history, Henry Reynolds (seated). Windschuttle claimed that historians such as Reynolds were responsible for 'the majority position that you can compare the Australian colonies of the nineteeth century with Nazi Germany in the twentieth'. He recommended they should 'stand back' and 'look at their creation with a criticital eye'. But whose creation was this 'position'? (Jacky Ghossein/Fairfaxphotos)

'genocide' is a symbol of mass *death*. In this case, the focus of those deploying the term is obviously upon an outcome and the victims. It is used to draw attention to the loss and suffering of a people or a racial group and, while it can be regarded as the outcome of killing rather than some other cause of mass death (such as disease), those using the term are not necessarily concerned with raising moral questions about any responsibility for those deaths. Windschuttle never defines the term but it is apparent that he follows popular usage in using the term in a subjective rather than a scientific sense, and that his focus is upon the question of mass killing and thus the Australian nation and not upon the matter of mass death and thus the Aboriginal people.[6] In reference to 'genocide', Windschuttle has said: 'It's a matter of symbolism and the definition of *Australian* history'.[7]

In *The Fabrication*, Windschuttle quickly cuts to the chase. He begins with the nation, complaining that many Australians did not celebrate its centenary in 2001 but instead focused on a great flaw at the heart of the nation: its treatment of Aboriginal people. He singles out a couple of gestures by the symbolic head of state, Governor-General Sir William Deane—a well-known champion of reconciliation—one of which was an apology he made to the Kija people for a massacre their people had apparently suffered. Windschuttle claims: 'A number of the cultural expressions produced for the centenary took up the same theme and candidly identified where the fault lay: Australia had committed genocide against the Aborigines'. In the space of a few short lines in Windschuttle's book, he has turned someone else's claim of a massacre into a claim of genocide.[8]

Windschuttle implies that during the centennial year there were many expressions of what he calls a 'genocide thesis',[9] but he only considers two examples at any length and his accounts of both can be questioned on one ground or another. The first is Phillip Knightley's *Australia: A Biography of a Nation*. Windschuttle claims it was written for the nation's centenary but, while the book's publicity refers to Federation, it was more likely penned by its expatriate author for a British publisher for an international event, the Sydney Olympic Games, the previous year, which was when it was published. Windschuttle claims that Knightley is one of those who have drawn an analogy between the Nazi genocide and colonialism in Australia. Windschuttle renders this argument thus: 'Australia was allegedly guilty of *conscious, wilful genocide* resembling the kind the Nazis perpetrated against the Jews'.[10]

Windschuttle's second example concerns the National Museum of Australia. He claims that Melbourne architect Howard Raggatt 'borrowed its central construction—shaped as a lightning bolt striking the land—from the Jewish Museum in Berlin, signifying that the Aborigines suffered the equivalent of the Holocaust'; that the Museum knowingly commemorated 'the genocide thesis' by adopting this design for its Aboriginal or 'First Australians' gallery; and that its founding director, Dawn Casey, accused the nation of 'the most terrible crime possible' by describing 'the opening of the institution as "a birthday gift to Australia"'.[11] Windschuttle's allegations rest on several assumptions, which can be faulted.[12] Most importantly, his argument assumes that the exterior appearance of a museum can be taken as a guide to its interior substance. This overlooks the point Dawn Casey made when the Museum opened: 'There is, of course, no mention of any link [to the Nazi German genocide] in our literature or in the content or texts of the museum . . . A diverse range of historians have worked with us creating the Gallery of First Australians . . . They, too, I think, make no association between [the subjects of] our museum and the Jewish one in Berlin'.[13]

Windschuttle claims that his expressions of the so-called genocide thesis occurred because 'the Governor-General, the journalist and the architect were all reflecting the consensus reached by the historians of Aboriginal Australia over the previous thirty years'. Following other Howard intellectuals, Windschuttle argues that this is 'a consensus that has largely been accepted by the country's intellectual and political classes'. These 'politically correct' or 'orthodox' historians, he contends, have 'created a picture of widespread mass killings on the frontiers of the pastoral industry that not only went unpunished but had covert government support. They created the intellectual framework and gave it the imprimatur of academic respectability. They have used terms such as "genocide", "extermination" and "extirpation" so freely that *non-historians* like Deane, Knightley and Raggart [sic] readily drew the obvious connection'. Here Windschuttle conflates radically different phenomena—mass killings, widespread killings and genocide—which follows his earlier transformation of a 'massacre' into 'genocide'.[14]

When Windschuttle proceeds to apply his argument regarding genocide to Van Diemen's Land (as Tasmania was called until 1855), he once more refers to the work of 'non-historians' to support the claim that frames his book. He singles out three journalists or writers: Phillip Knightley, Jan Morris and Robert Hughes. (He also makes reference to the work of others based overseas, such as the international genocide scholar Ben Kiernan.)[15] By repeatedly conflating popular and academic writings, Windschuttle's account leads his readers to assume that there is no difference between their writings and those of 'orthodox' academic historians in Australia, and he again attributes claims regarding genocide to the work of the academic historians who have specialised in Aboriginal history.[16]

Windschuttle gives just two examples to support his claim that academic historians in Australia have argued that Aboriginal people on the

Van Diemonian frontier 'were subject to "a conscious policy of genocide"'. Having first used this turn of phrase—'conscious genocide'—in the course of characterising a popular would-be centenary representation of Australian history (Knightley's), Windschuttle, in his introduction, applies it to the work of academic historians on Van Diemen's Land, explicitly referring to the research of Lyndall Ryan. In the first chapter he returns to the matter and implies that Henry Reynolds is another example of genocide talk of this nature.[17] In between times, Windschuttle co-opts another academic historian—myself—as a supporter of the 'genocide thesis'. Windschuttle provides no evidence for this claim. In my opinion, genocide is neither a necessary nor a useful concept for the task of understanding the nature of the white colonisation of this country.[18] What truth is there in Windschuttle's claims in respect of Ryan and Reynolds? As we shall see, the evidence for Windschuttle's claim that specialist academic historians have argued that Van Diemen's Land is an example of government pursuing a policy of genocide is threadbare.

If a historian presents a thesis (a major argument) about a particular subject, they usually provide a lengthy consideration of it, giving examples and evidence in order to persuade their readers of the case they are seeking to make. Does Lyndall Ryan do this in respect of genocide in Van Diemen's Land? It is quite clear that she does not. Windschuttle cites just two passages from her book, *The Aboriginal Tasmanians*, first published in 1981, to support his claim that she is 'the principal historian of the ruling [genocide] interpretation'. Let us consider both of these. Ryan, Windschuttle writes, 'compared the fate of the Tasmanian Aborigines under the British to that of the Jews under Hitler, noting Clive Turnbull's 1948 book *Black War* provided "a reminder that exterminating policies were not exclusive to Nazi Germany"'. However, Ryan made no such argument in her book. She *did* make reference to Turnbull's argument, but Windschuttle has misunderstood or misconstrued the point she was making. Ryan referred to Turnbull's analogy in order to describe and criticise what she called 'the myth of extermination', which had been propagated by writers such as Turnbull (who was a journalist). She then advanced the principal contention of her book, which was that Tasmania's indigenous peoples were *not* the victims of genocide, but had instead survived British colonisation. Ryan's focus was thus upon the Aboriginal people, not the British. Ryan was writing what has been called *Aboriginal* history. Windschuttle fails to recognise or at least acknowledge this, perhaps because he is preoccupied with trying to redeem the reputation of the *Australian* nation.[19]

What of the other piece of evidence Windschuttle provides to support his argument regarding Ryan's work? 'According to . . . Lyndall Ryan', he writes, 'these *tribal* people were "victims of a conscious policy of genocide"'. As we have noted, Windschuttle has already used this phrase—'conscious policy of genocide'—and he repeats it a few times in his text and has repeated it many times since. It would be reasonable for readers to assume that he has good cause for adopting it to evidence the argument he has chosen to frame *The Fabrication*. However, this is simply not the case. Let us examine carefully what Ryan actually argued in her book. In a chapter on Aboriginal people in Tasmania in the *twentieth* century, she stated: 'It is still much easier for white Tasmanians to regard Tasmanian Aborigines as a dead people rather than confront the problems of an existing community of Aborigines who are victims of a conscious policy of genocide'. It is quite clear that Ryan is *not* referring here to 'tribal people' in the era of the colonial frontier of the *1820s and 1830s*, as Windschuttle implies. Instead, she is referring to the policy of assimilation adopted in Tasmania after the Second World War, which, she argues, denied Aboriginal people their Aboriginality. Furthermore, Ryan called this 'cultural genocide', which is rather different to the 'genocide' Windschuttle attacks in his book, since it refers to an attempt to destroy or deny the identity of Aboriginal people, rather than to kill them. With both his pieces of 'evidence' from Ryan's book, Windschuttle has broken a golden rule by taking words out of their context. As a result, readers have undoubtedly been misled. It seems to me that no impartial reader of Ryan's *Aboriginal Tasmanians* could reasonably infer that her brief discussion of *cultural* genocide in Tasmania in the *mid-twentieth century* constitutes an argument for a conscious policy of *physical* genocide in Van Diemen's Land in the *1820s and 1830s*. In other words, in order for Windschuttle's account of Ryan's book to be regarded as plausible it requires an audience who is unfamiliar with the argument that Ryan actually makes in *The Aboriginal Tasmanians*. This, of course, will comprise most readers of his book.[20]

Inasmuch as Ryan could be said to have made any argument about genocide in respect of the Van Diemonian frontier in her book, she refers to it in its sense of mass death, not mass killing. (She mentions the near-extinction of Aboriginal people there in the nineteenth century, which no one disputes.) Ryan's discussion of government policy in the 1820s and 1830s, moreover, makes it clear that she does not argue that the colonial state in Van Diemen's Land pursued a 'conscious policy of genocide'. She notes that Governor Sir George Arthur, responsible for overseeing the colony during the period of the worse conflict between Aborigines and settlers, had a reputation as a humanitarian. She remarks: 'Arthur saw dispossession as a moral problem, which had to be solved by peaceful and compassionate means'. Furthermore, Ryan describes the various peaceful solutions Arthur tried in order to end the crisis caused by Aboriginal attacks on settlers. None of this is apparent to readers of Windschuttle's *Fabrication*. It should also be noted here that Windschuttle's own account of Arthur's policies basically resembles the one presented by Ryan.[21]

Are Windschuttle's claims regarding Henry Reynolds' work on genocide any more accurate? In his 2001 book, *An Indelible Stain?*, which is devoted to a consideration of the question of genocide in Australia's history, Reynolds in effect asks whether Van Diemen's Land was an example of conscious genocide: 'The question that must now be addressed is this: Did the administration of Governor Arthur adopt policies that had for their avowed or secret object the "extinction of the native race"? Were its senior members guilty of what we now call genocide?' Reynolds argues uncategorically that the answer is no: 'there is no available evidence at all to suggest that it was the intention of the colonial government to effect the extinction of the Tasmanians'. Furthermore, Reynolds challenges the long tradition of misrepresenting Van Diemen's Land as a site of deliberate extermination. In doing this, he critically surveys the work of many writers, including Raphael Lemkin (who coined the term genocide in 1944), before observing: 'Tasmania is usually counted as the site of one of the world's authentic cases of genocide despite the fact that few of the scholars display any first-hand knowledge of Tasmanian history. Indeed, ignorance appears to encourage sweeping and definite pronouncements'. Two pages later, Reynolds again remarks—this time in reference to the journalist Jan Morris' work—'That such an insubstantial piece should be included in a major international study of the history of genocide is an indication of how little is known about Tasmania by this community of scholars, the members of which almost automatically include Tasmania in their list of genocidal tragedies'.[22]

As we have seen, Windschuttle has no evidence for his claim that the leading historians of the *Van Diemonian frontier* have argued that Aboriginal people there were subjected to 'a conscious policy of genocide'.[23] Indeed, it is a furphy. If one were to adopt Windschuttle's rhetoric, one would describe his claim as a fabrication.[24] More specifically, Windschuttle has not provided any evidence for his imputation that academic historians have compared the British colonisation of this country to Nazi Germany's treatment of Jews or caused others to make such a comparison.[25] This is a figment of his imagination. Furthermore, as we have seen, Reynolds makes the very argument *against* genocidal histories of Van Diemen's Land (that is, against histories that allege this is an example of deliberate mass killing) that Windschuttle represents as his own. Windschuttle either fails to realise, or refuses to acknowledge, this. It is, of course, at odds with his principal argument that a politically correct or orthodox school of history led by Reynolds has besmirched the reputation of the Australian nation in this way.[26]

In summary, it is apparent that Windschuttle's treatment of the very matter that frames his book rests upon several fundamental errors and omissions in his account of the research done on the Van Diemonian frontier by scholars working in the field of Aboriginal history. In some instances it is unclear to me whether or not Windschuttle realised he was misrepresenting their work, but in most of the cases I presume he was unaware he was doing this. In the end, though, this is neither here nor there. The handling of the opening subject matter of his book casts considerable doubt upon whether or not readers can trust Windschuttle's rendition of the scholarship he attacks. Readers will recall that this problem was evident in his previous book, *The Killing of History*. In *The Fabrication*, his account might *appear* quite reliable as he discusses and quotes the writings of other historians, yet closer examination reveals that he has repeatedly distorted their interpretations, often by taking these out of the context in which they have been presented. This is only evident to readers who consult the work of the historians whom Windschuttle has attacked. (In the other chapters in this section, I will discuss other examples of Windschuttle's misrepresentation of the academic historiography in the field of Aboriginal history, as well as consider one particular example of Windschuttle's unsatisfactory treatment of historical sources: see Chapter 6, note 13.)

The flaws in what should be called *Windschuttle's* genocide thesis were drawn to his attention soon after the publication of *The Fabrication*. However, he chose to emphasise 'genocide' in a series of public debates following the publication of his book. He continued to imply that leading academic historians have compared Australia to Nazi Germany and to argue that they have supported the argument that colonial governments had '"a conscious policy of genocide"'.[27] Some time later he claimed that the 'principal advocates' of genocide in Van Diemen's Land had now 'walked away from the topic' and were unwilling to defend 'the charge of genocide' (even though they never made this argument in their books). In short, Windschuttle refuses to abandon his genocide thesis. He remains committed to an argument for which the evidence is, at best, tenuous.[28]

Beating up genocide

Following the release of Windschuttle's *Fabrication*, many Howard intellectuals accepted his genocide thesis and beat it up in the media (and newspaper journalists and editors accepted this). In essence, they repeated Windschuttle's account, failing to check what academic historians in the field of Aboriginal history had actually written. In November 2002, prior to the launch of Windschuttle's book, Paul Sheehan, a regular columnist for the *Sydney Morning Herald*, wrote: 'While the brutal dislocation of Australia's indigenous population has rightly become an acknowledged chapter of national shame, the accusation of genocide is something altogether different . . . The three volumes [of Windschuttle's work] will form a frontal assault on the accusation of genocide'. Two weeks later, Windschuttle published an opinion in the *Australian* in which he began by asserting that historians of Van Diemen's Land such as Lyndall Ryan 'claim the Tasmanian Aborigines were subject to "a conscious policy of genocide"'. A few days later, a report on ABC Radio National's current affairs program, *PM*, began: 'A Sydney historian is trying to overturn the conventional thinking on what's been widely accepted as one of the darkest moments in Australian history, the genocide of Tasmanian Aborigines'. Two days later, in a feature article on *The Fabrication* for the weekend

Canberra Times entitled 'Historian challenges the orthodox view of genocide in Tasmania', journalist Christopher Bantick asserted: 'Central to Windschuttle's claims is the view that a carefully planned and controlled program of genocide in Tasmania "is unsupported by historical evidence"'. At the same time, Michael Duffy, a regular columnist for the *Daily Telegraph*, claimed: 'History in Australia for the past two decades has been dominated by a negative view of this country based on allegations that European settlers committed a campaign of brutal genocide against the Aboriginal inhabitants'. The following Monday, the Melbourne *Age* headlined one of Robert Manne's regular columns (in which he attacked Windschuttle's book) 'Pale grey view of a genocide'.[29]

A few days later, Miranda Devine, a columnist for the *Sydney Morning Herald* and a member of the board of *Quadrant*, claimed that 'Ryan had compared the British treatment of Aborigines in Tasmania with Hitler's treatment of the Jews' in her book *The Aboriginal Tasmanians*. Another Howard intellectual followed suit a few days later. In an opinion piece for the *Australian*, Roger Sandall, a former editor of *Quadrant*, referred to 'Ryan's explicit assumption that Nazi Germany and colonial Tasmania were much the same'. On the same day, Andrew Bolt, a columnist for the *Herald-Sun*, asserted: 'The pack-attack of fashionable historians . . . shows how hard it is to tell the truth about our past. To say no—there was no genocide here . . . Some, like Professor Lyndall Ryan in her influential *The Aboriginal Tasmanians*, even liken our past to the Nazi genocide of the Jews'.[30]

A few days earlier, Michael Duffy had returned to the subject of politically correct historians in order to make their work on genocide a test of *their* integrity: 'Their current enthusiasm is the claim white Australians tried to commit genocide against Tasmanian Aborigines. Last week I said the response of historians to Keith Windschuttle's new book attacking this claim would tell us a lot about the honesty of academic life'. On Christmas Eve, P.P. McGuinness, the editor of *Quadrant*, drew attention to the issue of genocide in a discussion of Windschuttle's book in his regular column for the *Sydney Morning Herald*. A few days later, another columnist, Ron Brunton, led his readers in the *Courier-Mail* to believe that Ryan had argued in her book that Aboriginal people on the Van Diemonian frontier 'were "victims of a conscious policy of genocide"'.[31]

At the close of the month, the *Australian* weighed in editorially against the politically correct orthodoxy on genocide Windschuttle had invented: 'An orthodoxy entails intolerance of scepticism, and sooner or later provokes revision. Hence Keith Windschuttle's book *The Fabrication of Aboriginal History*. It offers a necessary re-examination of the nature and extent of violence between black and white on the colonial frontier. Did it amount to warfare, even genocide, as the orthodox view holds?'[32] In the same weekend edition, the *Australian* ran a feature article on the controversy stirred by Windschuttle's book and his supporters, which began by claiming that historians had emphasised 'guerilla warfare and genocide'. It linked this article with another feature on Robert Manne, originally published by another Murdoch (News Limited) newspaper eighteen months before (under its editor, Chris Mitchell, who had now assumed the chief editorship of the *Australian*), which began: 'The first full-scale intellectual war of 21st-century Australia is about one word: genocide'.[33]

Several months later, Howard intellectuals once more repeated Windschuttle's thesis. Michael Duffy referred to Windschuttle's book in these terms: 'In it he claimed some of Australia's leading historians had misconstrued or even invented evidence that genocide had been committed against the original inhabitants of Tasmania'. Andrew Bolt alleged that Windschuttle's book had 'told how Professor Lyndall Ryan . . . had claimed in her influential history *The Aboriginal Tasmanians* that 700 Aborigines were killed in a "conscious policy of genocide"'. A senior journalist for the *Australian*, Kate Legge, followed the line the Howard intellectuals had taken, alleging that 'Robert Hughes and Phillip Knightley . . . galloped off with Ryan's reference to genocide on the Tasmanian frontier'. (It was, of course, *Windschuttle's* reference to genocide that the *new conservative* critics of academic historians had 'galloped off with'.) A year later, Neil McInnes, a long-time contributor to the conservative American magazine *The National Interest*, claimed that some (unnamed) writers had called Van Diemen's Land 'a dry run for the Holocaust' and that Lyndall Ryan had 'authorised this rhetoric by declaring that the colonial government in Hobart had launched "a conscious policy of genocide"'. A few months later, Roger Kimball blogged: 'Eighteen months ago, Mr Windschuttle published *The Fabrication of Aboriginal History*, blowing the top off the received notion that Australia was founded on an act of "genocide" against the indigenous Aboriginal population'. Windschuttle promptly placed this on his website.[34]

In the meantime, the historian Geoffrey Blainey had repeated Windschuttle's genocide thesis in a review of *The Fabrication*, originally commissioned by Kimball for his *New Criterion* and later published by the *Australian*. It began: 'The island of Tasmania is now seen in scholarly and unscholarly circles as the setting for one of the most disgraceful episodes in the recorded history of the human race. According to this story, virtually a whole people was wilfully exterminated by the incoming British . . . Various historians and other social scientists have described it as a policy of genocide and a forerunner of what happened a century later in Hitler's Europe. In *The Fabrication of Aboriginal History*, the historian Keith Windschuttle inspects the evidence for this genocide'. One might have expected a historian of Blainey's calibre to have checked Windschuttle's claims against the specialist academic historiography. Instead, however, he went further than any other Howard intellectual had done in their characterisation of *The Fabrication* by describing Windschuttle's consideration of the question of genocide as 'the dominating theme of the book'. However, as I have demonstrated here, Windschuttle's treatment of this is fundamentally flawed.[35]

In beating up 'genocide', moreover, these new conservative intellectuals tended to lose sight of one of the other critical matters at stake in this controversy: the impact of British colonisation on Aboriginal people. On one occasion, one of these writers (Paul Sheehan) got so carried away in attacking an academic historian (Henry Reynolds) that he seemed to be oblivious to the fact that the historical sources he had quoted in order to point to a mistake in Reynolds' work amounted to evidence for contemporary apprehension about genocide in terms of the other meaning it has: mass *death* rather than mass *killing*.[36]

In the spring of 2003, the *Australian* was still beating the genocide drum. It editorialised: 'Windschuttle has managed to provide a powerful corrective to the view of the colonial administration as engaged in a genocidal war of extermination against the island's original inhabitants'. *Whose* view of the administration? It seems that none of the Howard intellectuals had ever consulted the few chapters of either Ryan's book or Reynolds' book covering the Van Diemonian frontier of the 1820s and

Shortly after the release of Keith Windschuttle's book *The Fabrication of Aboriginal History* in December 2002, the cartoonist Pryor imagined a future Aboriginal story-teller relating a tale of a white history war in which academic historians associated with Henry Reynolds were ambushed by aggressive forces led by Windschuttle and *Quadrant* magazine. (Geoff Pryor, *Canberra Times*)

1830s. Instead, they were content to rely on Windschuttle's erroneous account of these books. (Sadly, no journalist checked his claims against the specialist academic scholarship either.) Such are the costs of having history warriors careless of the truth about history. As so often occurs, truth is the first casualty when someone decides to fight a war.[37]

Globalisation and genocide

Since the Second World War, debates over national history have been shaped by the focus of global media on matters such as rights for indigenous or aboriginal peoples, but more recently they have been influenced by a focus on genocide. In the last decade or so, there has been a good deal of genocide talk in the world, not least in Australia. Some of this has concerned contemporary or near-contemporary examples, such as Cambodia, Rwanda and Bosnia, but most of it has focused upon the Nazi German extermination of European Jewry.

As a result of the globalisation of a discourse about the Holocaust, this has become *the* archetypal genocide. It has not only been invoked by many as the model to which any other genocides must be compared, however. It has also become the reference point more generally in discussions of any evil or trauma, whether historical or contemporary. In a context in which there is much anxiety about moral and political change or crisis, the Holocaust can fulfil a yearning for firmer moorings. But, as Andreas Huyssen and others have observed, in becoming the universal trope of trauma it can also simultaneously enhance and hinder other historical and memorial practices and struggles. In the Australian context, it has undoubtedly done both.[38] My concern here, though, is the way in which invoking the Holocaust has become, in some hands, a means by which other crimes are cast as minor by comparison to its absolute evil. As Peter Novick has argued, making the Nazi genocide the benchmark of atrocity and oppression can 'trivialise crimes of lesser magnitude'. This is not merely a distasteful mode of speaking, but a truly disgusting one, he points out. Yet, as he suggests, it is one that readily occurs when something like the Holocaust becomes the touchstone in moral and political discourse.[39]

Readers will recall that Nazi Germany was, by Windschuttle's own account, his point of entry into this controversy over Australian history. (This is also true for Robert Manne, one of Windschuttle's most publicly known critics. Significantly, neither had done any research or writing on the history of the Australian frontier prior to this.)[40] By taking the Nazi genocide as his reference point, Windschuttle is able to relativise and thus refuse the violence of British colonisation in his own country. Indeed, this is probably its primary function. In *The Fabrication*, his treatment of the matter is excessive. At the beginning he is emphatic: 'the Aborigines were *not* the victims of a holocaust. To compare the intentions of Governor Phillip or Lieutenant-Governor Arthur, or any of their successors, to those of Adolf Hitler, is not only conceptually odious but wildly anachronistic'; and at the end he is still insistent: 'To compare these figures [of Aborigines killed by whites in Van Diemen's Land] to the millions deliberately put to death in Pol Pot's Cambodia, Stalinist Russia and Nazi Germany is bizarre and offensive. It trivialises the experience of those peoples who have suffered genuine attempts at extermination . . . Van Diemen's Land was host to nothing that resembled genocide or any attempt at it'. Here, it is apparent that Windschuttle conflates and confuses the two definitions or dimensions of genocide: mass killing and mass death. Furthermore, it is evident that he uses the former definition to protect the Australian nation and that in doing so he dismisses the latter definition to the disregard of Aboriginal victims of British colonisation. Such are the consequences, one might argue, of an undue preoccupation with one's own nation.[41]

Windschuttle is not alone in invoking the Nazi German genocide as a marker of the real as a way of trying to provide a moral anchor for himself and his settler nation. Many settler Australians, like settler Americans, are quite happy to discuss the Nazi German genocide and other genocides. But, like settler Americans, they are deeply unhappy when such talk extends to *their* country. They work very hard to erect boundaries to stop the concept of genocide crossing over the temporal and geographical boundaries they have erected between the Old World and the New, and tampering with

History in the age of globalisation and the public intellectual? At the Melbourne Writers Festival in August 2003 Robert Manne and Keith Windschuttle did battle in a debate over Aboriginal history that attracted a sell-out audience. (Kelly Barnes/News Limited)

their sense of themselves and the settler nation. They patrol their nation's historical borders vigilantly, ordering any suggestions of a local genocide out of court. In this political work, a popular and populist account of the Nazi German genocide provides the means of settling down anxieties about the moral status of the Australian nation by creating an impenetrable border between the violence of the Nazi German genocide and the violence of the colonisation of this country. Anything that does not measure up to it (and little, if anything else, can) is treated as 'something altogether different' (to repeat Sheehan's words) and so 'nothing that resembled genocide' or a holocaust (to repeat Windschuttle's). Genocide happens over there, not here, and is committed by people like 'them' (Nazis), not people like 'us' (the British). This is to say that a story about the Nazi German genocide comes to be the guarantor of the virtue of Australia's colonial past. It can only play this role, of course, if the racism of the Nazi German nation state is detached from the wider milieu of racism in nation states throughout the nineteenth and twentieth centuries.[42] It is this very relationship between the ideals of race and nation in the nineteenth and twentieth centuries that conservatives such as the Howard intellectuals refuse, not by means of reasoned argument but by rhetorical outbursts, as we have observed.

The tendency to reject out of hand any consideration of the colonisation of Australia as an example of genocide does not only characterise the approach of radical conservatives such as Windschuttle. Inga Clendinnen, one of Australia's finest historians and the author of internationally famous studies such as *The Aztecs* and *Reading the Holocaust*, has criticised genocide talk in Australia. 'As an *academic*', she has remarked, 'I sympathise with the analyst's eagerness to assay such key terms [as genocide] . . . to see how far they can be stretched without tearing'. But, as *somebody else*, she continues: 'Nonetheless I am convinced that the persistent invocation of the term "genocide" by the authors of the [Human Rights and Equal Opportunity Commission inquiry into the separation of Aboriginal children from their parents] report and their later supporters to describe any phase of Australian policies to Aborigines was not only ill-judged, but a moral, intellectual and (as it is turning out) a political disaster'. Like many other writers, Clendinnen takes the Nazi German genocide as her primary reference point, observing: 'I am reasonably sophisticated in various modes of intellectual discussion, but when I see the word "genocide" I still see Gypsies and Jews being herded into trains, into pits, into ravines, and behind them the shadowy figures of Armenian women and children being marched into the desert by armed men. I see deliberate mass murder: innocent people identified by their killers as a distinctive entity being done to death by organised authority'. Clendinnen does not make clear why she regards references to genocide in the Australian context as a moral disaster, but she appears to speak as a *settler Australian* who finds it difficult to really confront her own nation's violent colonial history. It seems that she shares some of the outrage she has read or heard among other settler Australians over the use of that word 'genocide'.[43] Another liberal settler historian, Geoffrey Bolton, has recommended an end to genocide talk in Australia in language less ambiguous than Clendinnen's: 'We should discard the word genocide from discussion of the frontier conflict that took place in Australia . . . If we *get rid* of that we can *settle down* more exactly to see what happened'.[44]

Escaping the past

In the case of public intellectuals such as Keith Windschuttle, invoking the Nazi German genocide seems to perform the role of a screen memory— a means by which they create a screen or a block between themselves and some other trauma that they refuse to approach directly. By proclaiming the incomparable nature of the Nazi genocide as the real or the ultimate trauma, they can ignore another local, traumatic past that is more difficult—and therefore probably more useful—for settler Australians to face. As a result, they fail to find a proper way of remembering and memorialising historical trauma closer to home, which includes that of their own people, but more especially that of others, such as Aborigines. Furthermore, the focus on the Nazi German genocide works against a consideration among settler Australians of whether they have any historical responsibility for their nation's past, present and future in reference to Aboriginal people.[45]

The historian Alan Atkinson has discussed the problem of engaging Australia's colonial past in a somewhat different way. In the context of considering the excessive violence of frontiersmen in the 1820s and 1830s, he has suggested: 'There are several immediate responses we can make to this kind of unreality. We can ignore it, as the revisionist critics seem to do. We can turn away bewildered . . . [Or] we can feel, and wrestle with, a type of moral disgust. Only the last is really productive. More than any of the others, perhaps, the last proves we are human and that we can think'.[46]

In trying to turn away the question of genocide, the Howard intellectuals have refused to accept the point of a good deal of the genocide talk in this country. They have been so concerned with the character of the settler nation that they have failed to listen to what Aboriginal people—and those historians who have worked among them—have been saying, and to think about this. In the case of Tasmania, the Aboriginal spokesperson Jim Everett has asserted that a 'colonial holocaust' occurred there, while another leader, Michael Mansell, has claimed more generally that: 'The British had more impact on Aborigines than the Holocaust had on the Jews'. In insisting that Aboriginal people 'were *not* the victims of a holocaust', as writers such as Windschuttle do, they not only overlook the probability that many, perhaps most, of the 500–600 Aboriginal groups in this country prior to 1788 had no survivors within a generation or two of the British occupation of their land. In dismissing the claims of a genocide, 'revisionists' similarly fail to grasp that many Aboriginal people believe that 'genocide' is an appropriate word for remembering their historical *experience*.[47] It amounts to a truthful *myth*, and they tell this story in this manner. To treat the forms of history-making that Aboriginal people often adopt as though these are more or less the same as academic history is to misconceive, and thus misunderstand and misrepresent, their histories, and to subject these other ways of relating the past to the law (or rules) of the discipline of history. By insisting on the primacy of (white Australian) history, those such as Windschuttle are deaf to Aboriginal voices.[48] Consequently, they threaten to recreate the great Australian silence.[49]

WAR

 5

Keith Windschuttle continues *The Fabrication of Aboriginal History* in the manner in which he began it. Having beaten up genocide in his introduction, he beats up massacres in his opening chapter. Once again, he begins by claiming there is orthodox story (about some killings at Risdon Cove) that can be attributed to academic historians; once more, he proceeds to demolish that story by repeating the arguments his orthodox historians have actually made but which he presents as his own interpretation. He continues in this fashion, chapter after chapter. Some of the time he seems to know what he is doing; at other times he does not seem to know what he has done. Whatever the case, his fervent labour is shaped in large part by the project of the settler nation. At the turn of one century, Windschuttle repeats the fantastic claims nationalist historians made at the turn of the previous one: Australia was not like other colonies—it was an exception. Here British colonisation was relatively peaceful.

When he made his foray into the field of Aboriginal history, Windschuttle claimed that academic historians had helped create a sense that the foundations of Australia rested upon 'deadly violence against Aborigines'. He implied they had done so by constructing 'a story of widespread massacres on the frontiers'. (Windschuttle's use of the phrase 'widespread massacres' echoed a conservative spokesman, Hugh Morgan, who had attacked the new Australian history several years earlier.) In beating up massacres, Windschuttle confuses one of the matters at stake in the consideration of the colonisation of this country and in this historical controversy—the nature of settler violence—by failing to make critical distinctions. We noted in the previous chapter that

Windschuttle refers to widespread killings and mass killings, and massacres and genocide, as though they are one and the same. Such conflation has characterised his approach since he began work in the field. What is overwhelmingly important for Windschuttle is the emotional resonance of these terms today, not any precise historical meaning they might have.[1]

Significantly, in the course of conflating critical terms such as 'war', 'genocide' and 'frontier warfare', and 'massacres' and 'widespread killings', Windschuttle fails to distinguish between the writing on these subjects in different historical genres. As we noted in Chapter 2, Aboriginal history has become a very broad field in which people from many different backgrounds and disciplines make history in many different forms. As we also saw, the treatment of frontier killing differs enormously in the histories that have been created. Windschuttle knows these different historical registers exist but he overlooks their significance (unless it suits his argument), let alone any implications this has for his treatment of historical acts of violence. He mistakes the way settler violence has been cast in various forms of popular culture as well as Aboriginal people's history-making— which is that of mass killings, usually called massacres—for the way academic historians have characterised the violence—which is widespread killings on a small scale. Interestingly, in a good deal of his work Windschuttle has approached the past of the frontier in the same manner as the non-academic treatments he attacks, focusing on specific historical events rather than general historical processes, which is to say that he works more like a popular narrative historian and/or a myth-maker than an academic historian. This reflects his preoccupation with the symbolic that we noted in Chapter 4.[2]

Massacre, massacre

In the opening chapter of *The Fabrication*, Windschuttle considers an incident at Risdon Cove in 1804, the place where the British had first settled in Van Diemen's Land, in which several Aboriginal people were killed. He claims it provides 'a good case study of how the conflict between Aborigines and settlers has long been exaggerated by people far removed from the scene and by rumours and myths that have perpetuated themselves'. As in his response to popular claims that the colonisation of Australia was an example of genocide, he rails: 'To call the incident a "massacre" is to beat it up beyond credibility'.[3]

Windschuttle begins his account of this matter by describing the way several historical writers have treated Risdon Cove as a massacre. He then digresses to refer to other authors who have depicted 'Western imperialism' in its bleakest terms by using Van Diemen's Land as one of their most compelling examples before moving to imply that orthodox academic historians such as Lyndall Ryan and Lloyd Robson have treated Van Diemen's Land as an example of deliberate genocide. Finally, he claims that those who have done this treat the incident at Risdon Cove as a massacre, singling out (in a footnote) Henry Reynolds as his example. By framing the historiography of the conflict at Risdon Cove in this manner, Windschuttle has obscured a good deal. It should be observed that none of the authors Windschuttle first quotes in reference to a massacre at Risdon Cove or European imperialism is an academic historian who has specialised in Aboriginal history and conducted historical research on the Van Diemonian frontier: three are journalists (based overseas); one is an Aboriginal author (working in the form of myth or legend); another is an academic historian of genocide (writing in the popular press); another an art critic (penning a popular work of history); and so on. Windschuttle makes some of this clear. However, what he does not reveal is that none of these writers could have drawn their account of the incident at Risdon Cove from the principal academic historians of the Van Diemonian frontier. Why is this so? Because Henry Reynolds, Lloyd Robson and Lyndall Ryan have *not* argued that a mass killing occurred at Risdon Cove.[4] Windschuttle should know this but, as with his treatment of Ryan and Reynolds' writings in reference to the question of genocide, his account misleads readers.[5]

In his interpretation of what happened at Risdon Cove, moreover, Windschuttle has followed the account provided by Lyndall Ryan in her book *The Aboriginal Tasmanians* (1981). Windschuttle describes it as a defensive action by the British in which three Aboriginal people were shot dead and at least one—but perhaps more—was wounded, and he attributes this conflict to tension over kangaroos as a food source; Ryan concluded that, when some of the Moomaireremener, who were hunting kangaroos, visited the settlement, the acting commandant panicked and in the ensuing skirmish at least three Aboriginal people were killed, and she attributed such conflicts to competition over kangaroos as a source of food. Windschuttle's account does not reveal that his interpretation on this, and several other matters, mirrors Ryan's.[6] Instead it creates an impression in the reader's mind that the work of historians such as Ryan is so politically determined that it is more or less worthless.[7]

For one of his other arguments regarding Risdon Cove, Windschuttle follows another 'orthodox' historian. In *The Fabrication*, Windschuttle states: 'It was widely believed [from 1819] that this incident was the initial cause of the later hostilities'; in *Fate of a Free People* (1995), Henry Reynolds stated: 'from the 1820s onwards [the so-called Risdon Cove massacre] was believed to have been the major cause of Aboriginal hostility'. In other words, Windschuttle's argument is uncannily similar to Reynolds'. Once more, this is not apparent to the readers of Windschuttle's book.[8]

The first historian to wonder whether a myth had been forged about Risdon Cove was a colonial historian, James Bonwick. In *The Last of the Tasmanians* (1870), Bonwick introduces his treatment of the incident at Risdon Cove in this manner:

The composition of history makes us acquainted with the difficulties of learning the truth of a story. It is not merely the confusion of myth and fact. We are gradually arriving at the belief that all, or nearly all, the early history of nations has no reference at all to actual events or persons, but to statements of a foreign nature, mythological or astronomical . . . But when we leave, as we fancy, the region of myth, and come to very modern times—our own living era—other difficulties arise. Such are the conflicting accounts, such the various ways of regarding the same object or circumstance, such the influences of personal character and interests involved in the narrative, that we are often puzzled with what might have been supposed the plainest facts of modern history . . . The story of the first conflict of races in Tasmania [at Risdon Cove] is similarly involved in misty obscurity . . . All we positively know is that one day there appeared on the heights a large body of the Aborigines . . . The officer in command ordered the soldiers with him to fire upon the advancing hunters, and numbers were slain.

Bonwick then relates *eight* accounts of the incident. Windschuttle, however, misrepresents Bonwick's work by treating him as one of the makers of a myth about the Risdon Cove 'massacre': he relates to his readers only *one* of the stories Bonwick has told (which is the most excessive inasmuch as it claims that 'the whole was the effect of a half-drunken spree, and that the firing arose from a brutal desire to see the *Niggers* run'), and then proceeds to lambast Bonwick. Once more we see that Windschuttle's approach to a historiographical matter—that the story of Risdon Cove has become the subject of a myth—actually follows in the footsteps of those historians whose work he dismisses. Once more we see that Windschuttle fails to treat the writings of 'orthodox' historians in a fair and even-handed manner.[9]

In *The Fabrication*, Windschuttle repeatedly attributes massacre stories to so-called politically correct historians. He devotes his fifth chapter to a consideration, in his words, of 'several large-scale massacres of Aborigines, which [the orthodox school of Aboriginal history] allege were committed by British colonists in the period 1826 to 1830'. He calls this chapter 'Historical scholarship and the invention of massacre stories'. There he particularly singles out the work of Lyndall Ryan. Windschuttle's account of her book *The Aboriginal Tasmanians* suggests that she was primarily concerned to tell a story about settler violence, just as he has suggested that she was concerned to tell a story about genocide as mass killing. In particular, it implies that Ryan has written massacre history. However, if one reads Ryan's book impartially, one discovers that Windschuttle has misread, and so misrepresented her work, presumably because he has misunderstood and/or misconstrued her historical project. In the seven chapters of her book devoted to the period of the agricultural and pastoral frontier (1802–34), Ryan is preoccupied with telling a story of the conflict between settlers and Aboriginal people from the perspective of the Aboriginal people. In particular, she focuses on Aboriginal resistance to the white colonisers. Ryan's concern here is in keeping with her overall theme of the survival of people rather than their destruction. To a lesser degree, she is also concerned with the government response to Aboriginal attacks and settler attitudes. Ryan's focus on Aboriginal resistance is particularly evident in the way she frames her account of the frontier in Chapters 5–7, and it is either explicit or implicit on page after page. She discusses incidents of settlers killing Aboriginal people only occasionally, and in most of these instances she does so in the context of describing what she calls bloody skirmishes or a struggle between settlers and Aboriginal people, and/or settler reactions to Aboriginal resistance; and she hardly ever calls the settler killings 'massacres'. Inasmuch as a numerical count can reflect the content of a book, in only fourteen of the 213 paragraphs that comprise Chapters 4–10 of her book—or 6.6. per cent of the text—does Ryan refer to killings by settlers and the military. (A count of the number of sentences would yield an even lower proportion.)[10] In other words, Ryan's focus does not rest upon white violence, let alone upon massacres. Windschuttle gives the impression that Ryan is doing 'massacre history', but it is actually *he* who is creating massacre stories. This reflects his interest, not hers.[11]

Henry Reynolds does not write massacre history either. In *Fate of a Free People*, his book relating to the Van Diemonian frontier and its aftermath, he only refers to one settler killing of Aboriginal people as a massacre (and on another occasion he quotes a source referring to 'bloody massacres on both sides'). Over twenty years ago now, Reynolds cautioned against an 'overemphasis on the significance of massacres', arguing that this 'tends to throw support behind the idea that the blacks were helpless victims of white attack'; this assessment, he noted, ran 'easily along well worn channels of historical interpretation' and parodied 'the Aboriginal role in frontier conflict'. He extended this argument in *Fate of a Free People*: 'There is a tendency among writers sympathetic to the Aborigines to exaggerate the numbers killed in order to emphasise the brutality of the colonial encounter'. In other words, Reynolds anticipated—indeed, he articulated— the very argument Windschuttle now presents as his very own.[12]

A close reading of Windschuttle's work reveals that it is actually *he* who most uses the term 'massacre'. Indeed, he has used it repeatedly in his work on frontier conflict. He has done so much more than any academic historian in Aboriginal history whose work I know. For example, Windschuttle not only adopted 'massacre' for the title of the *Quadrant* essays in 2000, which marked his entry into this field; in the first of this three-part series he used 'massacre', 'massacres', 'massacred' and 'massacring' over twenty times, as well as 'mass killings', 'mass murder', 'mass terror' and 'mass grave', which is exceptional even for an article discussing this subject.[13] It is almost as though Windschuttle enjoys using the word. It seems that he is preoccupied with aggression, war and killing. These themes are evident in the argument and style of his earlier writing, in particular *The Killing of History: How a Discipline is Being Murdered by Literary Critics and Social Theorists*, as we noted in Chapter 3.[14]

It is also apparent, though, that Windschuttle is disturbed by the phenomenon of violence. As the historian Tim Rowse has noted, a notion of excess is built into terms such as 'massacre'.[15] This is also true, of course, of 'genocide'. Rather than trying to come to terms with this, though, Windschuttle seems to displace his own fearful fantasy about violence by projecting this onto others.[16] We have seen how he does this in respect of academic historians such as Henry Reynolds and Lyndall Ryan, but he also does it in reference to two of his historical subjects: missionaries and Aborigines. He accuses the missionary men of being obsessed with massacre stories and of inventing these. He charges Aboriginal men with being responsible for most of the violence that occurred on the frontier—indeed, he casts the latter as a senselessly lawless other. It is *they* (like the 'postmodernists' in *The Killing of History*) who are murderously violent, not the people with whom Windschuttle identifies himself: rational and enlightened white colonists. He also seeks to discharge the excessive violence he has brought into being by calling upon the discipline of the law and the discipline of history to play particular roles (as we will see).[17]

In fighting his own battle with violence—first beating up the violence by misrepresenting its treatment in the academic historiography and then beating it down—perhaps it is not surprising that Windschuttle has apparently failed to grasp the fact that most academic historians have written histories in which they have argued that the conflict on the frontier was widespread but *sporadic* and that in most incidents Aboriginal people were killed singly or in small numbers. He also ignores the fact that they have criticised 'massacre history', especially in popular historical discourse. Windschuttle will have none of this since he has convinced himself that academic historians are responsible for the popular focus on massacres. He claims that *he* is telling a new and true history when he proclaims that frontier conflict was *sporadic* rather than systematic. He presumes that this is some kind of revelation. But, as we have seen, he has, once more, simply repeated an argument that has already been made by the academic historians he denigrates.[18]

Windschuttle's treatment of the academic historiography in the field of Aboriginal history has obscured the fact that he makes many of the arguments its practitioners previously advanced. Windschuttle himself does not seem to realise that he has repeated the contentions of the very 'orthodox' historians whose work he has sought to discredit. This is ironic. At the end of the final chapter of the *The Fabrication of Aboriginal History*, Windschuttle declares that the academic historiography is 'all smoke and mirrors'. In reality, this comment describes his work, not theirs.[19]

A war on war

'It's no small thing what a culture makes of a war', American historian Tom Engelhardt has remarked. In Australian historical narratives, war has long had a central symbolic place in the making of the nation. There has been a good deal of remembrance about wars in the form of monuments and rituals. Memory of war has been used to construct national identity and create a cohesive national community. Indeed, it has become one of the cornerstones of Australia's nationhood and Australian popular culture regarding it. Yet the wars have always been those fought over there—Europe and Asia—and never here—Australia. The emphasis on the former has worked to displace the latter. In recent times, however, this has been challenged.[20]

In concluding *The Other Side of the Frontier* (1981), Henry Reynolds presented the burden of another history of war:

How, then, do we deal with the Aboriginal dead? White Australians frequently say that 'all that' should be forgotten. But it won't be. Black memories are too deeply, too recently scarred. And forgetfulness is a strange prescription coming from a community which reveres the fallen warrior and emblazons the phrase 'Lest we forget' on monuments throughout the land. If Aborigines are to enter our history 'on terms of most perfect equality', as [explorer] Thomas Mitchell termed it, they will bring their dead with them and expect an honoured burial. So our embarrassment is compounded. Do we give up our cherished ceremonies or do we make room for the Aboriginal dead on our memorials, cenotaphs, boards of honour and even in the pantheon of national heroes?

Fifteen or so years later, Reynolds returned to this matter in his *Fate of a Free People*, calling for changes in the Australian War Memorial and to ANZAC Day so that they no longer excluded commemoration of people killed in wars fought in this country. A few years later, Ken Inglis, another leading Australian historian, suggested at the launch of his book *Sacred Places: War Memorials in the Australian Landscape*, that the Australian War Memorial in the nation's capital should represent the wars between Aboriginal and settler.[21]

Inglis' words, which were attributed by many journalists and commentators to Governor-General Sir William Deane (who had launched Inglis' book), provoked outrage in some quarters, as Tom Griffiths has noted: 'It wasn't a war, wrote his critics. And even if it was a war, then it wasn't an officially declared war and both sides didn't wear uniforms. And even if it still rated somehow as a real war, then Aborigines were the other side, and they were the losers, and victors don't put up monuments to the losers. Aborigines are not Us'.[22]

In *The Fabrication*, Windschuttle sets his sights on this call for a memorialisation of the Aboriginal dead by attacking the story his so-called orthodox historians have told of the wars here. In doing so, he has repeated the claims conservative intellectuals such as Geoffrey Blainey have been making since the mid-1980s: there was no widespread killing; the rule of law was upheld; there was little Aboriginal resistance; and the Aboriginal death toll was almost all the result of disease and inter-Aboriginal violence. In fact, there has been a long colonial tradition of trying to distract attention from the violence of the frontier, and especially that of white frontiersmen. Windschuttle also tries to push away this settler violence and its cost in Aboriginal lives. In this attempt to discount rather than count the cost of British colonisation, he plays with both words and numbers.[23]

At the heart of the controversy over frontier conflict, Tom Griffiths has pointed out, there is a fundamental disagreement about the idea of war. Windschuttle denies there were any frontier wars by rejecting the contemporary language of conflict. In doing so, he resembles the 'postmodernists' he criticises: by playing with words, he tries to change the world. But this, of course, is also the role of the propagandist. Let us see how he does this.[24]

In *The Fabrication of Aboriginal History*, Windschuttle tries to get rid of war by getting rid of 'war'. This is critical, because there are many

references to 'war' in the contemporary sources created by government officials, settlers and others on that side of the frontier, and even more in some
academic histories. Rather than considering whether there was *a state of
war* between Aborigines and settlers, Windschuttle transforms consideration of the conflict by turning it into a matter about *a state of warfare.*
He claims that in order to have a state of war you have to have a state of
warfare. He then asserts that there was no conflict in Van Diemen's Land
that deserves the term 'warfare'. Only one side waged war. The British
fought a war against the Aborigines but the Aboriginal people did not do
the same. Consequently, there cannot have been a state of war. On what
grounds does Windschuttle decide this? To have a state of war, he says, you
must have two *military* forces confronting each other. Here, there was only
one: the British. Once again, Windschuttle has dictated a definition: a
warring party must be a *military* force. Having done this, he defines
military force on grounds that are inherently Eurocentric in nature. To have
a military force and so conduct warfare and so be at war, Windschuttle
determines, you must have political objectives and a form of organisation
to realise these, and these were lacking among Aboriginal people because
their culture did not resemble that of the British colonisers. They were too
different. They were not Us.[25]

To sustain this war game, Windschuttle has to do a considerable
amount of work. He does it in several ways, nearly all of them breathtaking
in their implications. First, he simply refuses to accept the conviction of
the colonisers themselves that Aboriginal people were engaged in a form
of warfare. Those such as Governor George Arthur, he has to concede, use
the term to describe Aboriginal attacks, but Windschuttle refuses to
count(enance) this: either Arthur's usage was merely 'a figure of speech, a
surrogate term for mere violence', which is very doubtful, or he 'had no
good reason to regard Aboriginal hostilities as genuine warfare', which is
rather condescending. At any rate, Windschuttle privileges his own authority over that of historical contemporaries. This hardly amounts to respect
for the historical record, something Windschuttle claims to have.[26]

Second, Windschuttle dictates who can be Aboriginal and who cannot:
the Aboriginal attacks counted by other historians as political were not
made by Aborigines because they were the work of just a few political
leaders who were not Aboriginal: Musquito, Black Jack and Black Tom.[27]

Musquito was not local to Van Diemen's Land, and he and the other men were not 'tribal Aborigines' but 'detribalised Aborigines' and 'Europeanised'. In making this argument, Windschuttle refuses to allow any historical process or change. Indigenes who once identified with a small local place, people and language (which we might call 'tribal') are unable to become 'Aborigines' who identify with a larger place (such as Van Diemen's Land) or acquire another language ('Aboriginal English' and English liberalism). Nor can Aboriginal spokespersons be 'genuine' when they claim 'rights'. 'The notion of "rights"', Windschuttle remarks, 'derives exclusively from the European political tradition, and has no meaning in traditional Aboriginal culture'. By contrast, Windschuttle allows colonisers who once called themselves Cornish or Londoners or English or British, and so on to become Van Diemonians or Tasmanians or Australians, to acquire new ways of speaking and to have rights to another people's place. In Windschuttle's lexicon, like that of so many settler Australians, *their* people are allowed to change and continue to be regarded as authentic subjects who have rights but Aboriginal people are not.[28]

Third, Windschuttle rules out of order any of the sources that suggest Aboriginal people might have had a political objective in attacking settlers. He insists that political statements have to be made directly by an Aboriginal person. Thus, when George Augustus Robinson (who was very well acquainted with Aboriginal people) declares that Aborigines 'have a tradition among them that the white men have usurped their territory', Windschuttle objects: 'this is Robinson speaking, not an Aborigine'.[29] Furthermore, statements have to be made by those whom Windschuttle defines as Aboriginal, which is to say they have to be 'tribal'. Finally, Windschuttle asserts the rule of the *written* word in historical research: 'Had a tribal native ever made a statement of this kind, we can be *sure* it would have featured prominently in both the contemporary and the historical *literature*'. We will return to this critical matter later.[30]

Guerillas and guerilla warfare

In *The Fabrication*, Windschuttle deploys yet another linguistic strategy to combat the world of war when he turns an argument that his adversaries *have* made for the presence of Aboriginal warfare into an argument for 'guerilla warfare'.[31] Windschuttle claims that there is a guerilla war thesis, indeed, he devotes a chapter to it.[32] Academic historians of Windschuttle's generation have undoubtedly used the term 'guerilla warfare' a good deal, but in their work it does not have the significance Windschuttle attributes to it.[33] One could readily delete 'guerilla warfare' and replace it with 'warfare' in passage after passage of their writings without really altering the essence of the argument they seek to advance.[34]

In claiming that academic historians, such as Henry Reynolds, have advanced a guerilla war thesis, Windschuttle attacks their work in the following manner: 'This is not history; it is the imposition onto Aboriginal history of an anachronistic and incongruous piece of ideology . . . In making this case [for guerilla warfare], these historians . . . have taken concepts derived from the political structures of the modern world and imposed them . . . onto the mental universe of a hunter-gatherer people'. And: 'the notion that the Aborigines of the 1820s and 1830s conducted anything resembling the anti-colonial guerilla warfare of Southeast Asia in the 1950s and 1960s is a romantic delusion'. Further: 'The most unseemly example [of anachronism] is the orthodox school's claim that the Tasmanian Aborigines of the early nineteenth century invented the same concept of guerilla warfare that was practised by very different societies in vastly dissimilar conflicts in Africa, Asia and South America in the mid-twentieth century . . . [Reynolds] imagines the Tasmanian Aborigine of the 1820s as the indigenous equivalent of a Che Guevara or Ho Chi Minh. This is not history: it is Sixties radical romanticism'.[35]

In this broadside Windschuttle ignores the fact that some writers at the time of the frontier wars used the term 'guerilla warfare' and that some historians prior to the rise of Aboriginal history in the 1960s did so too.[36] More importantly, his criticism of the historical use of this concept is disproportionate. This might betray the fact that Windschuttle has a particular relationship to this subject, albeit one that he is probably unconscious of.[37]

Discounting the dead

Windschuttle claims white settlers committed very little violence on the Australian frontier. In the case of Tasmania, he asserts that the British killed very few Aboriginal people. Indeed he goes further: 'In all of Europe's colonial encounters with the New Worlds of the Americas and the Pacific, the colony of Van Diemen's Land . . . was probably the site where the least indigenous blood of all was deliberately shed'. How does Windschuttle know this? Simply by counting up the number of such deaths in the contemporary historical record. He concludes that 120 Aborigines were killed by whites in Van Diemen's Land. As we have seen, Windschuttle plays around with words a good deal in his book but, most problematically, in seeking to portray the frontier he mistakes the written word for the world.[38]

Windschuttle's approach to the past is that of naïve realism. He works as though the contemporary historical sources are the past itself and assumes that they speak for themselves. He tells us how good the historical records are for Van Diemen's Land,[39] and he makes a point of telling us how many of these he has read. And he insists that his account rests on historical facts he has found there. His book could be mistaken for the work of an antiquarian fact-grubber and fact-worshipper. It is an approach that refuses to allow for the deep chasm between the past and the records and representations we have of it.[40]

The historical record for the frontier is much weaker than Windschuttle represents it to be. Aboriginal culture was an oral one, so there are no contemporary written historical sources *created* by Aborigines for the Australian frontier. All the contemporary literary record was created by non-Aboriginal people. There are some contemporary or near-contemporary Aboriginal accounts of the frontier as they were represented by whites, but these are relatively few. Many of the whites on the frontiers of settlement also belonged to an oral culture and few had much literacy. Much of the frontier was remote. Those who could have created a record of white violence were settlers—who often obfuscated their own violence since they were fearful they would be prosecuted for killing Aboriginal people—and government officials, policemen and soldiers, who often had an interest in obscuring the violence committed by settlers and their men as well as themselves. (In some instances, the evidence of white killings has since been destroyed.) In other words, the contemporary historical record of the frontier was created by relatively few people, and much of it by whites who had a vested interest in diminishing the evidence of settler violence. As a result, few if any historians have ever assumed they could produce a definitive record of Aboriginal deaths. Indeed, one of the founders of Aboriginal history, Charles Rowley, thought it was 'very difficult even to guess at the *scale* of violence'.)[41]

Windschuttle's interpretation of settler violence, however, does not only rest on the so-called historical record. It is determined primarily by his historical method, which is seriously defective. Windschuttle reduces settler violence by presuming that the number of recorded Aboriginal deaths represents more or less the number who were actually killed. This is a serious mistake. Let us consider how he calculates settler violence. First, he only considers this in terms of killings, so fails to consider other expressions of violence that cannot be quantified. Second, he reduces these to bodies found and so discounts any woundings that might have resulted in death. Third, he reduces the record of white killings by ruling out any historical accounts that were created by contemporaries who were not witnesses to killings, had not seen the bodies, or had not come into actual contact with the perpetrators. Fourth, he reduces the remaining record of white killings by rejecting story-tellers he chooses to regard as untrustworthy. Fifth, he takes at face value the euphemistic language colonists often used to obscure their violent acts. Windschuttle's method is more or less one that lawyers adopt to weigh up evidence in a court room. He thus adopts standards of proof that go far beyond those customarily used by scholarly historians.[42]

Windschuttle's account of settler violence is further weakened because he is unwilling to consider latter-day historical sources. In *The Fabrication*, Windschuttle argues: 'There might be rumours, gossip and legends that surface later but if there is no documentary evidence at all it is hard for the historian to determine the truth. This is not to argue that the lack of documents is of itself proof that nothing happened but, without reasonable evidence, the historian will find it difficult to sustain a case that something as dramatic as a killing did take place'. In other writings he has revealed that he is so attached to this way of doing history that he is willing to accept what are almost certainly false accounts of the past of other human beings:

> I am not arguing against writing the history of . . . any . . . group that a
> historian wants to define as oppressed. You can legitimately do this, by

all means, using the tools of traditional history . . . [But] if you pursue this objective, you have to conform to the traditional criteria of proof used by the discipline. You have to have documentary and other kinds of reliable evidence to support your case . . . If the subjects of your history genuinely are oppressed, then the historical evidence will establish this. But if you cannot support your case with sufficient evidence, you have to accept this too, and admit that the thesis about their oppression is not true.[43]

Basic to much historical work is a method that places emphasis on meaning as much as information, which treats historical sources as representational as much as referential, and which seeks to understand the past by reconstructing historical contexts as much as by reading texts. By doing this, historians begin to have some clues about how the world of the past works. They get a sense of how one event leads to another to another—a sense of consequence. But Windschuttle does not do this work. He prefers to read texts rather than render contexts. Doing the latter requires historical labour that demands a considerable amount of time, and he has been in a tearing hurry. He prefers to break up the past into singular details rather than deal with context and circumstance. He does not want to grapple with the messy reality of the past, with all its ambiguities, inconsistencies and contradictions. He wants certainty, not uncertainty.

Windschuttle has rejected the methodological advances made by historians over the last three or four decades. For example, whereas other historians have tried to tease meaning from the language of conflict that frontiersmen used, Windschuttle has taken refuge in these forms of silence. Another historian, Klaus Neumann, has put it like this: 'Windschuttle's obsession with facts that can be proven, paired with a remarkable lack of curiosity about an unknowable past, means that he has little time for stories that cannot be substantiated by recourse to hard written evidence . . . For Windschuttle, history is the account of a past that can be proven. He is not interested in pasts that cannot be reconstructed on the basis of firm historical evidence . . . The history he wants to tell is thus one that by default has to keep silent on much of what happened'.[44]

Alan Atkinson has reached much the same conclusion:

In a period when we have been struggling to make historical method stretch to comprehend the real diversity of human faith and understanding and the spiritual depth of human experience, and at the same time to communicate those issues to the world at large, the revisionist approach seems to lead in the opposite direction. This amounts to a failure of genuine, energetic curiosity and a failure of imagination, both of which are fundamental to good scholarship. Most of what revisionist critics such as Windschuttle have argued so far in their account of frontier violence is informed by these failures.[45]

Historical objects and objectivity

Windschuttle implies that he is being objective in adopting the historical methods he uses. He casts this as a way of achieving historical truth. But it is probable that Windschuttle's commitment to objectivity entails more than this. He represents himself in terms of an allegiance to an intellectual tradition, but it seems that his version of objectivity constitutes a means of countering what he sees as dangerous subjective forces. In the context of frontier history, it acts as a way of trying to keep the traumatic subject matter at bay. This leads to an extreme form of objectivism in his work—hyper-objectivity—rather than objectivity.[46]

Windschuttle's refusal of the subjective realm is especially apparent in his rejection of the role of compassion in historical work. In a profile on Windschuttle prepared in March and April 2003, journalist Jane Cadzow observed: 'That some still grieve over the fate of the original Tasmanians appears to genuinely puzzle him. You might say he regards it with complete incomprehension. "You can't really be serious about feeling sympathy for someone who died 200 years ago", he says'. Several months later, Windschuttle asserted in two debates: 'The responsibility of the historian is not to be compassionate, it is to be dispassionate'. How can we explain this?[47]

Windschuttle believes that being compassionate in historical work distorts a historian's judgement. It leads to the flaws he attributes to his orthodox school of historians. The historian, Windschuttle believes, must distance himself from the subjects of the past, otherwise he will not find the truth. There is some merit in this approach, but Windschuttle does not actually practise it. Furthermore, there is something oddly idiosyncratic about his approach. He treats 'compassionate' and 'dispassionate' as if they were antonyms, as though one cannot be both compassionate and dispassionate. Yet the moral philosopher Raimond Gaita has pointed out: 'A dispassionate judgement is not one uninformed by feeling, but one that is undistorted by it. This fact separates legitimate use of the words "emotive", "emotional" or "rhetorical" as terms of criticism from illegitimate insistence that objective thought must always be separable from feeling'. Windschuttle apparently assumes that one can only be dispassionate and so objective by denying compassion and subjectivity, no matter what the cost. (The author, he seems to insist, has to effectively extinguish his or her own self.[48]) As this suggests, the major weakness critics across the political spectrum have discerned in *The Fabrication*—its lack of a sense of tragedy—is actually the result of his commitment to the very objectivity that he and his sympathisers regard as his greatest strength. Arguably, a good historian should be passionate, compassionate and dispassionate in reference to as many of their historical subjects as they can.[49]

Windschuttle once apparently identified with the colonised—he claims to have written 'a bleak story about the destruction of Aboriginal society'— but now he identifies himself with the colonisers, or at least the 'respectable settlers'. He consistently identifies with their perspective—indeed, so much so that he seldom adopts a point of view that is not theirs, which is to say he lacks an objective stance. His account of the killing of the frontier plays down the impact on Aboriginal people while simultaneously playing up the impact on the settlers. Indeed, as Mark Finnane's consideration of this matter suggests, Windschuttle's account of the frontier conflict casts Aboriginal people as the perpetrators and the settlers as the victims. Most importantly, in his treatment of the frontier, Windschuttle tries to distance himself from the subjects most affected by the deathly past the frontier represents. He seems unable to accept the traumatic consequences of frontier conflict for Aboriginal people. As a result, he treats the Aboriginal dead as objects rather than as subjects.[50]

Windschuttle's attempt to distance himself from the historical reality of the frontier not only leads him to disavow the suffering of those most affected by colonisation—the Aboriginal people—but also to denigrate their most passionate champions—missionary men and other such figures as George Augustus Robinson, who held a mirror in front of the colonisers. In his work, Windschuttle attacks these men as much as he attacks Aboriginal people, and he attributes the same failings to them as he does to his orthodox historians.[51] He is dismissive of their compassionate embrace of the plight of Aboriginal people. He claims that their concern for Aboriginal victims was shallow and he accuses them of using Aboriginal people for their own aggrandisement (as he does 'orthodox historians'). There can be little doubt that the response of figures such as Robinson was excessive at times, as Windschuttle argues, though this has already been pointed out by historians such as Henry Reynolds. (Once more, we see Windschuttle has followed the interpretation of an 'orthodox historian'.)[52] However, Windschuttle's account of these men is in turn extreme, so much so that one might suspect he has unwittingly described himself more than he has depicted them. On occasion, missionary figures *did* allow their feelings of compassion to undermine their judgement or objectivity, but Windschuttle exaggerates the recurrence of this failing and hence its significance, and he ignores the fact that the objective conditions of the frontier often prompted their subjective response. This serves his need, which in the end seems to be one of refusing the traumatic reality to which these men bore witness, and which Windschuttle assumes, rightly or wrongly, he cannot witness.[53]

Relating, and relating to, the history of frontier conflict is, as we have observed, difficult work. One must have a strong stomach or heart to do this. Windschuttle does not seem to be up to the task. He is so discomforted by the historical reality of the frontier, which is primarily a story of how the Aboriginal owners of the country were dispossessed and destroyed, that he tells a story that distorts, denies and disremembers this past.[54]

It is hardly surprising that Windschuttle's history-making has been embraced by some settler Australians, especially perhaps those of his own generation, who grew up when there was a cult of forgetting or disremembering. You can almost hear their sighs of relief as they say something like this: 'The stories that those academic historians have been telling in recent years aren't true, you know. We didn't kill all those Aborigines. So, we can't be dispossessed'.[55]

LAW

 6

In any nation, the principal role played by many historians has been one of telling stories in order to legitimise that nation. This is done primarily by providing myths to suggest that the nation was founded on both moral and legal principles as a way to handle the historical reality that contradicts this.[1] In the Australian case, nationalist historians have long claimed that the country was not only colonised peacefully by the British, but that this occurred on the basis of civilised values and the rule of law. According to this fiction, the country was settled, not conquered. Nothing has dismayed and angered settler Australians more in recent years than Aboriginal political figures and radical historians pointing out that this is quite evidently nonsense. Like any nation, but especially a settler one, Australia's origins lie in the revolutionary overthrow of the sovereignty and order of another people or peoples, namely that of the Aborigines. It had no sanction in any law other than the laws of the conquering nation (and other European powers). Many settler Australians have not taken kindly to being reminded of this. Indeed, they wish to deny it. Since the mid-1980s, conservative public intellectuals in particular have made two moves. They have insisted on the relative absence of violence in the founding of the British colonies here; and they have insisted that these forerunners to the Australian nation had proper moral and legal foundations. These strategies go hand in hand. For his part, Keith Windschuttle has followed suit. In *The Fabrication of Aboriginal History*, he has presented an account of the colonisation of this country that is highly idealised and theoretical in nature rather than realistic and empirical.

Religion, philosophy, law

In his consideration of the moral and legal foundations of the British colonisation of this country, Windschuttle proceeds more or less in his usual manner. He misrepresents the work of his 'orthodox historians', beats their arguments up and then turns around and advances contentions they have already made. In doing so, he once more obfuscates the critical matters at stake.

Windschuttle claims that academic historians have cast the Van Diemonian frontier as an arena of unrestrained white violence. He returns to the furphy that frames his book, namely that an orthodox school of academic historians in the field of Aboriginal history have argued that the colonial government of the 1820s and 1830s administered 'a "conscious policy of genocide"'. As we have noted, this is a claim Windschuttle has repeatedly made, even though he does not provide any evidence in his book to support it. He also claims, however, that academic historians have not only propounded a genocide thesis (in respect of government), but also an extirpation one (in reference to settlers). Here he implies that academic historians have argued that there was a *universal* agreement among settlers that Aboriginal people should be extirpated or exterminated. Windschuttle fails to evidence this satisfactorily and cannot do so.[2]

Windschuttle's consideration of the work that so-called orthodox historians have done on colonists' attitudes and values is reckless in other ways. He alleges that they have been dismissive of religious belief: they refuse to consider whether it had any influence upon the behaviour of the colonists—indeed, they 'mock any suggestion that an appeal to Christian values might have carried weight'. According to Windschuttle, they also regard humanitarian sentiment as 'mere hypocrisy, worthy words that lacked substance because no action was ever taken by the authorities to back them up'. Similarly, they insist that 'neither Christian morality nor the rule of law had any force on the frontier'. Windschuttle barely evidences any of these claims, and where he does he once again refers to writers who are not academic historians. As we shall see, these are not contentions the majority of academic historians have advanced. It is another straw argument Windschuttle has created.[3]

Windschuttle presents this picture of colonial government and law:

The British colonies in Australia were founded under the rule of British law . . . A British declaration of sovereignty over a territory meant that all individuals within it, native and colonist, were subject to English law. Consequently, the instructions given by the Colonial Secretary in London to the various colonial governors required them not only to subject the Aborigines to the rule of law but to guarantee them its protection as well. As subjects of His Majesty, the Aborigines had to obey his law or suffer his punishment, but the same was true for anyone who sought to harm *them*. The instructions given to the first colonial officials required them to conciliate the natives but they paid as much attention to curbing violence by white settlers against them and punishing any offenders on this score. This was done not out of a sense of sympathy or kindliness but because the colonial governments had a legal foundation to which everyone, those in authority and those subject to it, were liable. It was this rule of law that made every British colony in its own eyes, and in truth, a domain of civilisation.

The final assertion aside, this account has long been advanced by academic historians in Australia, including those Windschuttle would regard as orthodox.[4]

In telling this story, Windschuttle emphasises the role played in the early Australian colonies by what he calls 'powerful social influences': 'Evangelical Christianity and Enlightenment humanism'. (Windschuttle eschews the term 'humanitarianism', which other historians have applied to this phenomenon.) He seeks to impress upon his readers the significance of these important religious and intellectual currents: 'The ruling ideas of the age, both at home and abroad, favoured the conciliation of the Aborigines. Van Diemen's Land was colonised at a time when British society and politics were strongly influenced by the revival of Christian Evangelicalism . . . and by the philosophy of the English and Scottish Enlightenment', which 'supported the unity of mankind and the belief that human beings had a common origin'. Furthermore, Windschuttle argues, the 'colonial governors and leading settlers not only held these ideas, they publicly expressed and acted upon them'. As a result, 'a demand to exterminate the Aborigines would not only have meant denying them the status of human beings protected by His Majesty's Laws, but would also have gone against the predominant religious and philosophical beliefs of the time'. There is nothing exceptional in this argument. Windschuttle has once more adopted the interpretation of other historians, including those he calls orthodox. At the same time, he has not alerted his readers to the critical issue. As Alan Atkinson suggests, every scholar who has done much work on the history of British imperialism, including the history in the Australian colonies, would admit that the Empire had moral ambition but they would also point to its serious, repeated failures.[5]

Windschuttle develops his picture of British colonisation in respect of Van Diemen's Land. He tells us twice that the colonial officers included men such as Governor George Arthur. Arthur had grown up during the religious revival of the late eighteenth and early nineteenth centuries, was a devout evangelical Christian, and had gained a reputation in the West Indies as an idealistic administrator. Windschuttle also tells us of the influence of William Wilberforce and evangelical Christianity on the campaign to abolish the transportation and ownership of slaves. He points out: 'In holding such views, Arthur was in accord not just with current sentiment in London but with the official policy towards indigenous people'. Similarly, he notes that colonial officials such as Arthur were not only issued with instructions requiring them 'to seek the goodwill of the natives but . . . also pa[y] as much attention to curbing violence against them and punishing any offenders on this score'. In making this argument about Arthur, Windschuttle has repeated a story already told by A.G.L. Shaw and Henry Reynolds. Windschuttle acknowledges Shaw's research, but not Reynolds'. On its own, this would be unremarkable but it reflects Windschuttle's general practice. He fails to acknowledge major points where academic historians have interpreted the past in a manner that does not accord with his picture of a 'historical orthodoxy'. In this case, Windschuttle has read Reynolds' account of Arthur's work, but he does not alert his readers to the implications of the considerable body of work Reynolds has done on the role played by humanitarians, such as Arthur, in Britain and the Australian colonies.[6]

Windschuttle realises that there is a stream of values and ideas other than Enlightenment humanism and Evangelical Christianity that he cannot ignore altogether. Not everyone shared the views of humanitarians like Arthur, he acknowledges: 'there were others who maligned the

Aborigines as "savages"'. Windschuttle proceeds by quoting the historian John Gascoigne: 'admonitions to accept Aborigines as fellow human beings were often prompted by an attempt to overcome a popular, untheoretical racism which equated indigenous people with the monkey or animal kingdom. In the first half of the nineteenth century such visceral, un-scientific racism was, *to some degree*, kept in check by elite opinion'. But Windschuttle does not seem to grasp the implications of Gascoigne's argument: such racism was only partially constrained.[7] Windschuttle provides evidence of this himself when he quotes a passage from the report of a government committee on Aborigines in Van Diemen's Land in 1830: 'It would indeed appear that there prevailed at this period too general a forgetfulness of those rights of ordinary compassion to which, as human beings, and as the original occupants of the soil, these defence-less and ignorant people were justly entitled. They were sacrificed in many instances to momentary caprice or anger, as if the life of a savage had been unworthy of the slightest consideration'. Windschuttle ignores this, intent as he is on focusing on 'the prevailing *ideas* about race relations'.[8]

The word and the world

This is by no means the weakest aspect of the account Windschuttle provides, however. More importantly, he fails to come to grips with the matter other historians have treated as absolutely critical: was there a discrepancy between the pronounced intentions of governments on the one hand and the actual outcomes on the frontiers of settlement on the other? To answer this question, the historian must attend carefully to any differences that exist between authority and power, between actions and outcomes, and between ideals, beliefs, opinions and intentions on the one hand, and actions, on the other. To do this, one must chart how religious beliefs, philosophical ideals and the rule of law actually functioned in Van Diemen's Land, and especially on the frontier.

Windschuttle does not do this. Instead, his approach is a highly idealistic one. He prefers to contemplate the frontier at an abstract level. He refers to 'the instincts of colonial culture' and 'a culture that fostered restraint in these matters' rather than demonstrating where and how these instincts or this culture were actually embodied in the *actions* of the human beings who lived on the frontiers of settlement. He is determined to maintain a focus on the realm of (philosophical) ideas and (religious) beliefs in metropolitan and colonial centres. He assumes that these were so powerful that they determined what happened in respect of colonists' attitudes and opinions as well as their actions and relationships with Aboriginal people. His account seldom grapples with what really happened when Aboriginal people and settlers encountered one another there.[9]

Most importantly, Windschuttle fails to consider how the rule of law worked in the circumstances of the frontier. 'It is', Martin Krygier and Robert van Krieken remark, 'a complicated matter to assess the extent to which the rule of law exists in any society at any time, though these complications do not appear to delay Windschuttle at all'. In their discipline—the sociology of law—Krygier and van Krieken observe that there is a truism that acknowledges the distance between 'law in books' and 'law in action'. This gap, they explain, is particularly apparent in frontier conditions—indeed, it is inherent in the very concept of a frontier. 'The rule of law must not only be proclaimed, or even endorsed by officials, for whether it exists and matters is a social matter', they point out. 'It must *count* in the social world'. Alan Atkinson has also made this point: 'As every good social historian knows, the law does not exist in a vacuum . . . The law is contingent on social relations, not the other way around'. But Windschuttle does not do social history. He assumes that he can point to the commitment a governor such as Arthur made to the rule of law and then claim that Aboriginal people were consistently safeguarded by it. This is poor historical practice.[10]

Windschuttle exaggerates the influence those such as Arthur had on the frontier. He confuses Arthur's authority—which was enormous—with his power—which was not. Windschuttle tells his readers: 'we need to realise that none of the early governors of the Australian colonies were politicians trying to woo a constituency by striking poses of moral rectitude or of statesmanship. Nor did they need to mollify the clergy or any other moral interest group . . . The Lieutenant-Governors of Van Diemen's Land were primarily administrators rather than politicians and they had little reason to be over-concerned about how well their public pronouncements were received locally. When they proclaimed a government order they expected it to be obeyed'. Quite, but this ignores the fact that the interests professed by government often clashed with those of the settlers, and that officials often lacked the power to ensure their will prevailed. Windschuttle incidentally provides evidence of this in his book. In 1830 the government committee reviewing the conflict between settlers and Aborigines observed: 'There is too much reason to apprehend that, as the white population spread itself more widely over the island, and the settlers came more frequently in contact with the Natives, many outrages were committed which no interposition of the government, however well disposed, could, with the means at its command, have been able to prevent'. Windschuttle ignores this, but other historians have pointed out that colonial governors were frequently unable to control the unruly actions of convict and other workers on the frontiers of settlement. A formal order forbidding the killing of Aborigines might be respected in places such as the main towns, where governmental authority was buttressed by power, but it could be treated with contempt in the countryside, which had areas that were often remote and where the power of government was relatively limited. Windschuttle also plays down the influence of the pastoral industry, which had become very important in the colonial economy; the largest pastoral landholders could wield considerable influence.[11]

In his account, Windschuttle also fails to pay attention to the nature of the white settlers. We learn little if anything about their moral and cognitive universe, as Krygier and van Krieken have pointed out. For example, he barely considers the social and cultural background of convicts or the conditions in which they worked and lived on the frontier, even though they comprised a large number of the whites who interacted with Aboriginal people on the frontier.[12] Indeed, a reader of Windschuttle's book can readily lose sight of the fact that he is dealing with a convict colony.[13] As Atkinson has remarked, Windschuttle overlooks the significance of a considerable body of historical sources that suggest many whites, especially those of humble status, were quite ready to kill Aboriginal people.[14]

At the same time, Windschuttle refuses to accept that his 'Evangelical Christianity and Enlightenment humanism' had little power to check the hatred that many of these frontiersmen felt towards Aborigines. He does not acknowledge properly that the frontier was often lawless, since it was a time and place where the usual restraints on men's behaviour were often weak. He retreats from this reality. At one or two points, Windschuttle admits that settlers had murderous impulses, but he seeks to justify these and to deny their significance by refusing to allow that their 'attitudes' or 'urges' might also have resulted in actions. After reviewing historical sources in which settlers volunteered their opinions on relations between Aboriginal people and themselves, he concludes: 'In *every* case, even the hardest attitudes were generated *solely* by the desire to stop the blacks from assaulting and murdering whites. They would have been a very peculiar people had they not felt the urge to retaliate. Despite the restraints of their culture and religion, and the admonishments of their government, the settlers of Van Diemen's Land were only human . . . The fact remains that *none* of the few who called for the extermination of the blacks acted out their sentiments, or had the power to do so'. (Every, solely, none? How does Windschuttle know? How can anyone know this?)[15]

By comparison, academic historians have long considered the ways in which the very conditions of the pastoral frontier in Australia tended to make settler violence likely if not inevitable: settlers sought to dispossess indigenous occupants of land and resources they held dear and Aboriginal people attacked stockmen, shepherds, hut-keepers and others, who often retaliated. This is not to regard frontiersmen as monsters. It is simply to acknowledge the point that many historians have made, including James Boyce in respect of Van Diemonian settlers: 'Even relatively sympathetic and sensitive men were prepared to kill once their own property and lives were directly threatened'.[16]

Windschuttle actually refers to a range of historical sources that suggest considerable violence occurred on the Van Diemonian frontier despite attempts by government to contain it. However, he is unwilling to recognise the significance of this historical record. He observes that governors issued proclamations warning settlers about committing acts of violence against Aborigines, but he does not inquire why they found it necessary to do so. Similarly, while he notes that officials and other colonists expressed considerable anxiety that Aborigines would or could be exterminated because of settler retaliation, he does not question why they entertained such fears. Windschuttle ignores these men's sense of reality as it threatens his ideal of a frontier governed by Enlightenment humanism, evangelical Christianity and the rule of law. He presumes to know their world much better than they did.[17]

Windschuttle's account of the work of high-ranking officials such as Arthur is a romantic one. As Alan Atkinson has observed, Windschuttle treats the humanitarianism they represent as though it was 'a simple, clear and unpolluted stream of idealism'. To recognise the true nature of humanitarianism one must pay attention to the context in which it operated, and read between the lines of the reports created by Arthur and others. Windschuttle does neither. 'Why did every statement Arthur make about Aboriginal violence talk about not only his responsibility to protect the colony but also his duty to have "every possible regard to humanity towards ignorant savages"?', Windschuttle asks. Why indeed? The answer lies partly in a phenomenon Windschuttle himself mentions. Officials like Arthur were highly conscious of the need to guard the moral reputation of the British Empire and they knew the Colonial Office was watchful. Windschuttle observes that 'the attitude of his superiors in the Colonial Office in London' was a 'factor weighing on Arthur's mind', but he backs away from the implications of this. He misses the critical point when he concludes: 'Arthur's own statements about his reluctance to deploy force against the Aborigines, and his orders to do so with as much humanity and as little bloodshed as possible, were all in accord with political feeling at home in Britain'. As other historians of humanitarianism have pointed out, officials like Arthur very much had an eye on the opinion of their imperial masters as well as the judgement of God and posterity when they formulated their statements of policy. Consequently, these should be treated cautiously. Windschuttle's reading of such statements is insufficiently critical or sceptical.[18]

Officials like Arthur had to negotiate a complex reality marked by different interests. As well as their need to protect the reputation of the Empire, they tried to protect some of the interests of the Aborigines (though, most importantly, *not* those they had in land), serve many of those of the settlers and, above all else, advance those of the colony as they conceived them. As numerous historians have pointed out, these interests were often in conflict, and colonial policy and practice would have been hugely contradictory if officials had sought to serve all these interests to the same degree, which they did not.[19] In many official statements, this is evident to the historian willing to read between the lines. Let us consider Windschuttle's treatment of a proclamation Arthur issued in 1828 authorising the magistrates and their deputies to capture and remove Aborigines from the areas of settlement. He notes that Arthur directed them to 'resort to whatever means a severe and inevitable necessity may dictate and require', but argues that Arthur 'emphasised that no civilians had the right to use force against the natives unless in self-defence or under the direction of the military or a magistrate'. Here Arthur spoke in two voices, as the Colonial Office and colonial officials so often did, but his meaning would nevertheless have been plain to colonists on the frontiers of settlement: he had accepted the necessity for prompt measures to end Aboriginal attacks by removing them from the settled districts by the best possible means. Windschuttle welcomes the appearance created by statements Arthur made. He is happy to accept their rhetoric as the reality. This simulacrum protects his ideal of the good British empire.[20]

This is also true of Windschuttle's approach to the way the legal system functioned in colonial society. He largely treats this matter at a theoretical level. He has pointed to the fact that the British proclaimed the principle of equality before law, and that unlawful killing of Aborigines was regarded as murder and carried the penalty of death.[21] At one point in his book, he actually considers this principle in practice. He claims that one man was charged and found guilty of the manslaughter of an Aboriginal man in Van Diemen's Land. However, one of his critics has cast doubt on this. (It seems the victim was a black immigrant rather than an Aboriginal man.)[22] More generally, though, the most Windschuttle is prepared to concede is the *possibility* that whites were not severely punished for assaults on Aboriginal people. He claims that not enough research has been done on this matter for us to know for sure. However, a recent study suggests that such research will not alter our general picture of the number of whites severely punished for murdering Aborigines.[23] Windschuttle also studiously avoids any discussion of the actual legal position of Aborigines themselves. Legal historians have argued that their status as British subjects was ambiguous during the first 50 or so years of white settlement, and that the British legal system seldom upheld their rights.[24]

Windschuttle seems to realise that his argument regarding the rule of law is weak. He tries to distract attention from the critical point in any historical debate about humanitarianism and the rule of law. 'Whatever the extent of their actions', he argues, 'there is no doubt that the colonial authorities genuinely believed that their responsibility was to curb any violence that settlers or convicts might commit against the Aborigines. They thought the colonial situation held considerable potential for conflict between ordinary settlers and the natives and it was their responsibility to keep it in check'. But, in the end, this is neither here nor there. What governments believed and thought is not the issue at stake. It is the extent of their actions that is crucial. This, more than anything else, determined the nitty-gritty reality of the frontier.[25]

As I have already noted, there is little difference between the accounts that Windschuttle and the so-called orthodox historians have provided of the ideals, beliefs and opinions of colonial authorities, or even the nature of government policy; there is, however, a fundamental difference between their accounts of government practice and what actually happened when policy was applied to what was happening on the frontier. Several academic historians have conducted research that has led them to conclude that colonial governors and other officials tried to implement their humanitarian ideals but were either foiled on the ground by settlers' opposition, the tyranny of distance, legal constraints (such as the disallowance of Aboriginal testimony), and a lack of government resources (such as police forces).[26]

Perhaps it not surprising that Windschuttle limits his consideration of this matter to the level of philosophy and policy rather than practice. His project is largely driven by a concern for the character of the settler nation. In his eyes, it is good enough to demonstrate that colonial authorities had benevolent intentions. The outcomes are less important. After all, he is trying to rewrite settler Australian history, not write Aboriginal history.

Windschuttle's history, Windschuttle's war

Why does Windschuttle paint an idealised picture of the role played by evangelical Christianity, humanitarianism and the rule of law that flies in the face of a historical consensus regarding the Australian frontier and historical common sense about frontiers in other settler societies such as the United States, Canada, South Africa and New Zealand? As we have noted, Windschuttle seeks to redeem Australia's reputation as a settler nation by resettling its history. But perhaps another factor has played a role, too.

It seems that Christianity, Enlightenment humanism and the law might have to play the role Windschuttle inscribes for them because of the very threat he unwittingly created in the first place by means of an act of projection. Having initially created a world of excessive violence (genocide and massacres) by constructing an 'orthodox' historiography, it becomes necessary to create another extremely powerful world (humanitarianism and the rule of law) in order to constrain this. Interestingly, the unrealistic battle that Windschuttle stages here between two diametrically opposed forces largely mirrors the one he had played out earlier in *The Killing of History*.[27]

More problematically, though, Windschuttle has scripted a historiographical drama in which a war between his two principal characters—the old 'orthodox' history and his 'new' history—holds centre stage, so much so that they displace the conflict that actually occurred historically. His present-day historiographical war takes the place of the real historical war. In fighting his war, moreover, Windschuttle repeats or re-enacts the very forces that are alive in his object of investigation: the aggressive violence of the frontier. Nowhere is this more apparent than in his attack upon Aboriginal culture and history.

CULTURE

 7

Keith Windschuttle's work, as we noted earlier, owes much to the culture wars American new conservatives began in the 1980s and which their Australian counterparts commenced some time later. In this war on the cultures of other peoples, they rely principally on historical theories that have long been deployed to justify colonialism. These have been especially important in the current context, in which settler societies have been confronted once again with the historical truth that they dispossessed and destroyed aboriginal peoples. This has proven very difficult in the Australian context. For a long time now, settlers here have lacked a story to explain satisfactorily why the land became the property of the new-comers, why another people and their culture largely ceased to continue, and how this revolution occurred.

'The course of history'

Representations of the relationship between European colonisers and aboriginal peoples have long been shaped by theoretical discourses that are inherently historical or historicist in nature. The disciplines we know as history, anthropology and archaeology largely emerged in the eigh-teenth and nineteenth centuries in the context of the encounter between Europe and other peoples—which is to say people Europeans regarded as 'other'. As noted earlier, these disciplines insisted upon a particular understanding of time or human history. This was conceived as the reason for the fundamental differences Europeans perceived between themselves and other peoples. The former constructed their culture as modern and civilised by constructing the culture of aboriginal peoples as ancient and primitive. That is, they claimed that cultures belonged to different periods of time or human history. Instead of regarding others, such as aborigines or indigenes, as peoples who were coeval or contemporaneous with themselves, Europeans claimed that they represented another time. According to this historical theory, there was a natural course of history beginning with the state of nature or antiquity, which was aboriginal, and progressing towards modernity, which was Europe's present. In this theory, peoples such as aborigines were always figured in terms of a lack or deficit.[1]

As Dipesh Chakrabarty has argued, historicism has had a very close relationship to political rule and political rights:

Historicism enabled European domination of the world in the nineteenth century. Crudely, one might say that it was one important form that the ideology of progress or 'development' took from the nineteenth century on ... Historicism ... posited historical time as a measure of the cultural distance ... that was assumed to exist between the West and the non-West. In the colonies, it legitimated the idea of civilisation ...

Historicism—and even the modern, European idea of history—one might say, came to non-European peoples in the nineteenth century as somebody's ways of saying 'not yet' to somebody else ... According to [liberals such as John Stuart] Mill, Indians or Africans [or aborigines] were *not yet* civilised enough to rule themselves. Some historical time of development and civilisation (colonial rule and education, to be precise) had to elapse before they could be considered prepared for such a task. Mill's historicist argument thus consigned Africans and other 'rude' nations [such as aborigines] to an imaginary waiting room of history. We were all headed for the same destination, Mill averred, but some people were [destined] to arrive earlier than others. That was what historicist consciousness was: a recommendation to the colonised to wait ...

Twentieth-century anti-colonial democratic demands ... on the contrary, harped insistently on a 'now' as the temporal horizon of action. From about the time of [the] First World War to the decolonisation movements of the fifties and sixties, anticolonial nationalisms were predicated on this urgency of the 'now'.[2]

In the eighteenth century, historicism was enunciated in a form of conjectural history by Enlightenment philosophers such as Adam Smith and Adam Ferguson, and was variously known as 'The History of Civil Society', 'The Natural History of Man' and 'The Course of Empire'. (More recently, scholars have called it stadial history, or a stagist theory of history.) They forged this story on the basis of reading accounts of antiquity in classical history, stories about indigenous peoples in North America and speculative works by philosophers such as John Locke. These philosophers held that human society developed through four historical stages, characterised primarily by hunting and gathering, pastoralism, agriculture and commerce respectively. Each was held to have particular ideas regarding law, religion, government and property. For example, nomadic hunter-gatherers were regarded as primitive peoples who either had none or lesser forms of these. This theory of historical change was constructed in Europe and so largely in the absence of actual aboriginal peoples. Nevertheless, it was critical in the colonisation of new lands such as *Terra Australis*. It played a major role in determining the historical and legal narratives that colonisers used to justify seizing the lands of aboriginal people and/or ruling them.[3]

The role of historical theories in the colonisation of other people's countries was not confined to European philosophers. By the mid-nineteenth century, British settlement was treated by imperial and colonial historians as the path of history. A liberal writer, John West—one of the first to tell the history of Van Diemen's Land and more sympathetic to the plight of Aboriginal people than most colonists—could sanction the British invasion in these terms in the 1850s:

> The original occupation of this county necessarily involved most of the consequences which followed: was that occupation, then, just? The right of wandering hordes to engross vast regions—for ever to retain exclusive property in the soil, and which would feed millions where hundreds are scattered—can never be maintained. The laws of increase seem to suggest the right of migration: neither nations nor individuals are bound to tarry on one spot, and die. The assumption of sovereignty over a savage people is justified by necessity—that law, which gives to strength the control of weakness. It prevails everywhere: it may be either malignant or benevolent, but it is irresistible.[4]

In the course of the following decades, it increasingly became a matter of common sense among colonists that Aborigines were either a race doomed to die out or a child race in need of European tutorship. This was largely due to the growing influence of historical theories of evolution. Among many, the demise of the Aboriginal race was regarded as a natural course of events. It was an outcome figured in human evolution rather than caused by the human agents of colonisation. In other words, according to the very logic of this theoretical history, an Aboriginal future was a contradiction in terms since Aboriginal people were deemed to be necessarily passing away. The death in 1876 of Truganini, the so-called last Tasmanian Aborigine, was hailed as proof of this. Among others, especially humanitarians, it was thought Aboriginal people might survive and could be uplifted so that eventually they, too, would be able to enter 'modernity' and even be deserving of the rights of citizenship—though not self-rule.[5]

In recent years, a few conservative intellectuals have continued to advance the theory of history outlined here. In the Australian context, the most important advocate has been the historian Geoffrey Blainey. In keeping with this conjectural history, he has repeatedly cast the history of the British colonisation of this country as a natural and thus inevitable process of evolution, and treated it as an encounter between the incompatible cultures or temporalities of European 'modernity' and Aboriginal 'antiquity'. The Europeans and Aborigines were 'probably as far apart as any societies thrust against each other in the history of the human race'; 'even with goodwill on both sides, they were incompatible'. '[T]he old way of life survived [before 1788]. But that way of life was doomed, even if the Papuans, the Javanese or the Maoris had been the first outsiders to settle in Australia. Such a form of land use was bound to be overthrown or undermined. The world's history has depended heavily on the eclipse of this old and wasteful economic way of life'. 'Here were the citizens and outcasts from the nation at the head of the world's latest economic revolution—the industrial revolution and the age of steam—confronting Aborigines who had not yet experienced the first economic revolution. Here were the inhabitants of the land that had just invented the steam engine meeting folk who could not boil water'. And so on. In cleaving to this speculative history, which has served imperialism and colonialism so well, Blainey has evaded a critical question: what responsibility do settlers bear for the plight of Aboriginal people since their colonisation of this country?[6]

Keith Windschuttle, as one might anticipate, prefers this theoretical history to any proper history. In the face of the realities of history, he takes refuge in theories of history. Windschuttle treats European colonisation of the so-called New World of the Pacific as though it were a natural occurrence caused by historical evolution, rather than one determined by human beings. That is, he treats examples of colonisation such as Van Diemen's Land as an inevitable historical process rather than a willed and wilful act whereby colonisers occupied another people's country. It was a moment, he says, when History intervened. At the same time, in order to argue that the quick demise of Aboriginal people was only to be expected, he emphasises their incompatibility with British civilisation and the fragility of their culture. Like John West, he claims that the British occupation witnessed the triumph of modern Western civilisation over primitive aboriginal culture. 'British colonisation of Australia', he has said, 'brought civilisation . . . to what was then a very primitive society . . . Primitive is a word you're not allowed to use any more, but I can't think of any other way to describe the kind of political, economic, [and] social organisation they had before the British arrived. All cultures are not equal'.[7]

We will now consider Windschuttle's argument and its sources in more detail.

A theoretical history

The Aborigines in Van Diemen's Land, Windschuttle claims—echoing the theoretical histories of the eighteenth and nineteenth centuries—were representatives of the most primitive human society Europeans had ever encountered. Their technology was simple: they lived off the land; they had no houses; they wandered from place to place; they had few possessions and these were crude; they went about naked; they could not make fire or boil water; and so on. They were not only backward in technology, they had regressed. They no longer ate the food they once consumed. This was because they were isolated, and so suffered the consequences of a lack of competition or innovation. Their society was also backward. It was extraordinarily violent, both among groups and between groups. Killing others was common, especially men killing women. Groups were destroyed by warfare. This was so common it threatened the survival of the Aborigines. They had no political leadership. Thus they failed to foresee the consequences of their behaviour and devise means to curb it. They numbered fewer than 2000 before the British came. Windschuttle concludes:

> The real tragedy of the Aborigines was not British colonisation *per se* but that their society was, on the one hand, so internally dysfunctional and, on the other hand, so incompatible with the looming presence of the rest of the world . . . They had survived for a millennia, it is true, but it seems clear that this owed more to good fortune than good management . . . Hence it was not surprising that when the British arrived, this small, precarious society quickly collapsed under the dual weight of the susceptibility of its members to disease and the abuse and neglect of its women.[8]

From what sources does Windschuttle derive this discredited account of precolonial Aboriginal culture? He draws on a range of material, but his description mostly relies on four kinds of information: anthropological texts published in the late nineteenth century; the writing of settlers in the mid- to late nineteenth century; archaeological speculation in the 1960s; and the speculative philosophy of history—that is, historicism (though he does not reference this). All these are highly problematical for one reason or another, and in using them Windschuttle has little concern for historical facts which, as I have already stated, he claims to respect.

For much of the nineteenth century, anthropological research in Australia did not comprise fieldwork among Aboriginal people of the kind conducted during the first half or so of the twentieth century in areas where they had not incurred the full force of British colonisation. It was done by anthropologists in Europe, whose work was primarily theoretical rather than empirical in nature. They worked in accordance with the framework of social evolution, which largely determined their lines of inquiry and the interpretations they advanced. Many anthropologists tried to prove evolutionary assumptions about the inferior nature of primitive indigenous peoples and the superiority of modern European peoples.[9] In their highly speculative work, anthropologists largely relied upon the *memories* of colonists who had first encountered Aboriginal people on the frontiers of pastoral settlement or even later—which was usually after their way of life had been severely disrupted by contact with sealers, whalers and settlers. Where he draws on their accounts, therefore, Windschuttle relies on a source that has the same nature as oral history even though he is loath to accept people's memories for any account of frontier conflict unless corroborated by contemporary historical sources.[10]

Windschuttle implies that his picture of precolonial Aboriginal culture is largely drawn from H. Ling Roth's *The Aborigines of Tasmania*, first published in 1890. Trained in natural science and philosophy, Roth compiled his book in England. It seems he may have never visited Tasmania. In some respects, *The Aborigines of Tasmania* was typical of the anthropological studies undertaken at this time. It carried the imprimatur of the famous British anthropologist E.B. Tylor, whose emphasis on questions regarding levels of civilisation and stages in evolution exerted considerable influence on anthropological studies carried out in Australia in the closing decades of the nineteenth century.[11] Windschuttle seeks to lend authority to this work on the grounds that Roth discusses 'the findings of all the original ethnographic studies'. This is misleading. Such work does not amount to scientific research; it mostly comprises the recollections of settlers who were untrained in the ethnographic observation of indigenous peoples. At best, Roth's sources might be described as ethnohistorical but, as the archaeologist Tim Murray has insisted for many years now, using such post-contact sources to create a picture of precolonial or 'traditional' Aboriginal cultures is a hazardous procedure. 'Given the strong likelihood that Aboriginal society had probably undergone drastic changes by the time [such] European observations were recorded', he and Christine Williamson have observed recently, 'it is extremely perilous to assume that all elements recorded are "traditional"'. Windschuttle compounds this problem, they note, by taking an uncritical approach to these sources. Yet in the end it seems that Windschuttle's anthropological account does not rest on Roth's text but upon other, mostly unreferenced historicist speculations, whose prejudices he accepts.[12] (Apart from anything else, Roth's approach to Aboriginal people was a compassionate one.) Perhaps is it not surprising that one critic has described Windschuttle's approach as 'DIY anthropologising'.[13]

To a much lesser degree, Windschuttle's account relies upon some of Rhys Jones' archaeological research. Jones' findings regarding Aboriginal food-gathering have been drawn into question by several other archae-ologists. (So, too, have the claims, which Jones repeats, that Aboriginal people could not make fire.)[14] However, Windschuttle either does not know or does not acknowledge this work. This is also true of the only rigorous attempt to construct the precolonial population, which suggests that earlier estimates of 3000–5000 Aboriginal people prior to European contact should be revised upwards. Not surprisingly, Murray and William-son have concluded that Windschuttle's account is 'based on a very partial and narrow understanding of the results of more than 30 years of archae-ological research into the history of Tasmanian Aboriginal society'.[15]

Windschuttle's claims regarding Aboriginal warfare and its toll in Van Diemen's Land prior to British colonisation probably have the least support of any he makes about Aboriginal culture. He has followed an argument Geoffrey Blainey made in his *Triumph of the Nomads* (1975) about the mainland, which rested on very few sources. For example, when Blainey repeated it in his *A Land Half Won* (1980), he seemed to provide just three relevant sources, one of which was his earlier book. Blainey's claims were controversial. Windschuttle knows this, but does not tell his readers that they were challenged on empirical grounds.[16]

On the basis of their familiarity with this field of research, Murray and Williamson point out that Windschuttle has made many errors in his portrait of precolonial society. Most importantly, they demonstrate that his negative account is informed by 'simplistic readings and progress and regression' and that these rest upon 'simplistic [historicist] assumptions'. They consider it extraordinary that Windschuttle attributes the survival of Aborigines in Van Diemen's Land to good luck. Research based on archaeological data, they note, emphasises the resilience and adaptability of their culture, not fragility and inability to change.[17]

Many have been shocked by Windschuttle's treatment of Aboriginal culture. It is deeply offensive to Aboriginal people, some of whom protested at the launch of his book. One Aboriginal woman remarked that she felt 'sick to the pit of my stomach'. Similarly, the academic historian Alan Atkinson has observed: 'there is very little "*humanised* knowledge"— knowledge imbued with human feeling and a feeling for humans'. Another white critic has remarked: 'There are passages in *Fabrication* that are genuinely hard to read because they seem so determined to deny the Tasmanian Aborigines a common humanity'. Windschuttle's book bears an uncanny resemblance to the thinking and attitudes that dominated in the second half of the nineteenth century and the first half of the twentieth. These were reflected in a national and racial consensus among historical writers. Windschuttle's work has threatened to revive this.[18]

Windschuttle's fatal impact

Windschuttle's treatment of the impact of British colonisation on Aboriginal people in Van Diemen's Land is as unsatisfactory as his treatment of precolonial Aboriginal culture, but its implications are probably more serious. Following in the footsteps of colonial and nationalist historians, he shifts responsibility for this away from the colonisers. To do this, he plays down the number of Aboriginal people killed by whites (as we have seen) and he plays up two other factors in the destruction of Aboriginal people. First, he stresses the role played by introduced diseases; and second, he blames Aboriginal men, claiming that their treatment of women rendered them vulnerable since their encouragement of sexual relations with white men resulted in venereal diseases, which caused both death and infertility.[19]

There can be no question that introduced diseases were the major killers of Aboriginal people. This was made clear in early academic studies. For example, in his first book—a collection of historical sources—Henry Reynolds devoted a chapter to disease and deprivation, which he introduced in this manner: 'Overshadowing all else in the history of post-settlement Aboriginal societies is the relentless decline in population which began in 1788 . . . Many of the causes of Australian depopulation are well known and can be readily illustrated. Exotic diseases like smallpox, measles, whooping cough and influenza decimated tribes all over the continent. Tuberculosis and other respiratory infections caused havoc [later] . . . Venereal diseases spread rapidly along the frontiers of settlement, undermining health and reducing fertility'.[20]

Windschuttle, however, exaggerates the impact of disease by arguing that Aboriginal people in Van Diemen's Land were dramatically affected by introduced diseases *before* permanent British settlement. Rather oddly, he lists influenza, colds, pneumonia and tuberculosis, which tended to affect Aboriginal people in the circumstances created by their dispossession and displacement, rather than diseases such as smallpox, which affected Aborigines in other colonies prior to contact, or measles, which affected them regardless of the circumstances in which they contracted it. Windschuttle's account contrasts with the picture other historians have presented regarding the pattern of introduced diseases in Van Diemen's Land and other Australian colonies.[21]

Windschuttle's argument regarding the relative impact of disease does not seem to rest on any research. Instead, it depends upon assumptions, which he extrapolates from other Australian colonial contexts, and on assertions, which he derives from arguments other historians have made about the impact of diseases in North America and the Pacific. (In advancing his case, he also misrepresents the writings of his 'orthodox historians'.)[22] In other words, Windschuttle's case—once again—is not an empirical one based on any pertinent historical sources.[23]

Other historians of Van Diemen's Land have presented a rather different account of the impact of disease in the colony on the basis of their historical research. They have argued that there is no evidence for a smallpox epidemic there, even though smallpox was the main killer of Aboriginal people in other colonies such as New South Wales. They have also contended that the Aboriginal population did not decline severely prior to the early 1820s, when large-scale pastoral expansion began. In their assessment, the Aborigines in Van Diemen's Land had a lower rate of venereal disease than those in other areas of southeastern Australia.[24]

Our understanding of the pattern of diseases other than smallpox and their precise impact in Australia still remains quite sketchy. Historians of other Australian colonies have pointed to the probability of a complex causal relationship between conflict, dispossession and displacement, and hunger, malnutrition and disease, which seem to have been major factors in the high rates of morbidity among indigenous peoples on other colonial frontiers.[25] Windschuttle refuses to accept this. Instead, he asserts: 'Their numbers were small to begin with . . . so it did not take much for the inevitable arrival of the outside world to cause the demise of such a fragile population'.[26]

The inevitable arrival of the outside world? Like Geoffrey Blainey and a host of earlier white historians, Windschuttle tends to displace any responsibility the British might have had for the consequences of a decision by their government to colonise Aboriginal lands. He rejects one, minor tradition in Australian colonial writing—a story of colonialism's disastrous impact on Aboriginal people—to repeat another, more influential one— a story of progressive British colonisation, which glosses over the invasion of Aboriginal land, the dispossession and destruction of the original owners and any responsibility of colonists for this.

The lie of the land

'Tasmanian Aborigines', Windschuttle asserts, 'did not own the land'. They had a notion of territory but no 'concept of land ownership' and no sense of 'possessing territory or of deterring trespassers from it'. Why is this so? Because they were 'nomadic hunter-gatherers', and 'the idea of "land" itself as property . . . derives from agricultural society, not that of hunter-gatherers'. Who says so? Those Enlightenment philosophers and their successors whose conjectural history has shaped the general way in which Windschuttle has represented precolonial Aboriginal culture more generally. In other words, Windschuttle once more advances an argument that is founded upon the assumptions of a speculative theory constructed in Europe rather than on empirical data from informed ethnographic or historical sources forged in Australia, or the arguments based on proper anthropological or historical research undertaken here.[27]

Windschuttle, furthermore, justifies the British possession of the land in much the same manner in which most settlers in the Australian colonies in the nineteenth century came to rationalise this during and after the time they were dispossessing Aboriginal people of their land. He conducts a discussion as follows: the British colonies were founded in accordance with contemporary international law, by which a European state could establish a colony in one of three ways: by purchasing or leasing the right from the indigenous inhabitants; by persuading these inhabitants to submit to their rule; or by unilaterally declaring possession on the basis of first discovery and effective occupation. The British, Windschuttle says, 'fell back on the third of the[se] means of legitimising a colony'. This was so because they were aware that 'James Cook and other navigators had indicated that there were no people there who had the kind of sovereignty over territory the British needed to conduct negotiations'. Nothing changed in 1788 because the colonists 'found the same problem'. That is: 'The nomadic hunter-gatherer Aboriginal society did not have a political or religious framework with which they could deal. There were no chiefs, no alliances, no military forces, no priests and no apparent permanent inhabitants of the territory'. Windschuttle continues: 'The principal fact that legitimised their colonisation was that the land was not cultivated and was thus open to annexation. Nomadic hunter-gatherers did not cultivate the land and hence did not possess it . . . Mere occupancy did not confer property rights; land had to be used. The first person to use it, which at the time meant some kind of agricultural cultivation, became its owner'. Windschuttle points out that these assumptions held true in the Americas as well: 'So when British eyes of the eighteenth century looked on the natives of Australia, they saw nomads who hunted but who had no agricultural base, and who therefore did not possess the country they inhabited. In contrast, the British colonists took up the land and "improved" it . . . By "improving" the land, the colonists thereby saw themselves as acquiring right of possession. They were not dispossessing the natives. Instead, colonisation offered the indigenous people the gift of civilisation, bringing them all the techniques for living developed by the Old World'. In the passage I have paraphrased and quoted here, Windschuttle does not make clear whether or not he endorses this rationalisation for dispossessing Aborigines of their land, but arguments he advances elsewhere suggest that he does.[28]

Windschuttle has followed the treatment of this matter presented by a leading Australian academic historian, Alan Frost. The conservative Frost made this argument in the early 1980s in a context in which a campaign for Aboriginal 'land rights' had drawn into question the moral and legal foundations of the Australian nation and provoked a crisis of legitimacy. Frost gave himself the academic task of trying to explain why the British had denied Aboriginal rights to land—which he performed by arguing that they did this in accordance with British law and the law of nations at the time Britain claimed the land of much of the Australian continent[29]—but he also had a political purpose, which was to justify this—which he performed not only by referring to the aforementioned legal conventions but also by holding the Aboriginal people responsible: they were too different ('too un-European') and so the British were unable to grasp that Aboriginal people *did* have a sense of land ownership. It should be noted that many liberal historians, such as Henry Reynolds, have in some respects endorsed Frost's treatment of this contentious matter inasmuch as they have tended to treat the denial of Aboriginal rights to land as a matter of (a lack of) British knowledge rather than a matter of having superior power.[30]

Even though Windschuttle apparently accepts this highly Eurocentric perspective on why the British denied Aboriginal rights to land in the Australian colonies, he lectures the so-called 'orthodox historians of Tasmania' for their failure to apply a cross-cultural approach to the conflict between Aborigines and settlers. He suggests that these historians have imposed their notion of exclusive use of private property on to the mentality of nomadic hunter-gatherers and assumed that the presence of the settlers on their land caused resentment and provoked violence. (He refers to Henry Reynolds' book on Tasmania and cites a passage Reynolds quotes there as though to prove his point.) As we might expect, Windschuttle once more fails to describe the academic historiography on this matter either accurately or fairly. Having beaten these historians up yet again, Windschuttle proceeds to advance his own argument regarding the response of Aborigines to the British intrusion. He claims there is no evidence that Aboriginal people had a concept such as trespass in reference to land. They clearly had a sense of proprietorial rights towards their game, he says, but just as clearly they did not have this in reference to their territory. He insists: 'If the Aborigines had a concept of preserving their own land against invaders, then this should have been evident right from the outset. It would have been at first contact when the intrusion would have been the most offensive to native sensibilities'. There are good reasons for concluding that this is nonsense.[31]

Let us consider these two matters in turn, taking the second one first. Windschuttle has misconstrued the critical issue by ignoring the fact that Aboriginal people did not necessarily object to the initial intrusion by settlers, but rather to settlers insisting later that the land (or control over it) was exclusively theirs. Henry Reynolds made this important point in his 1981 book, *The Other Side of the Frontier*: 'As a general rule [Aboriginal] clans did not react immediately to European trespass . . . Indeed the history of inland exploration indicates that local groups tolerated the passage of European expeditions provided they behaved with circumspection'. However, Reynolds points out, it is apparent that 'white and black perceptions of what was taking place were very wide apart'. Unless they had prior knowledge, it is unlikely that Aborigines had any appreciation of the fact that the whites were determined to stay indefinitely and own the land. He continues: 'If blacks often did not react to the initial invasion of their country it was because they were not aware that it had taken place. They certainly did not believe that their land had suddenly ceased to belong to them and they to their land. The mere presence of Europeans, no matter how threatening, could not uproot certainties so deeply implanted in Aboriginal custom and consciousness'. Reynolds goes on to argue: 'Aborigines reacted less to the original trespass than to the ruthless assertion by Europeans of exclusive proprietorial rights'. Since reciprocity and sharing were central to their culture, he contends that it was not so much the possessions that mattered to Aboriginal people but an affirmation of their principles of reciprocity and an anger over white possessiveness transgressing these. This was one of the motives for their attacks on settlers.[32]

In reference to the other matter—the question of property ownership—it seems that Windschuttle's understanding is fundamentally flawed. Les Hiatt, a leading Australian anthropologist who has considered the relationship of Aboriginal people to land for over 40 years, has questioned Windschuttle's treatment. He argues: 'If modern research on the mainland can be taken as a guide, what it implies is the existence in Tasmania of an ethic of reciprocal hospitality facilitating a sharing of resources while simultaneously affirming the right of hosts to give or withhold. The fact that Aborigines admired generosity . . . should not mislead us into thinking they lacked a concept of ownership'. He is reluctant to accept Windschuttle's assertion that Aborigines in Van Diemen's Land believed that (1) they held sole rights over natural food resources and yet (2) had no concept of property in land. 'How collectivities such as bands and tribes could have the first without the second is not explained', Hiatt points out. He observes somewhat wryly: 'If the indigenous Tasmanian polity placed no restrictions whatever on movement in pursuit of game or plant food, it was unlike any stable hunter-gatherer regime we know about'. How, one might ask, could it be that Windschuttle, who apparently has neither done any anthropological research nor read any recent research that challenges the interpretations offered by those such as Hiatt, knows better?[33]

In denying Aboriginal people their rights to land, Windschuttle once more makes an argument characterised by the idealism and relativism he despises. Aboriginal people cannot have had any sense of owning their country, he claims, because they had no word signifying land in the sense of property. They did not even have a word for land, or words for 'own', 'possess', or 'property'. Henry Reynolds has pointed out that they had many words relating to country, including words meaning 'my country'. But this is not good enough for Windschuttle. Only 'property' will do. We must respect their different conceptions of the world, he says. Here Windschuttle plays the game that has so often been played in colonial regimes: he claims to respect difference only when it serves the interests of colonial power.[34]

In a Eurocentric vein, Windschuttle also demands that evidence for an Aboriginal sense of land ownership be expressed by Aborigines in the form of words (rather than actions) and maintains that these have to be spoken by them and in their own precolonial or 'traditional' linguistic or political codes. Others cannot speak on their behalf because when that happens it is only whites who are speaking, and they cannot use words such as 'subjects', 'nation' and 'possessions' because these are only European concepts. Here, Windschuttle is being unrealistic. In any context, but especially a cross-cultural one, supplicants such as indigenous people have to speak the political language of the dominant order, translating their own concepts so that they make sense to the rulers and make a case in terms that they might accept.[35] Not surprisingly, Aboriginal people often relied on sympathetic colonists to perform this task.[36]

Historical denialism?

Windschuttle's treatment of the question of Aboriginal land ownership has the same fantastic quality as other colonial treatments of the matter have had, especially those found in the law where it seeks to turn the lie of this land into the law of this land. Windschuttle's work denies the reality that this country was the Aboriginal peoples' before it was colonised by the British. Any number of words should not be permitted to disguise this worldly reality.

In *The Fabrication of Aboriginal History*, Windschuttle also denies several other historical truths. This work denies that Aborigines were the original sovereign people of this country, and so denies that the British invaders usurped this; it denies that Aboriginal people engaged in warfare to defend their control of the country, and so denies that they resisted their dispossession; it denies that whites killed large numbers of Aboriginal people on the frontier; it denies the role the British invasion played in the displacement and depopulation of Aboriginal people, and so denies that the colonisers had some responsibility for this; and it denies the humanity of Aboriginal people and the value of their culture.

For quite some time, most of these historical assessments had been off limits among many settler Australians. The controversy surrounding Windschuttle's work has not encouraged thinking about the unthinkable, but it has provoked debate over what had passed out of consideration. One cannot deplore the fact that the British colonisation of this country might be regarded in different ways to those presented by most academic historians during the last three or so decades. 'Neither genuine questions nor good-faith answers should be placed off limits', Charles Maier, a historian who has considered the German *Historikerstreit*, has pointed out: 'When some knowledge is put off limits and received traditions are shielded from objective reconsideration', he remarks, 'we enter the realm of hallowing and sanctification—perhaps one necessary activity for communities, but not to be confused with scientific activity . . . [T]he validity of a historical interpretation or investigation is not to be measured by its political results'.[37]

Maier also offers this wise counsel: 'Let us accept that no question should be out of bounds'. Yet he goes on to ask: 'Does this mean that every answer must be honored?' The historical community, he suggests, is probably best to accept marginal historical projects as efforts done in good faith and subject these to thoughtful rebuttal rather than regard them merely as evil positions: 'Better to admit than to anathematise'. Yet many consider Keith Windschuttle's historical project to be a denialist one, and thus beyond the pale. Many have asked whether he has done his work in good faith, and whether he should be entitled to the privileges usually accorded to a historian by virtue of belonging to a scholarly community. Readers of his work have answered—and will continue to answer—these questions very differently.[38]

There should be less disagreement, I suggest, about whether we honour Windschuttle's answers—about whether we conclude that his work offers us something in the way of historical understanding. In response to Windschuttle's first writings in this field I argued that his intervention was essentially irrelevant in scholarly terms.[39] Little, if anything, in his later writings has given me cause to alter this opinion. I have discovered nothing significant in Windschuttle's writings that cannot be found in the large body of historical scholarship that preceded it. There are neither new arguments nor new insights. His work has not provoked professional historians to consider new questions; good polemical work can, of course, have this function. As we have observed, we have been presented with an account of the past that rests upon poor and faulty methods of historical scholarship. Most importantly, given that the impact of his work has primarily been historiographical, we have seen that his representation of the work of other historians is severely flawed, indeed, so much so, that his accounts simply cannot be trusted. In the light of these serious weaknesses, it is difficult to envisage how any research Windschuttle does in the future could play a significant part in deepening knowledge in the area of Aboriginal history.

Windschuttle is not, despite the appearance he and his supporters have created in the mass media, a controversial scholar who has been posing sophisticated questions about the past which must be addressed, and providing rich answers which add to our store of historical wisdom. It is lamentable that his work has been embraced by sympathisers who have not tested his claims carefully. Some of them should have known better. They are probably more culpable than he in placing historical truth in the public realm at risk.[40]

Finally, one might ask whether Windschuttle's work has served a useful purpose in some other way? It *could* have performed an important service in supplementing the work professional historians have done in order to draw attention to the excesses apparent in *popular* historical discourses. However, by performing this task in a crude and hyperbolic fashion

Windschuttle has threatened to throw the baby out with the bath water. His attack on popular historical representations has disguised the fact that sometimes—even quite often—they convey a germ of historical truth.

At most, Windschuttle's work has sent some of us back to pondering the question of how academic historians can best play the role of historical remembrancers in reference to what is undoubtedly the darkest, most painful chapter in Australia's history. In other words, how best can historians relate and relate to this past and its presence? What does this task involve? What does it require? And what could be the outcomes of doing this work better than most academic historians do it now? In the last part of this book, I will address these questions.

PART III

• • •

FUTURE

HISTORY

 8

How can professional historians better tell the history of colonialism in Australia, especially in a way that provides Aboriginal perspectives of it?[1] In recent decades, scholars have been considering this question and exploring new ways of undertaking this task. During the same period, as we have noted (in Chapter 2), other ways of relating the past and relating to the past—such as oral history, myth and tradition—have become increasingly popular and have become rivals for historical authority. It is now more apparent than ever that history, and particularly academic history, is only one way of understanding the past in the present.

Among academic historians, there has only been a partial acknowledgment of the enormous difficulties that arise when trying to represent British colonisation of this country—particularly its impact on Aboriginal people. At the same time, many academic historians have failed to recognise the limits of their discipline when they try to historicise this past. The nature of the difficulty faced by academic history can be made clearer by reformulating the question posed in my introductory sentence to this chapter: How does one relate disaster? More particularly, how does one relate a past in which the props of memory of one of the two peoples who could have registered it were mostly destroyed by the events of that past—either by the destruction or the dislocation of people and things—and when that people's perspective was barely recorded contemporaneously because they had an oral culture? In other words, how can you provide a reliable narrative of a cataclysmic event when the contemporary historical sources upon which academic history has conventionally relied are inadequate? Furthermore, how does one relate a *traumatic* past such as this one—traumatic for both

Aboriginal and settler peoples? That is, how does one relate a past that was only partially registered at the time it occurred because of its very nature? Taking these questions together, we might ask: do we require new historical concepts, new historical methods and new forms of historical narrative in order to be able to represent this past?

There is also a further problem, which academic historians in this field are yet to address in a comprehensive fashion: how does anyone relate *to* a traumatic past, and what are the implications of this for historical knowledge and historical method? This has probably become *the* critical issue as a result of the rise of oral history, myth and tradition, which are often regarded (for better or worse) as forms of memory—collective, public, social, cultural or otherwise?[2] There is, of course, a further question here for the practitioners of academic history. How should we respond to alternative ways of relating the past, such as myth, given that they have different regimes of knowledge and so have ways of realising truth that diverge from those championed traditionally by academic history?

The challenge posed by the task of doing Aboriginal history, I am suggesting, has several dimensions, nearly all of which intersect in some way or another. In the final part of this book, I address—mostly through particular examples of history-making—a series of questions. How have academic historians sought to relate and relate to the frontier past in recent decades? How do other stories, such as myth, relate this past? How have academic historians reacted to these other ways of relating this past, and how might they respond to other approaches to the past? Are new forms of history-telling required in order to include Aboriginal voices or perspectives that do not meet the discipline's traditional requirements regarding evidence? Finally, how can and should a democratic society handle different ways of relating (to) the Australian Aboriginal past? In tackling many of these questions, it should be apparent that there is an unavoidable link between the epistemological issues and the ethical issues at stake in the controversy over Aboriginal history.

A subaltern past

Before considering how academic historians have attempted to relate (to) the history of the frontier in recent times, the nature of the problem they encounter needs to be delineated somewhat further. The most significant aspect of the era of the Australian frontier was the destruction of Aboriginal people. They perhaps numbered between 750 000 and 1.25 million in 1788. Colonisation by another people or peoples brought devastation in its wake. Within a generation of first contact on the frontier, which occurred across the continent for over a hundred years, hundreds of Aboriginal groups had been destroyed completely. By 1901 there were only 100 000 or so Aboriginal people. The story of this terrible cataclysm has not been properly told historically. Indeed, the relative absence of this revolutionary event in the nation's history and culture testifies to its overwhelming impact. In trying to tell this awful history, one must contemplate the silence it has wrought.[3]

In order to grasp an understanding of an event of this magnitude, the voices of its principal victims are essential. Their testimony would best reveal what can be known of this past: the horrifying reality of life on this continent for Aboriginal people following the British occupation of their lands. The consistent presence of the voice of the sufferers in any telling of this story would put the actions of the colonisers into their proper perspective. But this is *the* historical problem. There are hardly any such voices in the contemporary historical record. This record is weighted very, very heavily in favour of non-Aboriginal accounts. This is an incontrovertible historiographical fact.

There are no contemporary or near-contemporary literary historical sources *created* by Aboriginal people. This is so because Aboriginal people had an oral culture rather than a literary one. In the absence of the technologies now available to record the spoken word, their perspectives of the events that occurred were never registered when they occurred or shortly afterwards. Other forms of representation, such as rock paintings, provide some sense of an Aboriginal perspective but few of these allow us to recreate much of their world of meanings. Later, some colonisers re-presented what Aboriginal people told them or what they assumed Aborigines told them, but this was nearly always in a language that was not their own, which is critical since conceptual frameworks are preserved in language and often there are words for which there are no real equivalents in another language.

Historians, in other words, have to rely on texts created by white people. We never have Aboriginal voices unless whites recount (and invariably reformulate) these in their writings. Observations the American historian Richard White has made about the North American frontier hold true for the Australian one: 'in Indian history at the earliest stages we are dealing with an imperial history whose documents are not produced by Indians . . . A large chunk of our early documents . . . are conversations between people who do not completely understand each other. Methodologically this has implications . . . We are connoisseurs of misreadings. We rarely know Indians alone; we always know them in conversation with whites. During early contact situations we never get transparent accounts that allow us to peer into a world of Indian meanings'.[4]

In the Australian case, the fundamental weakness in the contemporary historical sources is much greater than those for comparable colonial frontiers. This is so for several reasons. Rarely were any of the colonists who represented Aboriginal perspectives competent in the Aboriginal language(s) of their informants. Most of the violence took place in circumstances where there were few independent non-Aboriginal observers. The legal context in which colonisation took place meant that white violence could seldom be acknowledged officially or openly: this was not a conflict between nations but between British subjects. As such, colonial governments declared that there were severe penalties for settlers killing Aboriginal people. The army and police were only allowed to shoot Aborigines in particular circumstances. This discouraged truthful contemporaneous reporting of white violence, though it could not discourage representation of this violence in the form of unofficial rumours, accounts clothed in euphemisms or disingenuous official reports, both at the time and in the decades that followed.[5]

More than most historians of colonial frontiers, then, professional historians in the Australian case encounter a past whose traces do not allow them to relate it in the manner that has long been customary to their discipline. One might describe this problem in the terms suggested by Dipesh Chakrabarty. He has written:

> Some constructions and experiences of the past stay 'minor' in the sense
> that their very incorporation into historical narratives converts them into
> pasts 'of lesser importance' vis-à-vis dominant understandings of what

constitutes fact and evidence (and hence vis-à-vis the underlying principle of rationality) in the practices of professional history. Such 'minor'
pasts are those experiences of the past that always have to be assigned as
an 'inferior' or 'marginal' position as they are translated into the academic
historian's language . . .

Let me call these subordinated relations to the past 'subaltern' pasts.
They are marginalised not because of any conscious intentions [among
professional historians] but because they represent moments or points
at which the archive that the historian mines develops a degree of
intractability with respect to the aims of professional history.[6]

Historical realism

How have academic historians tried to relate the history of the Australian
frontier? Much of the work conducted in the 1960s and 1970s by historians such as Henry Reynolds, Michael Christie, Lyndall Ryan and Noel Loos
was conducted in terms of historical realism. In other words, it was
informed more or less by an assumption that there is a correspondence or
mimetic relationship between the actual past and history as represented
by texts. This has been called a referential illusion. It holds that the past is
indexed or mirrored by historical texts and so implies that the historian
can re-enter the past and grasp it in an unmediated fashion. It tends to
ignore the fact that in historical work one is concerned with a reality that
no longer exists other than in texts which mediate the past.

These historians presumed that the frontier could be known by
adopting conventional scientific methods. They assumed that historical
truth would be realised by doing a large amount of research and sifting
through the so-called historical record for historical facts (which they
regarded as 'hard historical evidence'). They asserted that their interpretations were grounded in the historical sources and historical facts, and
they provided accounts in which they amassed examples and detail as
documentary proof of the story they told. They often gave the impression
that little else was entailed in the production of historical knowledge.[7]

Many of these historians did not recognise, or at least acknowledge,
that the distinctive historical conditions of nearly every Australian frontier

exposed the very limits of their approach. In particular, they persistently ignored the problems these pose for historical reference or documentation. As such, they failed to accept that their historical methods and sources were inadequate to the task of representing this extreme past. It is now more apparent than ever that this was a profound mistake. It has left their work extraordinarily vulnerable to criticism. In the wake of the 'revisionist' assault, the consequences of this are now more evident than ever before. Most importantly, 'revisionist' critics have demonstrated that these academic historians lacked documentation for most of the killings represented in their accounts. However, this does not necessarily mean that the violence that their accounts point towards did not occur. (A lack of hard evidence does not mean the absence of a violent event.) It makes more sense to conclude that the approach of historical realism is not equal to the task of representing this past. To do otherwise is to conflate and confuse one way of representing the past—historical realism—with historical reality.

The best-known historian in the field of Aboriginal history, Henry Reynolds, has conducted his work in the tradition of historical realism. This includes his path-breaking study, *The Other Side of the Frontier*, in which he sought to understand the Australian frontier from an Aboriginal perspective. In the conclusion of that book, he wrote: 'It is clear, now, that the boundaries of Australian historiography can be pushed back to encompass the other side of the frontier. Stretches of difficult country remain but they will become increasingly accessible to our scholarship. The barriers which for so long kept Aboriginal experience out of our history books were not principally those of source material or methodology but rather ones of perception and preference'. Reynolds' book undoubtedly provided new insights into how Aboriginal people perceived and treated the newcomers.[8] However, it shed relatively little light on how they experienced the traumatic impact of the invasion.[9]

Reynolds, as we can see, did not question whether conventional historical sources or methods were suitable for the task of comprehending the frontier, especially from an Aboriginal perspective. He did not really acknowledge that the peculiar historical conditions of the Australian frontier (described above) affected the forms of knowledge available to the historian—that the real in a factual sense is largely absent from the contemporary historical sources.[10] Indeed, rather than come to terms with this problem, there was a naïve assumption, even a boastful declaration, that historians can comprehend this history by going about their business as usual. In Reynolds' history-making, there was a hasty attempt to achieve coherence and closure, to smooth over the gaps and absences in the historical sources, to create an effect of the real, which is typical of realist historical narratives.

To question the value of historical realism is not, of course, to deny the possibility of knowledge or understanding of the historical events of the Australian frontier. It is simply to acknowledge that, for the most part, this past cannot be represented by this approach and to accept that other ways of proceeding are required.

Reading the signs

Another approach has been evident in more recent historical studies of the frontier. It might be called 'reading the signs'. Whereas the earlier work was done by historians who did not doubt that the historical actuality of the frontier could be represented, the later studies were undertaken by historians who questioned whether it could be. They have treated the historical archive, like language more generally, as both referential and representational. While they have considered language as something that can and does refer to reality, they have also conceived it as something which represents and so shapes reality. Thus they have distinguished between what can be called the documentary and the work-like aspects of language. This is to say that they do not regard historical sources as just texts which simply document or index a basic reality, or divulge facts about it; instead, they also regard historical traces as texts that creatively process or rework reality in some way or another. As such, the task of the historian is not simply one of extracting information or quarrying facts from historical sources in order to reveal some reality. (Reading the signs regards this approach as necessary and crucial for historical research, but not as sufficient.) Instead, the role of the historian is also one of discerning meaning in historical texts by attending to their creative dimension in order to suggest what the reality might have been. In this, historians contend that much in historical sources *points* to the real rather than *reflecting* it. This is an approach which enables the historian to work with much more of the historical archive created by settlers on the Australian frontier.

Historians such as Tom Griffiths have read settler writings closely in order to understand the uneasy language of the frontier. Unlike realist historians, he and other scholars recognised that frontiersmen talked about settler violence in ways that both pointed to and pointed away from it. Griffiths has observed: 'The[ir] forms of language and description slip in and out of recognising the violence of the frontier. They reveal that many colonists accepted murder in their midst; but they reveal, too, their aware-ness that it could not be openly discussed'. (As he reminds us, they had good reasons to be silent, especially after several white men were hanged for a massacre of Aboriginal men, women and children at Myall Creek.) Griffiths has concluded that it is in such dissonances—the *gaps* between experience and language, the *chasm* between reality and representation—that the distinctive character of the Australian frontier lies. Unless one pays attention to this—and some realist and 'revisionist' historians have not—accounts of the frontier are prey to comic (or tragic) error.[11]

Reading the signs in the contemporary historical sources is a valuable means of understanding the Australian frontier, but on its own it is also limited and limiting. This is because it does not necessarily address one of the fundamental characteristics of academic historical work: distance.

Historical distance

It is generally recognised that any work about the past is done in the present. Where else could it be done, after all? It is also widely recognised that the past does not effectively exist unless it has remained present, just as it is recognised that historians cannot study the past without that engage-ment reflecting their present situation or location. Yet the discipline has struggled to acknowledge fully the implications of the relationship between past and present for its work. It has also insisted on making a rather arbi-trary distinction between times past and times present, which creates a sense of distance rather than proximity in the relationship between past and present. At one level, historians proceed from an unstated premise that there is a connection between past and present, but this is later disavowed as they tend to turn the past into something that is dead and gone. They reify it as an object of investigation rather than considering it as something with which they might have a living relationship. As Michel de Certeau has argued: 'Historiography . . . is based on a clean break between the past and the present . . . Historiography conceives the relation [between past and present] as one of succession (one after the other), correlation (greater or lesser proximities), cause and effect (one follows the other), and disjunction (either one or the other, but not both at the same time)'.[12]

The consequences of this are threefold. The practice of academic historians tends to deny the presence of the past—that is, the way in which the past often continues to be (in the) present; it tends to deny the presence of the historian or that of the present in their representations of the past; and it tends to deny historians' lived relationship with the subjects we treat and our implication in the ways we represent these. The refusal of the relationship between past and present in historical work has been such a marked feature of the discipline of the history, one scholar has remarked of late, that 'it has become difficult [for historians] to distinguish between the concept of historical distance and the idea of history itself'. Most importantly, I suggest, historians do not acknowledge openly the fact that our work is inherently dialogical—that it is necessarily the result of a dialogue between past and present, present and past, an exchange between the texted past and the historian (as well as between those historians who inquire into it), a fusion of the horizons of the past and the present. Were historians to grapple with the significance of this proximity, particularly the ways in which we are implicated in the histories we tell in representing the past, rather than merely trying to dispel these by creating historical distance, this would probably transform the way we conceive of history as a form of knowledge. This could also put an end to the misconception that tends to characterise many popular understandings of history: it is only about the past, not the present.[13]

In the past, several other characteristics of the discipline of history have served to accentuate or aggravate a sense of distance between past and present, or present and past. First, there was the discipline's preoccupation with progress—or at least change—which revealed the influence of the time in which history became a critical form of knowledge in Europe and its colonies. It reflected the drive of modernity to break continuously with the past. Academic historians strove to articulate the ways in which people in a past were different to those of the present, which inclined us to treat the past as past or at least to pay more attention to discontinuities between it and the present. Second, the discipline's insistence on a particular definition of historical objectivity (discussed earlier) led to an ideal of historical detachment from the past. Third, there was the historian's focus on explanation of events in terms of their causes or origins, which directed attention to what led up to a past rather than what led away from it (its effects). Fourth, the discipline had a tendency to subordinate experience and the emotional to the abstract, the conceptual and the analytical.

The influence of these factors has diminished over the last 40 or 50 years. The practice of 'history from below', especially its attention to *experience*, has challenged historical distance—at least to some degree. This has been evident in the practice of Aboriginal history. It can be illustrated by considering, once again, the work of Henry Reynolds. There can be no question that his research in this field was prompted by an encounter with the past in the present. Reynolds makes this clear in the introduction to *The Other Side of the Frontier*:

> I began this research because conventional Australian historiography seemed so inadequate to explain and illuminate the . . . experience of north Queensland. Nothing in my Tasmanian education had prepared me for the realities of race relations in what [Charles] Rowley called colonial Australia. It was not just the unaccustomed violence and hatred which grew as lush as guinea grass but the smaller more subtle things—expressions, phrases, jokes, gestures, glances[,] even silences[—]which sprang up out of local . . . experiences I knew little about. Among many things the reaction of Aboriginal children often disturbed me. When I walked in the gate of an Aboriginal house, as I often did in the late sixties, it was quite common for the children to suddenly stop playing and run for the sanctuary of the stumps under the high block houses. But one day a little girl of four or five did not run away. She stood in the middle of the path and stared at me in silence. She looked at me not as an individual, or as a male, or a well meaning academic, but as a white man, a *migloo*, with a fear that was not personal at all but historical and communal and unforgettable. Where did one go, what did one read in 1967 to understand that sort of experience?

Here we see that the distinction which historians usually contrive between past and present threatens to collapse, and that the connection between present and past becomes the ground upon which Reynolds does his work. However, historical distance is a powerful ideal and cannot just be shrugged off by an academic historian. Reynolds tries to resist the relationship between past and present. Arguably, he does so even in the passage you have just read, by employing the term 'historical'. It appears where I have inserted both the ellipses.[14]

Reynolds' resistance is all the more remarkable given his association with the very force that has probably done most to challenge historical distance—that is, memory in the form of oral history. (This matter will be discussed further in Chapter 9.) Prior to writing *The Other Side of the Frontier*, Reynolds had been involved in doing oral history—that is, interviewing people about their pasts, particularly Aborigines and Torres Strait Islanders. Significantly, he discusses this at some length in the introduction to his book and does so adjacent to the passage quoted above. He says, however, that the oral history he collected was less important for 'the factual material gained [than] for the stimulation of imagination and empathy'. Here, one senses a movement towards and then away from the realm of memory. Indeed, seldom in his book is an oral history quoted. It is evident that Reynolds cannot incorporate or assimilate oral histories into his historical work because the very proximity between past and present—upon which oral history, by its very nature, depends—transgresses the historical distance that lies at the heart of the academic conception of good historical practice. As he reflects in his intellectual memoir, *Why Weren't We Told?*: 'But as powerful and moving as Aboriginal stories were, the main research effort had to be with the European records. They carried the authority of the written word; they were put down at a set time and in a specific place'.[15]

Much of Reynolds' work makes reference to the tension that characterises most historical work, but which is especially strong in fields such as Aboriginal history. On the one hand, Reynolds acknowledges that his work is shaped by the present; on the other hand, he knows that the discipline of history remains uneasy about the implications of this. Reynolds expresses this ambivalence at the beginning of the introduction of *The Other Side of the Frontier*: 'It is based on extensive research among a vast array of historical records. Yet the book was not conceived, researched or written in a mood of detached scholarship. It is *inescapably political*, dealing as it must with issues that have aroused deep *passions* since 1788 and will continue to do so into the foreseeable future'. At the close of the introduction to his next book, *Frontier* (1987), he writes: 'While based on sound scholarship [*Frontier*] is inspired by *passion* about the past and concern for the future'. In *Why Weren't We Told?* (1999), he reflects on his North Queensland experience again: 'There was a history at work, a powerful all-important history which pressed heavily on the present . . . So [doing the] history of violence was never just an academic or a scholarly question for me. I could never completely separate in my mind past and present . . . It was also obvious to me at a very early stage in my research that what I was doing was *inescapably political*. It was work which, of necessity, engaged the world'. It is not really clear, I suggest, why Reynolds uses the term 'political' here. It seems to be a synonym for a much more dangerous word for historians: emotional. What Reynolds is really indicating here, I suggest, is that doing Aboriginal history is *inescapably emotional*. Alan Atkinson has commented recently: 'Aboriginal history is emotional history. Its usual purpose is to make an emotional point, or rather to make an intellectual point sharpened and coloured by emotion'. He points to other subjects in Australian history in which historians have dealt with comparable questions of feeling, of suffering, such as the trench experience of the First World War, the prisoner-of-war experience of the Second World War, and the experience of families during and after both these wars. [16]

While Reynolds and other historians in the field of Aboriginal history have acknowledged the influence of the present in history-making, very few have been able to accept the implications of this for the nature of historical understanding, let alone historical authority. Instead, like the vast majority of academic historians, they have retreated and continue to claim more or less that their knowledge of the past rests on some bedrock of which they are not really a part. As Peter Novick has remarked, the traditional ideal of historical objectivity has been modified in recent times, but in some way or another most historians cleave to its principles, at least when they try to account for the basis of their historical interpretations. [17]

Banishing the past

The costs of following this epistemological tradition are very high. By insisting on the concept of historical distance, professional historians necessarily lose a sense of the ways in which a past is present and they close down on ways of relating *to* that past. Several commentators in the field of Aboriginal studies have drawn attention to the consequences of this.

Patrick Wolfe has argued that academic history has represented colonisation as a past event rather than as a process that has continued and continues. This, he suggests, inserts 'a screen into Australian historical consciousness' that has the effect of insulating non-Aboriginal Australians from it. The anthropologist Gillian Cowlishaw has also remarked upon the way in which academic histories of the settler violence have filled a gap in our understanding of the Australian frontier violence, but have done so in such a way that racism is not seen to be 'an organic and ongoing part of colonialism'. More particularly, she has remarked: 'These histories seem to present with ease a view of our own past that fills us, as readers, with horror at the same time as it distances us from it. How is it that in reading these accounts we position ourselves on the side of the Aborigines and identify our forebears as the enemy? These violent and racist men could be our grandfathers and they certainly left us something, if not the land they took or the wealth they made from it, then the culture they were developing'. Klaus Neumann has similarly criticised this banishment of the past to a realm removed from the present. He, too, has pointed to the traces of the past in the present. Most of all, though, Neumann locates the tendency of historians to separate past and present in the way in which historians conceive of historical knowledge. The main problem lies, in other words, in our refusal to allow for the relationship between the present and past in their work.[18]

By holding on to the sense of history as a dialogical enterprise, one can acknowledge that almost any attempt to relate the past involves a relationship *to* that past. One can also challenge any claim that history is merely the past. In so doing, we are more able to represent history as work done in the present largely for the sake of the present. The rise of memory makes this clearer, at the same time as it complicates the traditional historical project of treating the nature of the past as forever past.

MEMORY

 9

In recent years, ways of representing and narrating the events of the frontier other than those traditionally adopted by academic historians have become increasingly apparent. The most common of these ways of relating the past—oral history, saga, myth, tradition and legend—are frequently described as *memorial* rather than *historical* in nature, because they do not rely on traces of the past contemporaneous to the past being recounted— or, to be more precise, they do not depend on traces whose provenance is unquestionably of that time. These histories have entered the public arena and have had a significant impact on the way in which many Aboriginal and non-Aboriginal Australians now know or understand the frontier past. They have presented an enormous challenge to the discipline of history, but also provide its practitioners with an opportunity to reconsider the ways in which they relate the past and relate to that past.

Other histories

Aboriginal people have long told stories of their encounters with newcomers in this country. Many of these tell of the violent conflict that occurred. Sometimes, these are stories that have been told by participants or witnesses; at other times they are not. Often the Aboriginal accounts have no counterpart in the contemporary written sources.

In many respects, these oral histories differ markedly from the manner in which contemporary sources, or academic histories which draw on these, narrate the violent conflict of the frontier. They are often generic rather than specific in their reference to protagonists, times and events, if not place. As Deborah Bird Rose has noted: 'In such stories a range of people are likely to coalesce into one or two people, and events that may have been relatively disconnected from the perspective of the participants are organised into connections based on a presumption about their intention'. These stories are often told through key figures such as Captain Cook (as we noted in an earlier chapter), while they often attribute a series of killings to one man (as, for example, in the Bowman stories told in North Queensland). As time passes, Rose has suggested, the stories tend to focus more on the intention of the participants rather than on the event itself.[1]

Oral histories and oral traditions regarding frontier violence have not been the preserve of Aboriginal people alone. It is evident that there has been a strong current of story-telling in settler communities during both the nineteenth and twentieth centuries that express uneasy recollections of the violence perpetrated by settlers.[2] One such oral tradition, related in a country town (Sofala) in New South Wales, tells of a large number of Aboriginal people being massacred at a place called Bells Falls Gorge. Many of its features resemble those of Aboriginal oral traditions of the frontier. It is not known precisely when this event is supposed to have occurred. Nor is there any explanation of why it had occurred, who the perpetrators were, or how many were killed. There are no accounts of such an event in the contemporary historical record of the mid-1820s. Nevertheless, the locals who relate this tradition consider the massacre to be a historical fact and reject any suggestion by academic historians that their story is not history: 'Locals objected to my using the terms "legend" or "myth" to describe the tradition', David Roberts has reported. 'They regarded it as a "local knowledge", and were untroubled by a lack of documentary evidence and were indifferent to the standards of proof required of scholarly history'.[3]

As well as oral traditions about frontier violence, there are also what might be called legends, which tend to be literary rather than oral accounts. These often have a much more tenuous relationship to events represented in the contemporary historical sources than oral traditions do. One such example is the story or stories told in recent times by some Aboriginal people about the killings at Risdon Cove in Van Diemen's Land (see Chapter 5). In these accounts something like a hundred or even two hundred people are said to have been slaughtered in a massacre. Aboriginal people have commemorated this event in several ceremonies at Risdon Cove in order to honour those who died. Their narrative is an allegory about the origins of colonisation in this area: the killings at Risdon Cove were 'the first massacre' and the event created the historical foundations of a relationship between the two peoples. It is a foundation or charter story, common in myth-making.[4]

Memorial discourses

Histories of this nature challenge academic history in at least two major ways. First, they involve a rather different relationship between past and present, or present and past, to the one that has long characterised the discipline of history. Second, they are often informed by different concepts of knowledge—particularly regarding truth—to those that have dominated in academic history. How have historians in the field of Aboriginal history responded to the rise of what has been called memory or memorial discourses, especially the most important one: oral history?

Oral history, which has been defined as a way of collecting memories through planned interviews or collaboration between two or more people, emerged as a trend in historical research in the 1960s. It was part of the move by historians to democratise the study of the past by recovering those peoples whose lives had been excluded from history, and particularly the oppressed: the working-class poor, women, gays and lesbians, migrants, blacks and indigenous peoples. Indeed, it was often central to the project of 'history from below', social history and subaltern history. It was also an attempt to change the practice, not just the content, of history. Interviewees or informants were regarded as fellow historians. Authority was shared. Several claims were made by its practitioners: it could supplement and/or correct the documentary record; it could provide new insights into the past; and it could change the content of history by providing information on those peoples whose culture was oral rather than literary and/or those whose perspectives were seldom presented in literary sources. More contentiously, some of the champions of oral history asserted that you could only undertake the history of some peoples by practising oral history (since they had not produced a documentary record of their own), while many claimed that it provided a truer, more reliable and more authentic history than other historical sources since interviewees or informants had seen what had really happened or knew what it was like because they were there, and they spoke rather than wrote their accounts.[5]

After the early wave of research in the field of Aboriginal history, which was when most of the classic studies of the frontier were researched,[6] historians began to use oral history as a way of revealing pasts 'hidden from history', and to uncover the perspectives and agency of their Aboriginal subjects. Particularly in northern and central Australia, where contact between Aborigines and settlers began much later than other parts of the country, historians followed anthropologists and linguists who had already recorded the testimony of Aboriginal people who had witnessed the frontier times. Oral histories were compiled by Luise Hercus and Peter Sutton, Bruce Shaw, Peter and Jay Read, and Grace and Harold Koch. Historical studies based on oral testimonies were undertaken by John Cribbin, Deborah Bird Rose, Howard and Frances Morphy, and Ann McGrath. Many of these demonstrated the potential of oral history, particularly where the documentary record provided at best a fragmentary account of what really happened.[7]

Most of these scholars were quite conventional in their approach to history. They treated oral history as another source for history—another means of uncovering historical facts or providing historical information. Some were naïve about the nature of the source they were using, as they tended to overlook the fact that memory can be notoriously unreliable. Some aspects of the past are remembered well, such as material conditions, everyday practices and routine occurrences; other dimensions, such as values, attitudes and feelings, are not. In many instances, memory is unreliable about an event in terms of when and how it happened and its relationship to other events. Indeed, memory is often littered with inconsistencies and distortions, silences and omissions. Notwithstanding this, historians using oral history for the conventional historical project (historical realism) have maintained that they are nevertheless able to distil a solid base of factual material from oral histories, and have sought to do this. Some have seemed reluctant to grapple with the problematic dimensions of oral history, or have done so superficially, compromising the integrity of their historical narratives accordingly. Many historians, similarly inclined to regard oral testimonies as potential sources of facts or information, have nonetheless been reluctant to rely on oral history because they have been concerned about its reliability. They realise that oral history is often of very limited use for discovering facts about what happened in the past. Some historians have gone further and dismissed or rejected oral history altogether.[8]

There can be little doubt that serious criticisms can be made of forms of memory work such as oral history and myth. Most importantly, many historians have pointed out that memory is ahistorical, even anti-historical, in some critical senses. Peter Novick, for example, has observed: 'Historical consciousness, by its nature, focuses on the *historicity* of events—that they took place then and not now, that they grew out of circumstances different from those that now obtain. Memory, by contrast, has no sense of the passage of time; it denies the "pastness" of its objects and insists on their continuing presence'. Yet historians such as Novick can go too far. They are inclined to construct memory as history's bad other and to demonise it. To quote Novick once more: 'To understand something historically is to be aware of its complexity, to have sufficient detachment to see it from multiple perspectives, to accept the ambiguities, including moral ambiguities, of protagonists' motives and behaviour. Collective memory simplifies; sees events from a single, committed perspective; is impatient with ambiguities of any kind; reduces events to mythic arche-types . . . Typically a collective memory . . . is understood to express some eternal or essential truth about the group'. This is no doubt so, but much the same could be said of many histories—especially public histories. This is not to argue that memory and history are identical, but nor is it to argue that they are opposites.[9]

Among those who worked in oral history, a more sophisticated approach to memory than the one adopted at first by academic historians soon became apparent.[10] Critical to such work has been a recognition that memory and history, far from simply complementing one another, can carry very different relationships to the past. Historians began to grasp the fact that the relationship of memory to the past was a complex one, mediated by many factors, and that its greatest value lay not in deriving facts about events in the past but in providing something other than factual or documentary knowledge. In doing so, they decided to embrace the challenge of enlarging our notion of what history can be, allowing or providing for ways of reckoning historical truth other than the realist. This work is informed by an assumption that something of the truth of past events and/or their aftermath is evident in the manner in which they have been remembered, and that memories—like dreams—tend to reveal hidden preoccupations in highly condensed symbols.[11]

In the field of Aboriginal history, several scholars have approached memorial discourses by adopting the frameworks that historians and anthropologists have used to understand myth and tradition in other historical contexts. They have considered oral histories and oral traditions not so much to recover past events of the frontier as to discover how these have been understood by Aboriginal and settler peoples since this time. In this mode, oral histories or traditions are treated as accounts *of* the past rather than accounts *from* the past. In the case of Aboriginal traditions, these have been regarded as the means by which Aboriginal people have sought to make sense of their situation.[12] As Jeremy Beckett has remarked, colonised peoples have not only had to endure colonisation; they have also had to comprehend it. The most famous example of these are the Captain Cook stories. These were discussed in Chapter 2, and there is no need to repeat this discussion here.[13]

The best known example of a settler tradition is probably the one regarding Bells Falls Gorge discussed earlier.[14] In his work, David Roberts has constructed a genealogy for this oral tradition. He found in literary sources that there were massacre stories similar to the one told by the settlers of Sofala regarding Bells Falls Gorge. In the 1880s a local settler related an incident in which Aboriginal people 'were shot down in a brutal valley'. This was based, Roberts suggests, on accounts told by this man's father and grandfather, who were prominent landowners in the area. As such, he speculates, the story of Bells Falls Gorge might have emanated from the time of the frontier (the 1820s), though he notes that we cannot be certain of this. The first published version of a massacre at Bells Falls Gorge appeared in the early 1960s. In a history of Aborigines in the area, serialised in a local newspaper, a local anthropologist and historian Percy Gresser made reference to this local tradition, having heard it from an old-timer in the Sofala–Wattle Flat district. Gresser was prepared to believe that this was 'a tradition with a solid basis in fact', but he thought the estimate of numbers killed was probably an exaggeration. Since Gresser published his account, Roberts demonstrates, the oral tradition of Bells Falls Gorge has undergone considerable change as it has been increasingly removed from its original form of story-telling and its original locality. In the early 1970s, the tradition became a regional story in an essay by T. Salisbury, *Windradyne of the Wiradjuri: Martial Law at Bathurst*, which was published in Sydney. In the late 1980s, the tradition was translated into the national realm by virtue of being told in a book by an Aboriginal historian, Mary Coe, *Windradyne: A Wiradjuri Koorie*, published by a national publisher, and in popular books prepared for the bicentenary of British settlement by Al Grassby and Marji Hill, *Six Australian Battlefields: The Black Resistance to Invasion and the White Struggle against Colonial Oppression*, and Bruce Elder, *Blood on the Wattle: Massacres and Maltreatment of Australian Aboriginals since 1788*. In the process of these changes in the genre of story and the context in which it was told, Roberts observes, 'detailed highly dramatised accounts of naked atrocity were produced, replete with descriptions of soldiers advancing in a pincer movement around an Aboriginal camp, of Aboriginal women grabbing their children and leaping over the cliffs, of broken bodies piling up on the rocks below and the water running red with the blood of murdered Wiradjuri'. As Roberts notes, the latter-day authors ignored Gresser's cautious remarks on the tradition and disregarded the fact that no contemporary historical evidence exists for a massacre at Bells Falls Gorge.[15]

In research of the kind Roberts undertook, the focus of scholars shifted from historical events to their aftermath and how they were represented in later narratives. As a result, the 'pastness' of the frontier past was diminished to some degree. As we have just noted, studies of oral traditions and myths can reveal the ways in which knowledge of violent colonisation has continued in both Aboriginal and settler communities, thus uncovering the ways in which past and present are connected. Yet the approach taken in historical analyses (such as Roberts') can also undermine the sense of that connection. This is largely because this work has been dominated by an interest in representation. Attention has been drawn to the ways in which stories about the past are derived as much from the present or from other pasts as they are from the one being represented. In this research, one of its keywords, 'invention', has played a critical role. The term can readily imply that traditions forged in the present are actually disconnected from the past they represent, though this was not the argument Eric

Hobsbawm made when he coined the term 'the invention of tradition' in a famous essay. J.G.A. Pocock has suggested recently, in the course of considering histories such as myth and tradition, that it would be more appropriate to use the term 'formation' instead of terms such as 'invention' or even 'construction' in respect of these. 'Formation', he argues, reflects the 'highly complex patterns of experience [that] are involved in [the] making [of histories]'. By using the concept of formation and allying it with the idea of experience, Pocock helps to draw our attention to the *connections* between past and present that are evident in history.[16]

Recently, several historians and anthropologists have responded to the rise of memorial discourses about the frontier by pointing towards another approach better suited than that of representation to preserving the importance of the events of the past *and* enabling us to grasp something of the continuing presence of this past, and hence its significance for us today. This approach might be called traumatic history. This is barely discernible in the research done in Australia so far, but it can be traced by discussing the work other historians have done on 'limit events'.[17]

Traumatic history

Tom Griffiths has argued in reference to the Australian frontier: 'We need history because some things cannot be recognised as they happen'. By history, Griffiths means both history and memory: *We need history and memory because some things cannot be recognised as they happen.* Griffiths does not spell out why he assumes this is so, but the context in which he made this argument suggests that he was referring to trauma.[18]

According to some clinical and theoretical work, trauma is an extraordinary event that cannot be experienced or assimilated fully at the time of its occurrence. It lies outside people's capacity to make cognitive and emotional sense of an event.[19] This means that trauma is inherently incomprehensible or unrepresentable in any realistic sense, that it can only be represented, inadequately, in highly symbolic terms that necessarily distort it in some sense or another, that it reveals itself in its belatedness, and that it returns repeatedly to haunt the psyches of those party to it—especially victims, but also perpetrators, bystanders, collaborators, and so forth. It can affect not only contemporaries but also those born later.

The concept of trauma has very important implications for historical work. It suggests that contemporary sources—upon which historians traditionally rely—are inadequate, as they cannot register the event properly. It also means that any memories of the event will be flawed in any empirical sense since the psyches of witnesses have been disturbed by it. Encountering unbearable pain, the mind constructs an alternative story. It might coincide at some points with the original event but for the most part this story will be a very different account of what happened, one marked by amnesia, exaggerations, chronological errors, repetition, and so forth. It is largely *because* of the trauma that memory makes such factual mistakes. Paradoxically, then, the fact that a memory misrepresents traumatic events can actually suggest that it is in some sense a truthful rather than a false account. As this suggests, the relationship of traumatic memory to events tends to be significatory rather than referential. Truth is rendered in figurative rather than literal terms.[20]

The temporality of trauma also affects historical work in other ways. Trauma throws into question any easy distinction between events and their aftermath and diminishes any sense of difference between past and present. In traumatic memory the distance between then and now collapses. The event or conditions seem to be both there and here at the same time. In other words, trauma challenges the very conception of time that informs historical scholarship by placing the past *in* the present rather than putting it before or behind it. Trauma resists the attempt of historians to historicise events—to place them in (an)other time, that of the past, not the present.[21]

At the same time, trauma challenges the emphasis historians tend to place on the knowingness of their historical subjects and therefore any sense of mastering the past. As Cathy Caruth has remarked: 'The traumatised, we might say, carry an impossible history within them, or they become themselves the symptom of a history that they cannot entirely possess'. Furthermore, because the very force of a traumatic event undermines understanding, people remembering it often feel deeply uncertain about the truthfulness of their own recollection.[22]

Trauma also poses challenging questions about how a historian should represent such a past and, in particular, what place they should give to the voices of victims or survivors. Similarly, it forces historians to ask how they themselves should and do relate *to* this past. It calls for both discursive and affective responses beyond those found in most historical work. More generally, traumatic events have ethical implications for national culture and politics, as they point up a significant ongoing relationship between past and present (and future).

There is no dominant view of how trauma should be addressed in art, in literature, in history or in politics. Here, one approach will be suggested. It is one that seeks to respect the protocols of scholarly history to a large degree, but also tries to expand academic history by engaging with memory or memorial discourses and addressing the ethical and political questions about the relationship between the past and present that they have highlighted. This could help bring about a more democratic culture and polity, which could command more public support. In the project of traumatic history, historical scholarship can play several roles. One might argue that professional historians should limit their role to that of testing the truth claims of memory by providing an appraisal of what is or is not factual in any remembrance of the past. This would lead to the emergence of a more accurate history in an empirical sense. However, academic historians can also delineate the ways in which such memories can produce knowledge about the past. For example, they can point out how, even though memories can contain silences, lapses, mistakes, distortions, and so forth, this does not necessarily invalidate them and so these traces can still be said to represent the past faithfully in some respects, even fundamental ones. Academic historians can also analyse the origins, production and circulation of memories so that they can explicate where these may or may not represent the past truthfully. In performing these tasks, professional historians can help in the transmission of critically tested memory and so influence what gets passed on as historical knowledge.

In Aboriginal history, those who have done oral history have not always performed these tasks. As Paula Hamilton has pointed out, doing oral history changes 'the relationship between past and present in historical research'. In the practice of oral history, the degrees of distance and proximity of the past are radically changed, most importantly in reference to the relationship the historian has with his or her sources of information or subjects. The source has a presence that contemporary historical sources seldom have. Most importantly, perhaps, historians usually forge a relationship with their interviewees, informants or collaborators. As Deborah Bird Rose has reminded us recently, not everybody wants to tell their story to academic historians and the like, and nobody has to do so: 'We are privileged to receive what we receive; there is no natural right to be told history'. Consequently, some scholars struggle to be critical because they feel the moral obligation they have incurred. This problem is likely to be deeper where the history narrated concerns a traumatic past. Indeed, in order for such a history to be shared, it usually requires a historian to identify with the past being presented in some way or another. The diminution in the historian's willingness or capacity to be sceptical is likely to be greater where they perceive the interviewee(s) to be oppressed and vulnerable. Many scholars have played an important role in enabling Aboriginal people to tell their stories, but their work has often not gone much beyond this. Generally speaking, historians have yet to work out proper or acceptable ways of working on or with Aboriginal testimonies for their own work of representing the past. As a result, few have really worked very productively with the considerable volume of Aboriginal autobiographies, life stories and oral histories now available.[23]

Academic historians might also consider not only how to *relate* this traumatic past, but also how they and other settlers might relate *to* it. Instead of defining history in narrowly professional terms and separating it off from matters of public memory or public history, professional historians might contemplate more deeply how they and other people in their settler culture today talk and write about this traumatic past, and how they do or do not live with it, rather than merely considering how others once wrote and talked about and lived in that past. Here, the role of these historians is not only one of acknowledging the presence of this past and our relationship to it rather than distancing ourselves from it by representing it as a past that has allegedly passed away; it is also a matter of encouraging a consciousness of this so that our readers might know of and acknowledge their relationship to a (post)traumatic culture and thus create an opportunity to work through the problems that continue in the present. This is an approach that could lead to a basic reconceptualisation of historical practice and historical knowledge, and so could transform the way we represent the work of history.[24]

History and transference

To play most of these roles—or to perform them better than is done at present—academic historians would be required to consider ways of going about our work that differ from those adopted traditionally in the discipline of history. Critical to this is a consistent acknowledgment by historians that they have a subjective relationship to the pasts they research. Historians usually have a transferential relationship to the past we study.[25] In other words, historians identify emotionally with something or other in the pasts or histories we research, and so we tend to be implicated in some way or another in our treatment of these. But this transference will be especially intense in the case of a traumatic history, particularly where historians work with testimony in some form or another and especially where we work with informants or interviewees. Trauma's very nature means historians are working on matters that are highly charged, and this is all the more so given that this past is a matter of contemporary social and political debate. (Here, readers might find it useful to have the example of the stolen generations in mind.) As such, historians should consider how we will deal with emotion (or affect) in any encounter or exchange with the human subjects manifest in our literary, visual and oral sources. Unless we reflect on this transferential relationship, we are likely to repeat some of the very processes that are active in our object of historical inquiry.

Contrary to what many might recommend, professional historians should not try to deny or circumvent any transferential relationship they might have to traumatic pasts or histories. To do this would not only serve to repress the traumatic memory, but would downplay the significance of their own relationship to this past. Instead, historians should seek to work through or handle their historical proximity critically, though not in such a way that they try to smooth over or harmonise the nature and the impact of the events they represent. Dominick LaCapra has recommended an approach in which the historian accepts or allows their empathic or empathetic response to one of the subjects in their object of inquiry, whether the participant be a perpetrator, collaborator, victim, resister or bystander. Indeed, he has insisted on the need for what he calls empathic unsettlement in responding to traumatic events or conditions, on the grounds that the historian must allow for this in order to have an experiential or empathic basis for working the past through. However, LaCapra also recommends that the historian must stop short of full identification with any one participant and strive to work through their transferential relationship, not to dispose of it but to realise the differences between our position and that of the historical subject, which will enable us in turn to grasp the ways in which we have a relationship with participants other than the one(s) with whom we have identified. In other words, the historian should try to attain different modes of proximity and distance with the various participants in an attempt to understand each one as well as the relations among them. By doing this, LaCapra suggests, the historian can attain a more complex subject position in relation to the past. This can provide for objectivity, though not in any transcendent (third-person) sense. By adopting this approach, historians can broaden and deepen our historical understanding of the past, but also acquire a richer sense of our relationship to this history.[26]

As historians work out how they might relate (to) traumatic pasts, more consideration should be given to whether new forms of historical narrative are required in order to represent these. Here, some other suggestions made by LaCapra might be considered. He observes: 'The problem that clearly deserves further reflection is the nature of actual and desirable responses in different genres, practices, and disciplines, including the status of mixed or hybridised genres and the possibility of playing different roles or exploring different approaches in a given text or "performance"'. In other words, works that cross boundaries between history and fiction—of, say, the monograph and the novel—might be contemplated as a way of trying to present a sense of the past. As noted at the beginning of this part, it is very difficult to present an account of the frontier from an Aboriginal perspective using the traces of the past that historians have traditionally relied upon. Consequently, it is difficult to conceive how Aboriginal-centred histories of the frontier can be told, at least by non-Aboriginal historians, unless history-makers combine genres. A recent book by Ross Gibson, *Seven Versions of an Australian Badland*, is an example of such an approach. Unless we have narratives of this kind, Aboriginal pasts such as that of the frontier will remain something that most Australians cannot really understand.[27]

Recognising this requires us, of course, to acknowledge the limits of history, to acknowledge that history is a limited good. Some pasts simply cannot be represented by using the traditional sources and methods of history. Only by accepting this can we hope to learn more deeply about the Australian frontier.

TRUTH AND RECOGNITION

•• • • • ● ● ● 10

The controversy over the truth about Aboriginal history has focused more attention on a very important problem: how can and should historical difference be handled? To be more specific, how can a nation's peoples best negotiate their different historical narratives about the past? And how can or should the Australian nation state and its peoples address or work through the burden of the Aboriginal past?[1] There need to be social, economic, cultural and political mechanisms that enable individuals and communities to perform these tasks.[2] National reconciliation provided a useful framework for a good deal of this work and could be renewed if some aspects of its approach were revised and others strengthened.

A shared history

In the decade-long work of the Council for Aboriginal Reconciliation (1991–2000), reconciliation and historical understanding were seen to go hand in hand, and so history work—primarily in the form of telling and circulating stories about the past—was regarded as one of the principal tasks of the Council. It defined its historical goal in these terms: 'A sense of all Australians of a shared ownership of their history'. This was usually represented as 'shared history'. The Council presumed that Australia could only become a reconciled nation if both Aboriginal and non-Aboriginal peoples more or less adopted the same historical narrative.

The Council conceived of history in rather simple terms, regarding it as a single body of historical knowledge. The story the Council told would include empirically testable facts, especially the ones previously excluded by Australian histories, which would be added together and assembled as an accurate and hence truthful account of the past. By being taught to all Australians, it would provide a basis for national reconciliation.[3]

This history comprised a historical narrative that largely followed the interpretation of the first wave of academic historiography. It told of the denial of Aboriginal rights to land; the dispossession, destruction and displacement of Aboriginal people; the formal racial discrimination that followed; and the marginalisation of Aborigines. This theme was accompanied by two minor ones: the points at which Aborigines and settlers had had harmonious relations; and the times when colonisers had raised a humanitarian voice against the treatment and plight of Aboriginal people and called for recognition of their rights.[4]

This project of 'shared history' was flawed in several respects. Its premise that there could be a reconciled history was unduly optimistic, even naïve. It did not allow sufficiently for difference. As Dipesh Chakrabarty has noted, both Aboriginal and settler peoples were expected to transcend the pulls of their respective group affiliations or identities in order to agree on the truth of historical injustice in the past. Yet, as long as any society contains at least two cultural traditions—one identifying with the colonisers or the non-Aboriginal, and another with the colonised or the Aboriginal—it is probably inevitable that there will be conflicting attitudes, opinions, beliefs and feelings about that very past. The Council for Aboriginal Reconciliation ignored the reality that different histories are told and upheld, in the public realm at any rate, because they are tied to collective identity, and that most such renditions of historical truth do not rest on empirically proven facts, especially when they concern matters of nationhood and national identity. As the Canadian-born historian and human rights commentator Michael Ignatieff has remarked in another context: 'The idea that reconciliation depends on shared truth presumes that shared truth about the past is possible. But truth is related to identity. What you believe is true depends, in some measure, on who you believe yourself to be . . . People . . . do not easily or readily surrender the premises upon which their lives are based . . . Resistance to historical truth is a function of group identity'.[5]

Another weakness accompanied this. As the New Zealand political philosopher Richard Mulgan has observed in his criticisms of reconciliation in Australia, a sense of one's collective self-worth is as important for dominant majorities as it is for subordinate minorities. However, reconciliationists gave little consideration to the impact their historical narrative might have upon those who identified closely with the original white colonisers. In other words, they failed to take into account the fact that the old settler history was the source of considerable meaning and value for many settler Australians. Not surprisingly, their attack on settlers' allegiance to this narrative fuelled resentment. There can be little doubt that some reconciliationists also tended to set themselves apart from other settler Australians, past and present, by expressing their moral revulsion at the values, opinions and actions of their predecessors. This, too, provoked anger.[6]

Too much of the history the council told was cast in oppositional terms. It could have drawn more attention to those occasions when friendly relations existed between Aboriginal and settler peoples, the moments when the ideals and values of both societies' cultures were upheld to the advantage of one or other or both, and the ways in which both peoples have drawn on the other's culture to their own advantage. In other words, the council could have done more to tell the story of compromise and convergence between Aboriginal and settler peoples that academic historians have been narrating for some time.[7]

Assessing histories

In its history work, the council also failed to consider a matter that has been raised as a result of the democratisation of history-making: whose forms of historical knowledge, or whose conventions of historical truth, were to be used in the process of reconciling the different histories that were being told? Would the 'shared history' of reconciliation be produced in accordance with the conventions of scholarly history or the conventions of a memorial discourse such as myth? The council seemed to presume that the protocols of the former would prevail, but it also assumed that Aboriginal people would tell their histories in other idioms. More importantly, the council did not suggest how the conflict between the truth claims presented by very different historical narratives might be resolved. This is a critical problem in contemporary democratic nation states.

Dipesh Chakrabarty has pinpointed its nature. In the discipline of history, he points out, enormous emphasis has been placed on the importance of being able to defend the narrative one presents on rational grounds: '[An] author's position may reflect an ideology, a moral choice, or a political philosophy, but the choices are not unlimited. A madman's narrative is not history. Nor can a preference that is arbitrary or just personal . . . give us rationally defensible principles for narration (at best it will count as fiction and not history)'. Furthermore, Chakrabarty notes, there has been considerable investment in a particular kind of rationality and a particular notion of the real. In settling disputes about the past, history has insisted on certain procedures for assessing historical narratives according to whether or not they meet its secular conception of the real and its evidentiary rules for determining what is reality—rules which privilege scientific rationality and facticity. As a result of a democratisation of history, hitherto neglected groups such as Aboriginal people have been encouraged and urged to tell their histories, but they do not always tell these in ways that conform to the protocols demanded by the discipline of history, or meet its condition for rationality and that of the democratic nation state it serves. In the case of Aboriginal peoples in Australia, as we have noted, this is so because of their traumatic experiences of the past, the absence of a literary culture, a lack of power and their practice of other ways of narrating stories about the past. Readers will recall that their history-making is an example of what Chakrabarty has called subaltern pasts. These 'minority histories' provide narratives (such as Captain Cook stories) that do not meet the dominant understandings of what constitutes fact and evidence, and so history's particular principle of rationality. Hence they are assigned an inferior position in historical discourse. Often they are not treated as history at all, but cast out as a narrative other, as mere myth, legend, tales, and so forth. Chakrabarty observes: 'These are pasts that are treated . . . as instances of human "immaturity", pasts that do not prepare us for either democracy or citizenly practices because they are not based on the deployment of reason in public life'.[8]

Here we come to the nub of the problem: 'If minority histories go to the extent of questioning the very idea of fact or evidence, then, the [traditionalists] ask, how would one find ways of adjudicating between competing claims in public life? Would not the absence of a certain

minimum agreement about what constitutes fact and evidence seriously
fragment the body politic [of the nation state], and would not that in turn
impair the capacity of the nation to function as a whole?' Traditionalists
insist that a shared, rational understanding of what constitutes historical
facts and evidence *must* be maintained in order for national institutions
to be able to adjudicate between conflicting historical narratives and to be
able to operate effectively.[9]

Their apprehension is not unreasonable. But in the interests of repre-
sentative democracy and social justice, is it appropriate to insist that
minority peoples present histories that meet the epistemological requirements of the dominant group when they are often unable to do so? Some
traditionalists, of course, fear that the abandonment of history's particular rules for determining what is real and unreal, true and untrue, will lead
to an outbreak of 'relativism' or 'postmodern' irrationalism, which will then
sweep through Historyland and the nation. As Chakrabarty suggests, these
fears are probably extreme. Historical practice in both the academy and
the public realm still respects the objectivist impulses of the instruments
of executive government, the bureaucracy and the judiciary. This is to
suggest that some traditionalists exaggerate the deleterious consequences
of multiple narratives. It is significant that they seldom describe these in
any detail, or provide much evidence to justify their fears. They appear to
lack confidence and trust that other people can handle difference and
the conflict it often causes. They seem to be unduly anxious about what
might befall their people or the nation as a result of *their* story or *their* way
of telling a story no longer being accepted as *the* truth or the only way of
representing the truth.[10]

This said, it probably makes sense for there to be some commonly
understood ground rules to guide the reception of multiple historical
narratives in most circumstances and contexts.[11] The overarching principle here might be that narrators make clear to their audiences the
genre(s) or form(s) in which they are telling their account of the past, and
that audiences should receive these narratives in accordance with their
conventions of knowledge and truth. The conventions of forms such as the
academic monograph and the novel, say, are widely known, but the criteria
by which one might assess forms such as myth might not be any longer.
According to Deborah Bird Rose, the following criteria are used by

Aboriginal people in the Northern Australian communities she knows for discerning the truthfulness—or what she calls the faithfulness—of stories. *Place*: knowledge of the place of an event. *Presence*: being an eyewitness, coupled with the general reliability of the narrator. *Genealogy*: if the speaker was not present, a statement is required regarding who told the story and whether that person was an eyewitness. As Rose notes, these criteria are not inconsistent with the kinds of criteria used traditionally by academic historians: 'In both there is a strong desire to separate faithful accounts from what is colloquially termed "bullshit"'. Guidelines such as these will not always meet any need to adjudicate between competing historical narratives, but they could assist cross-cultural communication and so both increase the chances of historical understanding between peoples and lessen the degree of conflict that occurs.[12]

Sharing histories

There was another strand in the Council of Aboriginal Reconciliation's history work, which was called 'sharing histories'. Its premise differed somewhat to those informing the project of 'shared history', as Heather Goodall has pointed out. Whereas 'shared history' largely conceived of history as a body of historical facts presented as a singular story compiled by an anonymous narrator, 'sharing histories' tended to regard history as a collection of narratives told by differently situated or positioned peoples, and hence contingent on who the teller is, what their purpose is, the context in which they tell their story and who their audience is.[13]

In conceiving history in this way, 'sharing histories' highlighted the conjunction between past and present as the ground upon which all history-making occurs. It thus countered the tendency of academic history to create a sense of distance rather than proximity between present and past. In doing this, it performed the useful function of prompting people to reflect on the nature of the relationship they have to the history they are telling, hearing, reading or seeing.

In this approach, there is an acceptance that much historical knowledge is a matter of perspective and interpretation. This is not a relativist position, contrary to what is sometimes claimed. It does not hold that all historical accounts are true or equal, that anything goes. It merely acknowledges that the most significant parts of historical narratives are always contingent, limited and partial. In 'sharing histories', furthermore, a narrator will assert vigorously the value of their interpretation and challenge those of others, but also acknowledge that some other interpretations have value, too. In this way, 'sharing histories' can be a forum in which there is an exchange of knowledge between differently situated or positioned people—a place where they both tell their histories and listen to others, and a place of robust but courteous debate. Here, the vital work of cross-cultural communication can occur, so that people might understand and respect other people's histories and history-making even though they will probably continue to differ about the interpretations presented.

'Sharing histories' assumes that democracies such as Australia will continue to be peopled by groups with diverse histories and identities; it presumes that there will continue to be contestation and conflict; and it recommends that this situation be accepted. National communities do not require that all conflicts be resolved and full consensus be reached on all matters. As Richard Mulgan has argued, one should not expect reconciliation between Aboriginal and settler Australians to involve agreement on every aspect of the histories that are told. It is more sensible to admit the ongoing presence of different pasts or histories and seek to accommodate these through a shared commitment to certain democratic principles. Most importantly, these should allow for different forms of historical knowledge and their ways of telling the past. It would thus provide for a measure of equality between academic history and other ways of relating the past.[14]

Working through the past

Aboriginal and settler Australians have a common problem: a lack of legitimacy. Their moral status, and hence their identities and rights, are denied by the other group. Many settler Australians refuse to acknowledge that the status of Aboriginal people as the first peoples of this country should bestow upon them any special rights; many Aboriginal people refuse to acknowledge the right of settler Australians to belong in what Aborigines regard as their country. This impasse is not uncommon in settler societies—consider Israelis and Palestinians, for example.[15]

The refusal of either group to accept the legitimacy of the other's rights is reflected in the histories that have been formulated for a long time now. Many Aboriginal people, and those sympathetic to their plight, have told a story about the foundation of the Australian nation that seems to forever condemn settlers to the status of invaders. This history implies that the nation state, and the laws upon which the rights of its settler citizens depend, can never be legitimate because the nation's origins were fundamentally unjust. In effect, the nation is deemed to suffer from an original sin that it can never expunge or redeem. For their part, many settler Australians—and particularly new conservatives—articulate the traditional foundational narrative of the nation. This refuses to acknowledge properly that British colonisation entailed the abrogation of aboriginal sovereignty and rights, and tends to deny that Aboriginal people today have any legitimate moral and political claims on the basis of being aboriginal.

How might this impasse be addressed, if not resolved? To begin, we must clarify the very nature of this conflict. In the final analysis, it is not a conflict about the past—no truly important historical dispute ever is— but a conflict over *the past in the present*. More particularly, it is a conflict regarding the moral relationship of settler peoples to this history—to this relationship between past and present, present and past. As we have observed, there are few nation states that do not have morally problematic origins. However, this has proven to be a particularly significant problem in the Australian case. There might be several reasons for this. One seems to be especially important, however. In other settler colonies founded by the British, treaty agreements were made between the two peoples. In recent years, some of these treaties, which had been moribund for a long time, have been mobilised as a moral and political basis for the legitimate interests of both aboriginal *and* settler peoples. These provide a constitutional mechanism for entrenching the status of both. This has been evident in New Zealand. This option is not available in Australia, of course. In other Anglophone settler countries, though—most notably Canada—treaties have been forged recently between states and aboriginal peoples. In these contemporary agreements, the state does not seek to address the problem of its origins so much as attempt to redress the problems that followed from the original act of colonisation.

A treaty or treaties might provide a way of working through the

Australian impasse in mutually advantageous ways by laying down a broad framework of principles that would govern the relationship between Aboriginal and settler peoples. At a national level, such an agreement could include the following. For their part, settler Australians would acknowledge that Aboriginal people are the original owners of this country; that they were dispossessed, displaced and devastated as a result of British colonisation; that the consequences of this continue to the present day and are the primary reason for the plight of Aboriginal people today; that previous generations of settlers, and particularly their governments, bear considerable responsibility for this, especially where they denied Aboriginal people their rights as a sovereign people and their rights as citizens; that settler Australians and their national government today should acknowledge this injustice and the suffering it caused by means of an apology; that the current generation of settler Australians are the beneficiaries of the dispossession of Aboriginal people and so have a responsibility (relative to their means) to support policies and practices today that seek to redress the impact of this and prevent any further acts of dispossession; that Aboriginal people have a right to reparations in some form(s) or another until such time as the vast majority have recovered. For their part, Aboriginal people might acknowledge all the rights of citizenship the Australian nation has bestowed upon settler peoples; the legitimate presence of settlers; and the responsibilities they have as citizens of the nation state. Such an agreement would depend on an ongoing commitment of each party to its terms, and would last only as long as this was present.

A treaty seems to be the best means of establishing a constitutional basis for addressing the problem both peoples have. There are, though, other means of entrenching Aboriginal rights, so they are not so vulnerable to changes in government and what seems to be a cycle in which, every generation or so, programs for reform swing from one approach to Aboriginal difference to another.[16] It has been suggested that the most important political and legal document of the nation, the Australian Constitution, might be the means of recognising the status of Aboriginal peoples by enshrining certain principles regarding their constitutional position. Fundamental changes to the constitution would be required, of course. A renewed constitution could form a new contract of Australian democracy, as historian Mark McKenna has suggested.[17]

Constitutional reform has been on the agenda of Aboriginal leaders for more than a decade now.[18] The reforms that have been advocated include: a new preamble to recognise the occupation and ownership of the country by Aboriginal people, and to acknowledge the historical fact of their dispossession; guaranteeing freedom from racial discrimination by replacing section 25 of the Constitution with a general clause prohibiting this; and the amendment of section 51 (xxvi), the so-called race power, to ensure that the power of the Commonwealth to legislate on matters specifically relating to Aboriginal people can only be used for the benefit of Aboriginal people. In addition to constitutional reform, there have been calls for a bill of rights. In such a legal document, special rights for Aboriginal people in accordance with their status as Australia's aboriginal peoples could be entrenched. The rights demanded have included those for land, customary law and traditions, and forms of Aboriginal self-government.[19]

In considering measures such as these, it should be emphasised that they alone cannot perform the task of working through the consequences of colonialism. As the Canadian legal scholar Jeremy Webber has wisely observed: 'Such dramatic initiatives [as a national treaty] may indeed be essential as a way of marking new beginnings, of accomplishing a material change in the protection of rights long denied, and of achieving some practical conciliation between indigenous rights and non-indigenous interests. But we should not pretend that they can solve these issues once and for all, at one moment in time. The redefinition of the relationship [between Aboriginal and settler peoples] is a matter for the long haul, and indeed is likely to be a matter of continual adjustment'. This is a lesson that people right across the political spectrum might well learn. The task of reform, Webber argues, is one that requires a restructuring of the relationship between Aboriginal and settler people so that it enhances the conditions upon which they interact. In the end, it is the nature of that relationship more than the vindication of Aboriginal rights, however important this is, that will offer the best means of working out solutions over the long term.[20]

Other ways of working through the past (than those involving the state) are also critical. In recent years, corporations, companies, schools, universities and churches, for example, have sought to use their often considerable resources in ways that can help to renew Aboriginal capital (in the broadest sense of that term) and lead to Aboriginal recovery. Here, a recognition of the moral claim that Aboriginal people make upon settler Australians can become a response in which moral connection can lead to a commitment to purposive action.[21]

In work of this kind, which acknowledges the past in the present in order to make a new future, the key word should probably not be *reconciliation*. Reconciliation implies that historical difference can somehow be transcended. It implies that there can be some kind of final (re)solution, which brings the history of conflict between settlers and Aborigines to an end. It is more appropriate to assume that there will continue to be difference and differences but to continue to strive to moderate these. This suggests more of an ongoing process and an ongoing relationship in which Aboriginal and settler Australians recognise and respect the interests of the other as they struggle towards a truly just society. This, of course, entails a battle for life, not fighting a 'history war' to the death.

Days of mourning, days of celebration

However, the problem of the dead has to be considered too. As many scholars have noted, they are an important part of a community. Death has lain at the heart of the formation of many nations. Stephen Muecke, a professor of cultural studies, has argued: 'States can be set up as political entities, but they only become nations through the magical or spiritual agency of death. Mythologists and anthropologists can tell us why. A people recognises itself as a people . . . through the symbolic treatment of its dead'. In the case of Australia, though, it has remembered and mourned only those who fought wars elsewhere (as we noted earlier). It has not developed ways of remembering and mourning the victims of the wars here, particularly the Aboriginal people who lost the most as a result of these wars. In other words, their losses have never been recognised properly by the settler nation; indeed, the settler state has never acknowledged that they are worthy of recognition.[22]

As a result of its failure to work through this and other such traumatic events in the white colonisation of this country, the Australian nation has been unable to grapple with the wounds of the past and the divided legacies it has left. Instead, it has repressed them, which has only made them worse. As Henry Reynolds more or less noted over 30 years ago, popular historical discourse in Australia swings between exaggerating and under-estimating the extent of bloodshed. In other words, it can be argued that the failure to recognise the Aboriginal dead and dispossessed is responsible in large part for the excesses in both the directions discussed earlier in this book, such as those who beat up genocide (in its sense as mass killing) and those who beat down genocide (in its sense as mass death). What is required is an effective social process of mourning this event and its aftermath. This would constitute a means of engaging its trauma and achieving a reinvestment in life. As Dominick LaCapra has observed: 'Through memory-work . . . one is able to distinguish between past and present and to recognise something as having happened to one (or one's people) back then that is related to, but not identical with, here and now'. There can also be other beneficial outcomes, not least for the settler nation. 'Recognition', anthropologist Stephan Feuchtwang points out, 'is a mirror-structure'. That which recognises can itself command and demand recognition.[23]

The work of mourning required in Australia cannot occur unless there are effective rites of passage in reference to the wars fought over this country. Physical and ritual memorials provide a mechanism for this. It is the function of the memorials to those who fell in the First and Second World Wars, and the annual days such as ANZAC Day that commemorate this loss. What is required in Australia are appropriate memorials in the form of monuments throughout the land and an annual day of mourning to commemorate the dead of the wars fought here.[24] In the national capital, Reconciliation Place—which lies between Parliament House, the Aboriginal tent embassy and the Australian War Memorial, and alongside the High Court, the National Library and the National Gallery—could be reconstructed and made the site for such a memorial and for an annual ceremony. And so we could remember them. By means such as this, the Australian nation could recognise the reality of the past and work through its aftermath.

It seems to me that there is no other alternative to telling the truth about Aboriginal history and working through its consequences. What should be done instead? Re-enact the oppression and indignities of the past simply because some settler Australians find it difficult to admit the failings of the Australian nation? Try to build national pride by a deliberate denial of that past? If anyone is going to take pride in what is truly good about their nation's past, they must also be prepared to accept what is truly bad in it. One can celebrate as well as mourn. Acknowledging the bad does not diminish the good. On the contrary: telling the truth about Aboriginal history can actually help us to pinpoint just what was good in the past, the conditions that enabled this good to be achieved, and the lessons this has for us today.[25] This would be a history to help realise a better future.

● ACKNOWLEDGMENTS

I wish to thank the many people who have helped me with this book. Several colleagues and friends commented on the first draft, and I am grateful to them for their critical comments and suggestions: Alan Atkinson, Dipesh Chakrabarty, Graeme Davison, Tom Griffiths, Paula Hamilton, John Hirst, Mark McKenna, Peter Read, Liz Reed, Bill Schwarz and Elizabeth Weiss. Stephen Foster, Claudia Haake, Paula Hamilton, Mark McKenna, Shanti Narayanasamy and Liz Reed read either some or all of the revised manuscript and provided a good deal of useful advice. I am especially indebted to Dipesh Chakrabarty, Eleanor Hancock, Mark McKenna and Liz Reed for their advice, and my parents for their counsel and encouragement. In writing this book, I have also learned much from other scholars who have considered the historical and historiographical matters it discusses. I also want to acknowledge the research work of Marina Bollinger and Meighen Katz, the assistance of Jane Cadzow and Susan Tonkin, the help provided by archivists at the Archives Office of Tasmania and the National Archives of Australia, and librarians at the National Library of Australia, and the financial assistance of the School of Historical Studies, Monash University.

At Allen & Unwin Elizabeth Weiss was a superlative publisher from beginning to end, while Angela Handley and Sue Jarvis were fine editors. I am thankful for the advice a defamation lawyer engaged by Allen & Unwin gave on an earlier version of this book. My thanks to Peter Nicholson and Geoff Pryor for allowing me to reproduce their cartoons, and to Fairfax and News Limited for permission to reproduce the other illustrations.

● NOTES

In this book, the references to the sources that have been used for each point have generally been provided in notes at the end of each paragraph, rather than in notes at the end of each sentence.

Introduction

1 David Thelen, 'History After the *Enola Gay* Controversy: An Introduction', *Journal of American History*, vol. 82, no. 3, 1995, 1033.
2 In the case of the United States, another problematic race history, that of slavery, seems to have largely displaced that of aboriginal peoples in the historical consciousness of most non-aboriginal Americans.
3 In an era where the political landscape has changed so much, it no longer makes as much sense to apply terms (such as 'the left') to characterise positions on a political spectrum. This is evident in the increasingly common use of the term 'left liberal' (which confuses what are still very different political philosophies and programs). Throughout this book, I use 'new conservatives' to refer to historical 'revisionists' and their supporters, since the contradiction implied by this term conveys the ways in which their position has some aspects of conservatism and others that depart radically from this political tradition.
4 Since Windschuttle's first writings on Aboriginal history were published, some major public debates have occurred, mostly in Melbourne and Sydney. They include: Gould's Book Arcade, Sydney, 12 November 2000; *Lateline*, ABC TV, 16 April 2001; National Press Club, Canberra, 19 April 2001; 'Social History, Aboriginal History and the Pursuit of Truth', Blackheath Philosophy Forum, 1 March 2003; 'White Settlement in Australia: Violent Conquest or Benign Colonisation?', Melbourne Trades Hall, 5 March 2003; 'Telling Histories', Dechaineaux Theatre, Hobart, 29 March 2003; 'Roundtable on

Tasmanian Aboriginal History: Fact or Fiction?', Queen Victoria Museum and Art Gallery, Launceston, 16 May 2003; 'Contesting the Frontier: Truth and Method in Australian History', University of Sydney, 28 May 2003; 'The Construction of Aboriginal History: Fact or Fiction?', University of New South Wales Speakers' Forum, Sydney, 29 May 2003; 'The Manne–Windschuttle Debate', Melbourne Writers Festival, 27 August 2003; 'History Wars Forum', State Library of Victoria, Melbourne, 3 September 2003; *Lateline*, ABC TV, 3 September 2003. Most of these featured Keith Windschuttle and the leading historian in the field of Aboriginal history (at least in the public eye), Henry Reynolds.

5   Bernard Lane, 'Publisher Discusses Defects Claims with Historian', *Australian*, 11–12 January 2003; Michael Christie (Reuters), 'History War Hits Aussies', *Dominion Post* (Wellington), 5 March 2003; Jane Cadzow, 'Who's Right Now, Then?', *Age Good Weekend Magazine*, 17 May 2003, 18; Matthew Ricketson, in 'Footnotes to a War', *Sydney Morning Herald*, 13 December 2003; Ean Higgins, 'Who's Still Afraid of Keith Windschuttle?', *Australian*, 22 July 2004.

6   The favourable critical reception of this novel, which largely concerns the Jewish Holocaust, dismayed those who considered it historically ignorant, culturally insensitive and anti-semitic. Some saw it as a marker of an enormous cultural change and anticipated a national crisis. See, for example, Robert Manne, *The Culture of Forgetting: Helen Demidenko and the Holocaust*, Text, Melbourne, 1996.

7   See Eve Vincent and Claire Land, 'Silenced Voices', *Arena Magazine*, no. 67, 2003, <www.arena.org.au/Archives/Mag%20Archive/Issue%2067/against_the_current_67.htm>; Chris McConville, 'Writing Australian History: Fact or Fabrication?', *History Australia*, vol. 1, no. 1, 2003, 104; Aileen Moreton-Robinson, 'The Whiteness of Windschuttle's Worries: Aboriginal History and the National Character', in Phillip Adams and Dale Spender (eds), *The Ideas Book*, University of Queensland Press, St Lucia, 2005, 51–67; Angela Blakston, 'Pointing Fun at the Write Stuff', *Age*, 19 March 2005.

8   Iain McCalman, 'Flirting with Fiction', in Stuart Macintyre (ed.), *The Historian's Conscience: Australian Historians on the Ethics of History*, Melbourne University Press, Melbourne, 2004, 155.

9   In my opinion, Macintyre's treatment of Windschuttle's work (*The History Wars*, Melbourne University Press, Melbourne, 2003, especially Chapter 9) is more satisfactory than that offered by most of the historical contributors to Robert Manne's compilation: *Whitewash: On Keith Windschuttle's Fabrication of Aboriginal History*, Black Inc., Melbourne, 2003. Rather oddly, the principal new conservative response to criticisms of Windschuttle's work has focused only on those made of his book and has concentrated almost exclusively on those made by the contributors to Manne's *Whitewash*: John Dawson,

Washout: On the Academic Response to The Fabrication of Aboriginal History, Macleay Press, Sydney, 2004. This ignores many other commentaries on Windschuttle's *Fabrication* and his writings on Aboriginal history, some of which have offered more telling criticisms. See, for example, Alan Atkinson, 'Honey and Wax: A Review of Keith Windschuttle, *The Fabrication of Aboriginal History, Vol. 1*', *Journal of Australian Colonial History*, vol. 4, no. 2, 2002, 20–34.

10   My approach here is informed by observations that the American historian Dominick LaCapra has made in reference to the German historians' dispute, or *Historikerstreit*. See his 'Revisiting the Historians' Debate: Mourning and Genocide', *History & Memory*, vol. 9, nos 1–2, 1997, 80–112.

1 Nation

1   J.H. Plumb, *The Death of the Past* (1969), Penguin, Harmondsworth, 1973, 11, 14, 15.

2   Saul Friedlander, *Memory, History and the Extermination of the Jews of Europe*, Indiana University Press, Bloomington, 1993, 58–59; Raphael Samuel, *Theatres of Memory, Vol. 1: Past and Present in Contemporary Culture*, Verso, London, 1994, 25; Meaghan Morris, *Too Soon Too Late: History in Popular Culture*, Indiana University Press, Bloomington, 1998, 4.

3   Raphael Samuel, 'The Return of History', *London Review of Books*, 14 June 1990, 12; Andreas Huyssen, 'Monument and Memory in a Postmodern Age', in James E. Young (ed.), *The Art of Memory: Holocaust Memorials in History*, Prestel-Verlag, New York, 1994, 12, 'Trauma and Memory: A New Imaginary of Temporality', in Jill Bennett and Rosanne Kennedy (eds), *World Memory: Personal Trajectories in Global Time*, Palgrave, New York, 2003, 24; Michael S. Roth, *The Ironist's Cage: Memory, Trauma and the Construction of History*, Columbia University Press, New York, 1995, 8–9. For further consideration of the growing significance of the past, see Huyssen's thought-provoking essay, 'Present Pasts: Media, Politics, Amnesia', in Arjun Appadurai (ed.), *Globalisation*, Duke University Press, Durham, 2001, 57–77.

4   Benedict Anderson, *Imagined Communities: Reflections on the Origin and Spread of Nationalism*, rev. edn, Verso, London, 1991, 4, 6.

5   Ernest Renan, 'What is a Nation?' (1882) (trans. Martin Thom), in Homi Bhabha (ed.), *Nation and Narration*, Routledge, London, 1990, 11; Eric Hobsbawm, *On History*, Abacus, London, 1998, 6, 357.

6   Morris, *Too Soon*, 19.

7   For a survey of the treatment of relations between Aborigines and whites in historical and other texts during the first half or so of the twentieth century, see Richard Broome, 'Historians, Aborigines and Australia', in Bain Attwood

(ed.), *In the Age of Mabo: History, Aborigines and Australia*, Allen & Unwin, Sydney, 1996, 56–68. For the theme of victimhood, see Ann Curthoys, 'Constructing National Histories', in Bain Attwood and S.G. Foster (eds), *Frontier Conflict: The Australian Experience*, National Museum of Australia, Canberra, 2003, 185–200.

8   Walter Murdoch, *The Making of Australia: An Introductory History*, Whitcomb and Tombs, Melbourne, [1917], 9; John La Nauze, 'The Study of Australian History, 1929–59', *Historical Studies*, vol. 9, no. 33, 1959, 11.

9   W.E.H. Stanner, *The 1968 Boyer Lectures: After the Dreaming*, ABC, Sydney, 1969, 24–25. (These lectures were modelled on the BBC's Reith Lectures.) Chris Healy, Henry Reynolds and Geoffrey Bolton have pointed out that this silence characterised national histories more than local and regional ones: Healy, *From the Ruins of Colonialism: History as Social Memory*, Cambridge University Press, Melbourne, 1997, 123; Reynolds, *Why Weren't We Told? A Personal Search for the Truth About Our History*, Viking, Melbourne, 1999, 12; Bolton, 'Reflections on Comparative Frontier History', in Attwood and Foster (eds), *Frontier Conflict*, 165–66. Keith Windschuttle has claimed that 'the great Australian silence' is 'a myth' (*The Fabrication of Aboriginal History, Vol. 1, Van Diemen's Land 1803–1847*, Macleay Press, Sydney, 2002, 406–11), but S.G. Foster has pointed out that his account is marred by 'misrepresentation, inaccuracy and distortion' ('Contra Windschuttle', *Quadrant*, vol. 47, no. 3, 2003, 25–28).

10 Stanner, *After the Dreaming*, 17, 25, 27.

11 Some of this work appeared in major books, such as Ronald and Catherine Berndt's *The World of the First Australians*, Ure Smith, Sydney, 1964; D.J. Mulvaney's *A Prehistory of Australia*, Thames & Hudson, London, 1969, and Mulvaney and J. Peter White (eds), *Australians to 1788*, Fairfax, Syme & Weldon, Sydney, 1987; Charles Rowley's trilogy, *Aboriginal Policy and Practice*, which included *The Destruction of Aboriginal Society* (1970), Penguin, Melbourne, 1972; and Noel Butlin's *Economics and the Dreamtime: A Hypothetical History*, Cambridge University Press, Melbourne, 1993. The claims regarding the impact of Aboriginal people firing the land have since been questioned by archaeologists.

12 D.J. Mulvaney, *A Prehistory of Australia*, 12, 'Discovering Man's Place in Nature', *Proceedings of the Australian Academy of the Humanities*, vol. 2, 1971, 55, 'Beyond 1788: A Personal Exploration', in Bain Attwood (comp.), *Boundaries of the Past*, The History Institute, Victoria, Melbourne, 1990, 10.

13 Henry Reynolds, 'History from the Frontier', in Attwood (comp.), *Boundaries of the Past*, 23, 26.

14 The Australian constitution, it should be noted, makes no reference to citizenship rights. For a consideration of why the referendum was represented in these

terms, see Bain Attwood and Andrew Markus, *The 1967 Referendum, or When Aborigines Didn't Get the Vote*, Aboriginal Studies Press, Canberra, 1997.

15 See my *Rights for Aborigines*, Allen & Unwin, Sydney, 2003, Parts III–V, for a discussion of this shift from an emphasis on equal or civil rights to indigenous rights.

16 Judith Brett, *Australian Liberals and the Moral Middle Class: From Alfred Deakin to John Howard*, Cambridge University Press, Melbourne, 2003, 197, 200–01.

17 See John Chesterman, 'Defending Australia's Reputation: How Indigenous Australians Won Civil Rights', *Australian Historical Studies*, vol. 32, nos 116 and 117, 2001, 20–39 and 201–21; Stuart Ward, *Australia and the British Embrace: The Demise of the Imperial Ideal*, Melbourne University Press, Melbourne, 2001; James Curran, *The Power of Speech: Australian Prime Ministers Defining the National Image*, Melbourne University Press, Melbourne, 2004, 37–39.

18 Ibid., 45–47, 56.

19 Howard Morphy, *Aboriginal Art*, Phaidon, London, 1998, 35–37; Jim Davidson and Peter Spearritt, *Holiday Business: Tourism in Australia Since 1870*, Melbourne University Press, Melbourne, 2000, xxx, 80–81, 205–06, 248–49, 356–57.

20 See Andrew Lattas, 'Primitivism, Nationalism and Individualism in Australian Popular Culture', in Bain Attwood and John Arnold (eds), *Power, Knowledge and Aborigines*, La Trobe University Press, Melbourne, 1992, 45–58; and Bain Attwood, 'Introduction', in Attwood (ed.), *In the Age of Mabo*, xxvii–xxviii.

21 See Lee Sackett, 'Promoting Primitivism: Conservationist Depictions of Aboriginal Australians', *Australian Journal of Anthropology*, vol. 2, no. 2, 1991, 233–46; Janice Newton, 'Aborigines, Tribes and the Counterculture', *Social Analysis*, no. 23, 1988, 53–71.

22 See Attwood, 'Introduction', xxviii–xxix.

23 David Lowenthal, *The Past is a Foreign Country*, Cambridge University Press, Cambridge, 1985, 53.

24 See Attwood, 'Introduction', xxix–xxxi.

25 Morris, *Too Soon*, 5, 212, 220.

26 See Jeremy Beckett, 'Aboriginality, Citizenship and Nation State', *Social Analysis*, no. 24, 1988, 3–18.

27 Curran, *Power of Speech*, 15.

28 Graeme Davison, *The Use and Abuse of Australian History*, Allen & Unwin, Sydney, 2000, 2–4; Curran, *Power of Speech*, 191, 199, 201–02, 209, 212–13, 220, 223–24, 227, 230, 233.

29 Paul Keating, 'Redfern Speech' (1992), in Michelle Grattan (ed.), *Reconciliation: Essays on Australian Reconciliation*, Black Inc., Melbourne, 2000, 60–62.

30 See Attwood, 'Introduction', xxxiii.

31 Elizabeth Povinelli, 'The State of Shame: Australian Multiculturalism and the Crisis of Indigenous Citizenship', *Critical Inquiry*, vol. 24, no. 2, 1998, 579.

32 David Carter, 'Working on the Past, Working on the Future', in Richard Nile and Michael Peterson (eds), *Becoming Australian*, University of Queensland Press, St Lucia, 1998, 12.

33 Ken Gelder and Jane Jacobs, *Uncanny Australia: Sacredness and Identity in a Postcolonial Nation*, Melbourne University Press, Melbourne, 1998, 17, 22.

34 Gyanendra Pandey, *Remembering Partition: Violence, Nationalism and History in India*, Cambridge University Press, Cambridge, 2001, 152. It should be noted that some earlier histories had used the term 'invasion' to describe British colonisation. See, for example, Thomas Dunbabin, *The Making of Australasia*, A. & C. Black, London, 1922, 33.

35 Geoffrey Blainey, 'They View Australia's History as a Saga of Shame' (1985), in *Eye on Australia: Speeches and Essays of Geoffrey Blainey*, Schwartz Books, Melbourne, 1991, 46–51; Hugh Morgan, 'A Day to Remember Realities of History', *Age*, 28 January 1985, '1770 Cook Annexation of Australia was Quite Legal', *Age*, 29 March 1986; Ken Baker, 'The Bicentenary: Celebration or Apology', *IPA Review*, vol. 38, no. 4, 1985, 175–82, 'The New History', *IPA Review*, vol. 42, no. 3, 1988–89, 50; Leonie Kramer, 'The Rocky Horror History of Australia', *IPA Review*, vol. 38, no. 4, 1985, 183–85; Peter Coleman, 'Great Australian Death Wish', *Quadrant*, vol. 24, no. 5, 1985, 7–8.

36 See Attwood, 'Mabo, Australia and the End of History', in Attwood (ed.), *In the Age of Mabo*, 106–07. For Blainey's historical writings, see for example his *Triumph of the Nomads: A History of Ancient Australia* (1975), Sun Books, Melbourne, 1976, 103–11, and *A Land Half Won*, Macmillan, Melbourne, 1980, Ch. 6.

37 See Andrew Markus, 'Between Mabo and a Hard Place: Race and the Contradictions of Conservatism', and Attwood, 'Mabo', in Attwood (ed.), *In the Age of Mabo*, 88–99 and 100–16. Significantly, Keith Windschuttle's writings about conflict on the Australian frontier were immediately preceded by an article attacking what he considered to be Aboriginal separatism and the championing of this by academic historians: 'The Break-Up of Australia', *Quadrant*, vol. 44, no. 9, 2000, 8–16.

38 *Future Directions: It's Time for Plain Thinking—Liberal National*, Liberal and National Parties, Canberra, 1988, 7.

39 John Howard, 'Some Thoughts on Liberal Party Philosophy in the 1990s', *Quadrant*, vol. 38, nos. 7–8, 1994, 21, 24–25.

40 Blainey, 'Drawing Up a Balance Sheet of Our History', *Quadrant*, vol. 37, nos 7–8, 1993, 15; Mark McKenna, 'Metaphors of Light and Darkness: The Politics of "Black Armband" History', *Melbourne Journal of Politics*, vol. 25, 1998, 71–72; Curran, *Power of Speech*, 241–63.

41 Howard, in 'An Average Australian', *Four Corners*, ABC Television, 19 February 1996.

42 See Haydie Gooder and Jane Jacobs, 'Belonging and Non-Belonging: The Apology in a Reconciling Nation', in Alison Blunt and Cheryl McEwan (eds), *Postcolonial Geographies*, Continuum, New York, 2002, 200–13.

43 Howard, Sir Thomas Playford Memorial Lecture, 5 July 1996, typescript, 1–3, The 1996 Sir Robert Menzies Lecture, 18 November 1996, typescript, 2, 4, 9–11.

2 Democracy

1 Joyce Appleby, Lynn Hunt and Margaret Jacob, *Telling the Truth About History*, W.W. Norton & Company, New York, 1994, 28–29.

2 Ibid., 2, 200.

3 C.D. Rowley, *The Destruction of Aboriginal Society*, Australian National University Press, Canberra, 1970, 5, 8–9; Henry Reynolds, *Why Weren't We Told? A Personal Search for the Truth About Our History*, Viking, Melbourne, 1999, 245.

4 See Bain Attwood, *The Making of the Aborigines*, Allen & Unwin, Sydney, 1989, 135.

5 See some of the introductions to the books listed in note 7 below.

6 Peter Novick, *That Noble Dream: The 'Objectivity Question' and the American Historical Profession*, Cambridge University Press, New York, 1988, 1–2; Robert F. Berkhofer, Jr, *Beyond the Great Story: History as Text and Discourse*, Belknap Press, Cambridge, MA, 1995, 48.

7 See Rowley, *Destruction*; Henry Reynolds (comp.), *Aborigines and Settlers: The Australian Experience*, Cassell Australia, Melbourne, 1972; R.H.W. Reece, *Aborigines and Colonists: Aborigines and Colonial Society in New South Wales in the 1830s and 1840s*, Sydney University Press, Sydney, 1974; Raymond Evans et al., *Exclusion, Exploitation and Extermination: Race Relations in Colonial Queensland*, ANZ Book Co., Sydney, 1975; Henry Reynolds and Noel Loos, 'Aboriginal Resistance in Queensland', *Australian Journal of Politics and History*, vol. 22, no. 3, 1976, 214–26; M.F. Christie, *Aborigines in Colonial Victoria, 1835–1886*, Sydney University Press, Sydney, 1979; Lyndall Ryan, *The Aboriginal Tasmanians*, University of Queensland Press, St Lucia, 1981; Reynolds, *The Other Side of the Frontier*, Department of History, James Cook University, Townsville, 1981; Noel Loos, *Invasion and Resistance: Aboriginal–European Relations on the North Queensland Frontier 1861–1897*, Australian National University Press, Canberra, 1982.

8 For example, the work done by humanitarians like Mary Bennett, William Morley, Frederic Wood Jones and A.P. Elkin in the 1920s and 1930s; Aboriginal

leaders such as William Cooper, William Ferguson and Bill Onus in the 1930s and 1940s; journalists, or former journalists, such as Paul Hasluck, *Black Australians* (1941) and Clive Turnbull, *Black War: The Extermination of the Tasmanian Aborigines* (1948); the novelists Eleanor Dark, *The Timeless Land* (1941) and Katherine Susannah Prichard, *Coonardoo* (1943); the political scientist E.J.B. Foxcroft, *Australian Native Policy* (1941); the geographer, A. Grenfell Price, *White Settlers and Native Peoples: An Historical Study of Racial Contacts Between English-speaking Whites and Aboriginal Peoples in the United States, Canada, Australia and New Zealand* (1949); and the anthropologists Ronald and Catherine Berndt, *From Black to White in South Australia* (1951).

9 Reynolds, *The Other Side*, 1.

10 Reece, 'The Aborigines in Australian Historiography', in John A. Moses (ed.), *Historical Disciplines and Cultures in Australasia*, University of Queensland Press, St Lucia, 1979, 262–63, 'Aboriginal Community History: A Cautionary Tale', Paper delivered to the Australian Historical Association Conference, Sydney, 1982, 6, 'Inventing Aborigines', *Aboriginal History*, vol. 11, no. 1, 1987, 16–17. Ironically, no other major academic historian had referred to massacres more than Reece did in his *Aborigines and Colonists*.

11 Diane Barwick, 'This Most Resolute Lady: A Biographical Puzzle', in Diane Barwick et al. (eds), *Metaphors of Interpretation: Essays in Honour of W.E.H. Stanner*, Pergamon, Sydney, 1985, 221; D.J. Mulvaney, *Encounters in Place: Outsiders and Aboriginal Australians 1606–1985*, University of Queensland Press, St Lucia, 1989, 154; Attwood, *The Making*, 137; Richard Broome, 'Aboriginal Victims and Voyagers: Confronting Frontier Myths', *Journal of Australian Studies*, no. 42, 1994, 71.

12 Beverley Nance, 'The Level of Violence: Europeans and Aborigines in Port Phillip, *Historical Studies*, vol. 19, no. 77, 1981, 532–52; Noel Butlin, *Our Original Aggression: Aboriginal Populations of Southeastern Australia, 1788–1850*, Allen & Unwin, Sydney, 1983, *Economics and the Dreamtime: A Hypothetical History*, Cambridge University Press, Melbourne, 1993; Reece, '"Laws of the White People": The Frontier of Authority in Perth in 1838', *Push From the Bush*, no. 17, 1984, 2–28, 'Inventing Aborigines'; Ann McGrath, *'Born in the Cattle': Aborigines in Cattle Country*, Allen & Unwin, Sydney, 1987, especially Ch. 1; Marie Fels, *Good Men and True: The Aboriginal Police of the Port Phillip District 1837–53*, Melbourne University Press, Melbourne, 1988; Mulvaney, *Encounters in Place*, especially Chs 4, 6, 11 & 23; Jan Critchett, *A 'Distant Field of Murder': Western District Frontiers 1834–1848*, Melbourne University Press, Melbourne, 1990, especially 2, 23; Reynolds, *With the White People*, Penguin, Melbourne, 1990; Judy Campbell, *Invisible Invaders: Smallpox and Other Diseases in Aboriginal Australia, 1780–1880*, Melbourne University Press, Melbourne, 2002.

13 Reece, *Aborigines and Colonists*, 2; S.G. Foster, 'Aboriginal Rights and Official Morality', *Push From the Bush*, no. 11, 1981, 68–98; Reynolds, *The Law of the Land*, Penguin, Melbourne, 1987; Mulvaney, 'Review of . . . Henry Reynolds, *The Law of the Land*', *Overland*, no. 111, 1988, 93–95; A.G.L. Shaw, 'British Policy Towards the Australian Aborigines, 1830–1850', *Australian Historical Studies*, vol. 25, no. 99, 1992, 265–85; Bain Attwood, 'Aborigines and Academic Historians: Some Recent Encounters', *Australian Historical Studies*, vol. 24, no. 94, 1990, 130–31.

14 Peter Read, 'Review of *A Picnic with the Natives* [et al.]', *Australian Historical Studies*, vol. 24, no. 97, 1991, 483. Keith Windschuttle has tried to dismiss the significance of this work by claiming that it merely amounted to a few mutterings in the 1990s ('Foreword', in John Dawson, *Washout: On the Academic Response to the Fabrication of Aboriginal History*, Macleay Press, Sydney, 2004, x). This is obviously incorrect.

15 For a consideration of this work, see my 'Aboriginal History', in John A. Moses (ed.), *Historical Disciplines in Australasia: Themes, Problems and Debates*, a special issue of *Australian Journal of Politics and History*, vol. 41, 1995, 33–47.

16 'Dedication', *Aboriginal History*, vol. 11, 1987 (a special volume in honour of Diane Barwick), 1–2.

17 See Reynolds, *The Other Side*, especially Chs 1–3.

18 See Fels, *Good Men and True*, especially Ch. 4.

19 The Working Party of Aboriginal Historians for the Bicentennial History, 1788–1988, 'Preparing Black History', *Identity*, vol. 4, no. 5, 1981, 8; James Miller, *Koori: A Will to Win. The Heroic Resistance, Survival and Triumph of Black Australia*, Angus & Robertson, Sydney, 1985, xvii.

20 Working Party, 'Preparing Black History', 7–8; Marcia Langton, '*Well, I Heard it on the Radio and I Saw it on the Television . . .*': *An Essay for the Australian Film Commission on the Politics and Aesthetics of Filmmaking by and about Aboriginal People and Things*, Australian Film Commission, Sydney, 1993, 33.

21 Peter Sutton, 'Myth as History, History as Myth', in Ian Keen (ed.), *Being Black: Aboriginal Cultures in 'Settled' Australia*, Aboriginal Studies Press, Canberra, 1988, 260–61.

22 Ibid., 265.

23 Kenneth Maddock, 'Myth, History and a Sense of Oneself', in Jeremy R. Beckett (ed.), *Past and Present: The Construction of Aboriginality*, Aboriginal Studies Press, Canberra, 1988, 19.

24 For a discussion of these stories, see ibid., *passim*, and Deborah Bird Rose, 'The Saga of Captain Cook: Morality and European Law', *Australian Aboriginal Studies*, no. 2, 1984, 24–39.

25 See, for example, Bain Attwood and John Arnold (eds), *Power, Knowledge and Aborigines*, La Trobe University Press, Melbourne, 1992; Tom Griffiths,

Hunters and Collectors: The Antiquarian Imagination in Australia, Cambridge University Press, Melbourne, 1996; Patrick Wolfe, *Settler Colonialism and the Transformation of Anthropology*, Cassell, London, 1999.

26 Shoshana Felman, 'Education and Crisis, or the Vicissitudes of Teaching', in Cathy Caruth (ed.), *Trauma: Explorations in Memory*, Johns Hopkins University Press, Baltimore, 1995, 16; Jay Winter, 'The Memory Boom in Contemporary Historical Studies', *Raritan*, vol. 21, no. 1, 2001, 56, 66; Homi Bhabha, quoted in Dipesh Chakrabarty, *Provincialising Europe: Postcolonial Thought and Historical Difference*, Princeton University Press, Princeton, 2000, 18; Dipesh Chakrabarty, 'Reconciliation and its Historiography: Some Preliminary Thoughts', *UTS Review*, vol. 7, no. 1, 2001, 11; Paula Hamilton, 'Sale of the Century? Memory and Historical Consciousness in Australia', in Katharine Hodgkin and Susannah Radstone (eds), *Contested Pasts: The Politics of Memory*, Routledge, London, 2003, 136–37.

27 For a discussion of the Wilkomirski case see, for example, Stefan Maechler, *The Wilkomirski Affair: A Study in Biographical Truth* (trans. John E. Woods), Random House, New York, 2001; for an account of the Demidenko affair see, for example, Andrew Riemer, *The Demidenko Debate*, Allen & Unwin, Sydney, 1996; for a summary of the Khouri case see <www.randomhouse.com.au/norma.htm>.

28 David Carter, 'Introduction: Intellectuals and their Publics', and 'The Conscience Industry: The Rise and Rise of the Public Intellectual', in David Carter (ed.), *The Ideas Market: An Alternative Take on Australia's Intellectual Life*, Melbourne University Press, Melbourne, 2004, 1, 15, 23.

29 Ibid., 3, 22, 34–35; Carter, 'Public Intellectuals, Book Culture and Civil Society', *Australian Humanities Review*, <www.lib.latrobe.edu.au/AHR/archive/Issue-December–2001/carter2.html>, 15. See Gillian Whitlock, 'Becoming Migloo', in Carter (ed.), *The Ideas Market*, 236–58.

30 Chakrabarty, 'Reconciliation', 9.

31 Reynolds, *Frontier: Aborigines, Settlers and Land*, Allen & Unwin, Sydney, 1987, viii, 4, 9, *This Whispering in Our Hearts*, Allen & Unwin, Sydney, 1998, xvi, 6, 31, 67, 178–200, 247, 280, *Why Weren't We Told? A Personal Search for the Truth About Our History*, Viking, Melbourne, 1999, 170. For other histories, see for example Evans et al., *Exclusion, Exploitation and Extermination*, 28, 34, 51, 71; Christie, *Aborigines*, 45, 50; Loos, *Invasion and Resistance*, 46, 95, 131–32; Richard Broome, *Aboriginal Australians: Black Response to White Dominance 1788–1980*, Allen & Unwin, Sydney, 1982, 42–43; Ann McGrath, 'Sex, Violence and Theft', in Patricia Grimshaw et al., *Creating a Nation*, McPhee Gribble, Melbourne, 1994, 135, 'Introduction', in McGrath (ed.), *Contested Ground: Australian Aborigines Under the British Crown*, Allen & Unwin, Sydney, 1995, 18–19.

32 Christie, *Aborigines*, 79, note 117; Mary Coe, *Windradyne: A Wiradjuri Koorie*,

Aboriginal Studies Press, Canberra, 1989, especially 57–60; David Roberts, 'Bells Falls Massacre and Bathurst's History of Violence: Local Tradition and Australian Historiography', *Australian Historical Studies*, vol. 26, no. 105, 1995, 615–33; Mark McKenna, *Looking for Blackfellas' Point: An Australian History of Place*, University of New South Wales Press, Sydney, 2002, 41–45.

33 Bruce Elder, *Blood on the Wattle: Massacres and the Maltreatment of Australian Aborigines since 1788*, Child & Associates, Sydney, 1988; Phillip Knightley, *Australia: Biography of a Nation*, Jonathan Cape, London, 2000; Roger Milliss, *Waterloo Creek: The Australia Day Massacre of 1838, George Gipps and the British Conquest of New South Wales*, Penguin, Melbourne, 1992; Neville Green, *The Forrest River Massacres*, Fremantle Arts Centre Press, Fremantle, 1995; *Frontier: Stories From White Australia's Forgotten War*, ABC Television, Sydney, 1997. Most of the books cited here were the subject of much critical commentary by academic historians. See, for example, Broome, 'Massacres', in Graeme Davison, John Hirst and Stuart Macintyre (eds), *The Oxford Companion to Australian History*, Oxford University Press, Melbourne, 1998, 415; Tom Griffiths, 'The Language of Conflict', in Bain Attwood and S.G. Foster (eds), *Frontier Conflict: The Australian Experience*, National Museum of Australia, Canberra, 2003, 148, and the references there (149 note 16).

34 Rodney Smith, *Australian Political Culture*, Longman, Sydney, 2001, 141–43. See, for example, Grace and Harold Koch (comps), *Kaytetye Country: An Aboriginal History of the Barrow Creek Area*, Institute for Aboriginal Development Publications, Alice Springs, 1993. I wish to thank Helen Irving for an email exchange that stimulated me to consider some of the matters discussed in this section.

35 Richard J. Evans, *Telling Lies about Hitler: The Holocaust, History and the David Irving Trial*, Verso, London, 2002, 7.

3 Politics

1 There are several commentaries on the *Historikerstreit*. See, for example, Charles S. Maier, *The Unmasterable Past: History, Holocaust, and German National Identity*, Harvard University Press, Cambridge, MA, 1988. The controversy over Daniel Goldhagen's *Hitler's Willing Executioners* is considered by Ian Kershaw, *The Nazi Dictatorship: Problems and Perspectives of Interpretation*, 4th edn, Arnold, London, 2000, 251–62. For the *Enola Gay* controversy (over an exhibition about the American bombing of Hiroshima and Nagasaki proposed by the Smithsonian Institution's National Air and Space Museum in Washington, DC), see *Journal of American History*, vol. 82, no. 3, 1995, and Edward T. Linenthal and Tom Engelhardt (eds), *History Wars: The Enola Gay and Other Battles for the American Past*, Metropolitan Books, New York, 1996.

2   This said, there were similarities between the dispute in the mid-1990s over Daniel Goldhagen's *Hitler's Willing Executioners* and the one over Keith Windschuttle's *The Fabrication of Aboriginal History*. For example, neither Goldhagen nor Windschuttle had a track record as academic historians; their books were combative, provocative and aggressively argued; their messages had a stark simplicity; they demonstrated certitude about their interpretations; they appealed to a popular audience and to prejudice; and most specialist academic historians agreed in their lines of fundamental criticism of the argument and methodology of these books. However, this seems to have had little impact on much of the public consideration of them.

3   See David Carter, 'Introduction: Intellectuals and their Publics', in David Carter (ed.), *The Ideas Market: An Alternative Take on Australia's Intellectual Life*, Melbourne University Press, Melbourne, 2004, 8.

4   Why these figures have been keen to support a historical 'revisionist' whose work is obviously flawed and ill-judged is a question that deserves more consideration than I can give it here. It already seems evident that his supporters will try to distance themselves from Windschuttle's work now that their backing is no longer required. See, for example, Gerard Henderson, 'The Trouble with Keith Windschuttle', *Age*, 7 December 2004; Peter Coleman, 'Between Facts and Fudges', *Australian*, 24–26 December 2004.

5   For a discussion of the political work Pearson and another Howard appointee, his biographer David Barnett, did there, see Stuart Macintyre and Anna Clark, *The History Wars*, Melbourne University Press, Melbourne, 2003, Ch. 10.

6   Mark Davis, *Gangland: Cultural Elites and the New Generationalism*, 2nd edn, Allen & Unwin, Sydney, 1999, 32, 'Great White Noise', in Carter (ed.), *The Ideas Market*, 190–91.

7   Davis, *Gangland*, 230; Sean Scalmer and Murray Goot, 'Elites Constructing Elites: News Limited's Newspapers 1996–2002', in Marian Sawer and Barry Hindess (eds), *Us and Them: Anti-Elitism in Australia*, API Network, Perth, 2004, 140, 142, 146–47, 149. Having fuelled the conflict in the most recent episode in the controversy over Aboriginal history by casting it as a struggle between two war-like forces, it is rather odd to find the *Australian* newspaper's editor-at-large, Paul Kelly, concluding an opinion piece: 'Our national maturity will come only when we transcend both the triumphalist and black armband stereotypes' ('Our Rival Storytellers', 27–28 September 2003). This ignores the nature of the academic historiography over the last twenty or more years.

8   For further discussion of this, see Hindess and Sawer (eds), *Us and Them*, especially the introduction by the editors and the essays by Sawer and Damien Cahill.

9   *Commonwealth Parliamentary Debates*, House of Representatives, 29 October

1996, 5976; John Howard, Sir Robert Menzies Lecture, 18 November 1996, typescript, 2.

10 See Guy Rundle, 'The New Social Conservatism and the Myth of the Elites', and Paul Gillen, 'The Conversational Turn and the Conservative Revisionists', in Carter (ed.), *The Ideas Market*, 40–62 and 63–79. For a discussion of American new conservatives in the *Enola Gay* affair, see Linenthal and Engelhardt, 'Introduction', and Mike Wallace, 'Culture War, History Front', in Linenthal and Engelhardt (eds), *History Wars*, 1–7, 171–98.

11 It should be noted that neither Clark nor Blainey were necessarily party to this combat. (Clark died in 1991.)

12 For a discussion of these controversies, see Macintyre and Clark, *History Wars*, Chs 4 and 5.

13 Catharine Lumby, 'Outside in: Journalists and Academics in the Public Sphere', in Carter (ed.),*The Ideas Market*, 202, 212.

14 Apparently this university does not hold copies of their MA theses from this period. A member of the faculty in which Windschuttle did his thesis suggested to me that Windschuttle's dissertation was a study of un-employment (personal communication, 15 February 2004).

15 Too much significance has been attributed to Windschuttle's shift from one end of the political spectrum to the other. Curiosity about this change has distracted some observers from what are actually more important *continu-ities* in his politics over 40 years. Less attention should be paid to the content of Windschuttle's political beliefs in terms of 'left' and 'right', and more to their common structure (which would entail a consideration of the rigid and doctrinaire way in which he has held his beliefs and the polemical manner in which he has espoused his opinions) and the common source or well-spring of those beliefs (which would entail a consideration of the role the politics of *ressentiment* has played in his work).

16 ASIO reports, 9 and 25 February 1971, National Archives of Australia, Series A6119, item 3246, <http://naa12.naa.gov.au/scripts/Imagine.asp?B=4269 838&I=1>, see pp. 6 and 8; biographical statements, Windschuttle, *Unemploy-ment*, 1st and revis. edns, Penguin, Melbourne, 1979, 1980, iii; Windschuttle, *The Media: A New Analysis of the Press, Television, Radio and Advertising in Australia*, Penguin, Melbourne, 1984, author's note; Windschuttle, *The Killing of History: How a Discipline is Being Murdered by Literary Critics and Social Theorists*, Macleay Press, Sydney, 1994, dustjacket; Windschuttle, 'The Cultural Cold War', *Quadrant*, vol. 43, no. 11, 1999, 37; David Myton, 'Windschuttle's Way', *Campus Review*, vol. 12, no. 2, 2002, 10; Windschuttle, letter to the editor, *Australian*, 15 January 2003; Jane Cadzow, 'Who's Right Now, Then?', *Age Good Weekend Magazine*, 17 May 2003, 21, 24; Ann Curthoys, personal communi-cation, 1 March 2005.

17 Keith Windschuttle, 'Exposing Academic Deception of Past Wrongs', *Sydney Morning Herald*, 19 September 2000, 'The Myths of Frontier Massacres in Australian History', Part II, *Quadrant*, vol. 44, no. 11, 2000, 22, 'Selected Readings', *Australian Review of Books*, vol. 6, no. 3, 2001, 5, 'The Fabrication of Aboriginal History', *New Criterion*, vol. 20, no. 1, 2001, <www.newcrite rion.com/archive/20/sept01/keith.htm>, 3, 6–7; Windschuttle, paraphrased and quoted by Andrew Stevenson, 'A Voice From the Frontier', *Sydney Morning Herald*, 22–23 September 2001; Windschuttle, *The Fabrication of Aboriginal History, Vol. 1: Van Diemen's Land 1803–1847*, Macleay Press, Sydney, 2002, 2–3, 5–7, 9–10, 28, 116, 401–03.

18 This charge—and so the very title of Windschuttle's book—is an ambiguous one. Windschuttle has not really made it clear whether he is arguing that Aboriginal history is a fabrication because historians have consciously fabricated accounts or because their political commitment has influenced their approach to such a degree that they have unintentionally fabricated the past. He implies that they have done both, but this is somewhat contradictory.

19 It has been suggested by some of his contemporaries that Windschuttle resents elites. One student friend from their days at the University of Sydney has recalled: 'He was conscious of privilege and wealth, and that he didn't have it'. Another has remembered: 'He had a chip on his shoulder about all the privileged young kids at university . . . There's always been that resentment against an entrenched elite' (quoted by Cadzow, 'Who's Right?', 21).

20 In the 1960s and 1970s, a one-time friend has claimed, Windschuttle had both 'a considerable understanding of the powerfully manipulative impact of the tabloid media' and 'a deep hatred of the ruling class who owned the newspapers' (Bob Gould, 'Deconstructing the Sixties and Seventies: An Open Letter to Keith and Liz Windschuttle', <http://members.optushome.com.au/ spainter/Windschuttle.html>).

21 In his earlier work, which owed much to the influence of the New Left of the 1960s and 1970s, Windschuttle was especially concerned to attack the myths (i.e. falsehoods) of the ruling class, but he has continued to have a penchant for assaulting myth in much the same terms. For example, he devotes the opening chapter of *The Fabrication* to an attack on the myth of a massacre at Risdon Cove in Van Diemen's Land.

22 Windschuttle, *Unemployment*, rev. edn, vi, see Ch. 8; 'Preface', 'Part I, Introduction' and 'Drug Menace Turned on by Press', in Keith and Elizabeth Windschuttle (eds), *Fixing the News: Critical Perspectives on the Australian Media*, Cassell Australia, Sydney, 1981, v, 2, 169; Windschuttle, 'Drug Menace Turned on by Press', in ibid., 169; Windschuttle, *Media*, ix, see Ch. 10; Windschuttle, *Killing*, 36, *Fabrication*, 6, 9, 116; Windschuttle, quoted in Stevenson, 'Voice'.

23 Margaret Jacobs, 'Review of . . . *The Killing of History*', *Journal of American History*, vol. 85, no. 2, 1998, 627; Tom Griffiths, 'The Language of Conflict', in Bain Attwood and S.G. Foster (eds), *Frontier Conflict: The Australian Experience*, National Museum of Australia, Canberra, 2003, 136. Other writers have pondered whether several features of Windschuttle's work might not have personal roots. In undertaking a major profile on Windschuttle in which she interviewed friends and members of his family, the journalist Jane Cadzow learned that there was little 'grey' in his life. 'He doesn't go in for shades of grey', one had observed; with Windschuttle, 'it's black and white', another had remarked. Cadzow heard this comment on many occasions, so much so that she began to wonder about his choice of pets: 'Kingpins of the [Windschuttle] Paddington household are Bobby and Teddy, two bouncy dogs he walks daily and clearly adores. A Scottish terrier and a West Highland terrier. One black and one white'. Those close to Windschuttle, Cadzow also reported, 'say the only thing that hasn't changed [over the years] is his certitude'. Some recalled this as well as his dogmatism. For example, one remembered Windschuttle as 'one of the most rigid kinds of Marxists you could imagine'; another referred to his 'refusal to countenance opinions that differ from his own' ('Who's Right', 19, 21). In *The Fabrication*, things tend to be completely this or completely that or always this and never that, and so on (5, 8, 9, 19, 26, 41, 42, 80, 85, 86, 89, 98, 99, 100, 101, 102, 103, 104, 112, 114, 115, 118, 129, 130, 133, 146, 152, 153, 166, 169, 184, 194, 198, 209, 219, 226, 227, 230, 231, 233, 234, 247, 251, 269, 271, 276, 285, 300, 303, 326, 327, 331, 341, 353, 370, 377, 399, 402, 403, 406, 408, 412, 415, 419, 424, 426, 427, 430, 431). My focus here is upon understanding Windschuttle's work even though, as Alan Atkinson has remarked, '[a] book like *The Fabrication of Aboriginal History* forces the reader . . . to wonder, as he moves from page to page, about the character and intentions of the author . . . It has a sinewy, uncompromising tone . . . which makes it hard to ignore the man behind the writing' ('Honey and Wax: A Review of Keith Windschuttle, *The Fabrication of Aboriginal History, Vol. 1*', *Journal of Australian Colonial History*, vol. 4, no. 2, 2002, 21).

24 Jacobs, 'Review', 627; Graeme Davison, 'A Premature Post-Mortem?', *Agenda*, vol. 2, no. 3, 1995, 383; Alan Atkinson, unpublished letter to the editor, *Australian*, 12 February 2003 (quoted with permission of the author); Inga Clendinnen, quoted Miriam Cosic, 'Dangerous Journey', *Australian*, 4–5 October 2003; Clendinnen, 'Despatches from the History Wars', *Australian Financial Review*, 31 October 2003.

25 Dominick LaCapra, 'Review of *The Killing of History*', *American Historical Review*, vol. 103, no. 1, 1998, 148–49, 'Communications', *American Historical Review*, vol. 104, no. 2, 1999, 710; Jacobs, 'Review', 626; Daniel Gordon, 'Capital Punishment for Murderous Theorists?', *History and Theory*, vol. 38,

no. 3, 1999, 378. Even those very critical of 'postmodernism' have noted the crudity of Windschuttle's treatment of it. In the course of discussing an article by Windschuttle ('Cultural History, Western Imperialism, and the Case of Edward Said') in the journal of the Historical Society, Elizabeth Fox-Genovese remarks in her editorial: 'From the beginning, a number of our members—and readers of *The Journal*—have been eager to have us declare war upon the literary turn in particular and postmodernism, including post-colonialism, in general. One may readily sympathise with the temptation, not least because such ferocious blows against what Marc Bloch called "the historian's craft" have been inflicted in their name. The issues nonetheless remain more complex than many of the uncompromising anti-postmodernists acknowledge, and serious engagement with them demands something more than *slash-and-burn guerilla tactics*' ('Introduction', *Historical Journal*, vol. 1, nos 2–3, 2001, <www.bu.edu/historic/journal_spring00.jpg>, my emphasis).

26 Readers might investigate for themselves another, simpler example: an article in which Windschuttle misrepresents an argument made by the historian Graeme Davison. See Davison, 'National Museums in a Global Age: Observations Abroad and Reflections at Home', in Darryl McIntyre and Kirsten Wehner (eds), *National Museums: Negotiating Histories Conference Proceedings*, National Museum of Australia, Canberra, 2001, 12–28, and Windschuttle, 'How Not to Run a Museum', *Quadrant*, vol. 45, no. 9, 2001, 11–14. See also Davison's response: 'Conflict in the Museum', in Attwood and Foster (eds), *Frontier Conflict*, 201–04.

27 LaCapra, 'Review', 149, 'Communications', 710; J. Bradford DeLong, 'Anti-Post-Modernism', <www.j-bradford-delong.net/email/antipostmodernism. html>; Gordon, 'Capital Punishment', 381, 383. The point of DeLong's 'joke' is this, of course: 'If I'm supposed to line up on "their" side or on that of Keith Windschuttle, it is no decision at all' ('Anti-Post-Modernism').

28 Too much can be made of credentials. Several eminent historians of Windschuttle's generation do not have PhDs. This includes Henry Reynolds. There is some evidence to suggest that Windschuttle is anxious about his lack of academic qualifications as a historian and is troubled by what he apparently sees as his failure to do a PhD, which requires a dissertation or a thesis (Cadzow, 'Who's Right', 19, 22, and note 28 below). In *The Fabrication*, Windschuttle uses the term 'thesis' a good deal: 2, 4, 6, 63, 64, 65, 77 (2), 79, 88, 95, 99, 100, 102, 105, 114 (2), 115 (2), 116, 118, 119, 125, 126, 129, 197, 307, 308 (2), 327, 328, 341, 353, 356, 360, 372), as well as in two of the chapter headings (4 and 9). Usually, a 'thesis' (or major contention) is something that an author advances him or herself, but Windschuttle describes his own arguments in these terms on one or two occasions only (115–16). There is a general expectation that a PhD student would advance a thesis or argument in their

dissertation. Windschuttle not only repeatedly attributes a thesis or theses to other historians; he also claims that each of these fails (just as he failed to complete his PhD thesis).

29 See Christopher Pearson, 'Scholars Skirmish on the Frontiers of History', *Age*, 17 December 2001; Myton, 'Windschuttle's Way', 10; Windschuttle, *Fabrication*, back cover; Peter Coleman, 'The Windschuttle Thesis', *Quadrant*, vol. 46, no. 12, 2002, 80; Michael Duffy, 'Once Again, Goal Posts are Moved', *Daily Telegraph*, 21 December 2002; Gerard Henderson, 'The Battle is Not to be Left Behind', *Age*, 24 December 2002; Ron Brunton, 'Fabrication Fury, but the Rest is History', *Courier-Mail*, 28 December 2002; P.P. McGuinness, 'History, Lies and Imagination', *Quadrant*, vol. 47, no. 3, 2003, 2; Claudio Veliz, 'History as an Alibi', *Quadrant*, vol. 47, no. 3, 2003, 21–24. Others supported this ruse by reproducing the claim that Claudio Veliz, one of Windschuttle's greatest boosters, is a senior historian (Bernard Lane, 'British Arrival a Benign "Picnic"', *Australian*, 10 December 2002; Miranda Devine, 'The Book Launch, Bluster and Backdowns', *Sydney Morning Herald*, 19 December 2002).

30 Statement of Claim in the Supreme Court of the Australian Capital Territory, 25 March 2002. In the course of considering the politics of expertise in one of her regular columns for the *Bulletin* in 2002, Catharine Lumby, director of media studies at the University of Sydney, questioned Windschuttle's credentials and experience as an historian. For example, she observed that he had no PhD in history ('The De-Skilling of History', *Bulletin*, 12 February 2002, 41). Windschuttle began legal proceedings against the *Bulletin*, alleging that Lumby's article had defamed him as a historian (Statement of Claim). In September 2004, the publishers of the *Bulletin* issued a statement saying that it accepted that Lumby's allegations were incorrect (*Bulletin*, 7 September 2004, 7).

31 For reviews, see those cited above (by Davison, Gordon, Jacobs and LaCapra) and Stuart Macintyre, 'Review of . . . *The Killing of History*', *Australian Historical Studies*, vol. 28, no. 109, 1997, 191–92.

32 According to a search I had conducted of *APAFT*, the database that indexes the major Australian academic journals, and *Historical Abstracts*, which does the same for the international academic history journals, Windschuttle had published at best one article on historiography ('Foucault as Historian', *Critical Review of International Social and Political Philosophy*, vol. 1, no. 2, 1998, 5–35) in a refereed journal (according to the criteria used by *Ulrich's International Periodicals Directory*), and none on history. Prior to publication of *The Fabrication*, Windschuttle had authored a book on history and theory (*The Killing of History*) but no book of history.

33 Paul Sheehan, 'Our History, not Rewritten but Put Right', *Sydney Morning Herald*, 25 November 2002; Lane, 'Stripping the Armbands', *Australian*,

6 December 2002; Roger Sandall, 'Mr Windschuttle Versus the Professors', *Australian*, 23 December 2002.

34 Windschuttle, *Fabrication*, 294.

35 For a discussion of the similarities between some American new conservative writings and Windschuttle's, see Davis, *Gangland*, Ch. 9, especially 187, 192.

36 Windschuttle, *Fabrication*, 403, and see especially Chs 2–4 of the Australian edition of *Killing* and Ch. 9 of the American edition (Free Press, New York, 1997).

37 Windschuttle, 'Cultural History and Western Imperialism: The Case of Edward Said', *Journal of the History Society*, vol. 1, nos 2–3, 2000–01, 169–206; Roger Kimball, endorsement on the back cover of Windschuttle, *Fabrication*; McGuinness, 'History'; Veliz, 'History'; Geoffrey Blainey, 'Native Fiction', *New Criterion*, vol. 21, no. 8, 2003, <www.newcriterion.com/archive/21/apr03/blainey.htm>; Windschuttle, '*Whitewash* Confirms the Fabrication of Aboriginal History', *Quadrant*, vol. 47, no. 10, 2003, 8–16. For his *New Criterion* articles, see <www.sydneyline.com/Anti-Westernism.htm> and <www.sydneyline.com/Intellectuals.htm>.

38 Gordon, 'Capital Punishment', 379; Windschuttle, 'About the Sydney Line', <www.sydneyline.com.About.htm>; Brian Kennedy, *A Passion to Oppose: John Anderson, Philosopher*, Melbourne University Press, Melbourne, 1995, 5, 8–9, 16, 37, 45, 58, 65, 83, 90, 92, 95, 98, 101–02, 109, 112, 124, 141, 146, 148, 152, 169–70, 179, 191–92, 194, 200, 202, 209–10. Kennedy points out that 'in his understanding of reality, Anderson always emphasised complexity both in the things themselves and in the minds that perceive them' but that there were 'camp followers who, disregarding the master's subtleties and complexities, applied his teaching indiscriminately' (ibid., 66, 152).

39 Davison, 'Premature Post-Mortem?', 382; Macintyre, 'Review', 191; LaCapra, 'Review', 149; Windschuttle, *Fabrication*, 40, 45, 46, 49, 85, 88, 89, 100, 102–03, 114, 116, 122–23, 130, 133, 139, 143–44, 148, 149, 153, 154, 166, 177–79, 192, 226, 254–55, 260, 262, 271, 274–77, 280, 283, 303, 308, 312, 327, 367, 399, 403, 404, 406, 414, 415, 437; Windschuttle, 'White Settlement in Australia: Violent Conquest or Benign Colonisation?', debate, Melbourne Trades Hall, 5 March 2003, <www.sydneyline.com/RMIT%20debate%20with%20Grimshaw.htm>; Cadzow, 'Who's Right', 19, 22–24; Martin Krygier and Robert van Krieken, 'The Character of the Nation', in Robert Manne (ed.), *Whitewash: On Keith Windschuttle's Fabrication of Aboriginal History*, Black Inc., Melbourne, 2003, 83; Windschuttle, in *Lateline*, ABC Television, 3 September 2003, transcript, <www.abc.net.au/lateline/content/2003/s938399.htm>. Cadzow reported: 'Those who know [Windschuttle] say he has always been a polemicist and provocateur—the type who wakes up in the morning spoiling for a fight'— and someone who gets 'pretty personal' in arguments ('Who's Right', 18–19).

40 Windschuttle, *Killing*, 117, 'How Not to Run', 12, *Fabrication*, 3, 401–02.

41 Ibid., 3; Cadzow, 'Who's Right', 22; Krygier and van Krieken, 'Character', 83.

42 Windschuttle, in History Wars Forum, State Library of Victoria, broadcast *Late Night Live*, ABC Radio National, 3 and 4 September 2003, recording transcribed by author, emphasis reflects the original.

43 As a result, in my opinion, his perception of external reality is distorted.

44 Windschuttle, quoted in Lane, 'Stripping'; Windschuttle, in 'White Settlement in Australia'; Windschuttle, quoted in Cadzow, 'Who's Right', 22.

45 Mark McKenna has argued in reference to some of Reynolds' work: 'This way of packaging history, as if it were a legal contest to be settled in a court of law, implied that the nation awaited sentence if it were found guilty. In lending itself naturally to the media, it also created a framework for the public discussion of frontier history which would later be adopted in a much cruder fashion by conservative commentators who would attempt to prove Australia "not guilty"' (*Looking for Blackfellas' Point: An Australian History of Place*, University of New South Wales Press, Sydney, 2002, 47).

46 Stuart Macintyre, 'Events of the Day: Review of Robert Manne, *The Way We Live Now*', *Australian Book Review*, no. 202, 1998, 8; Manne (ed.), *Whitewash*, back cover. In keeping with the new culture of public intellectuals, this occurred by means of well-organised publicity for *Whitewash*, which comprised the now customary publisher's hyperbole, which played to the combative tone of the 'history wars'; a former Liberal prime minister, Malcolm Fraser (who has become one of the Howard government's most despised critics), and a former head of the Council for Aboriginal Reconciliation, Pat Dodson, launching the book at the Melbourne Writers Festival; a well-advertised debate between Manne and Windschuttle at the same forum, which was later made available on the websites of the *Age* and *Sydney Morning Herald*; a column by Manne in both those two newspapers; and publication of his contribution to the aforementioned debate in the magazine *Eureka Street*; (Malcolm Knox, 'It's No Joke as Historians Flunk "Loyalty Test"', *Sydney Morning Herald*, 25 August 2003; Manne, 'Aboriginal History: A Few Facts', *Age*, 25 August 2003; Debate, <www.smh.com.au/specials/historywars>; Kate Legge, 'The History Wars', *Australian*, 30–31 August 2003; Manne, 'Windschuttle's Whitewash', *Eureka Street*, vol. 13, no. 8, 2003, 23–27).

47 Windschuttle acknowledges that academic historians do not always agree on every matter but he seldom points out the frequency of their disagreements (*Fabrication*, 28). These include: the relative significance of various causes of conflict; the relative importance of disease, settler violence and inter-Aboriginal killings as causes of depopulation; the form that settler violence commonly took; the role played by racism on the frontier; the nature of the Aboriginal response to the settler intrusion; the forms of Aboriginal resistance and its effectiveness; and the significance of humanitarian endeavour.

48 It seems Windschuttle knows this as he fudges the matter by employing an ahistorical term, 'leftish', rather than 'the left' here (*Fabrication*, 401).

49 For example, Windschuttle alleges that 'many historians and their publishers now forbid the use of "massacre" to describe any mass killing of whites by indigenous people', but he only cites some American publishing guidelines as evidence (*Fabrication*, 269).

50 In response to criticisms of Windschuttle's work, his new conservative supporters and sympathisers have alleged that his critics have resorted to *ad hominem* arguments (see, for example, Christopher Pearson, comments made in question time, *Frontier Conflict: The Australian Experience* forum, National Museum of Australia, 14 December 2001; McGuinness, 'History', 3). This, it might be argued, betrays an ignorance of this concept. First, it refers to a device that is intended to divert attention from a critical examination of the substance of an author's argument, and to discredit that argument by introducing irrelevant considerations to do with the character or motives of its author. Those who have referred to Windschuttle's 'standing' as a historian (by commenting on his apparent lack of training or experience), his motives (by observing his politics) and his polemical style (by noting his background as a journalist), for example, have tried to draw attention to matters they believe, rightly or wrongly, are relevant to a consideration of his work. By describing these criticisms as *ad hominem*, Windschuttle and his supporters might be said to have diverted public attention from matters of some import. However, if we accept that these arguments are *ad hominem* and hence should be disregarded, so too, it seems to me, must the particular claims that the new conservatives have put about the political character or motives of the academic historians they criticise. In a second definition, *ad hominem* refers to an author's argument that appeals to his or her hearer's or reader's personal feelings or prejudices rather than their intellect or reason. Some of Windschuttle's work, and most of the devices he uses to frame his book and some of its chapters, could be described in these terms.

51 See my consideration of one of Reynolds' books in '*The Law of the Land* or the Law of the Land? History, Law and Narrative in a Settler Society', *History Compass*, vol. 2, 2004, 1–27. As I argue there, it is difficult to discern how any political purpose determined the interpretative core of his most important research on the Australian frontier—the famous trilogy of *The Other Side of the Frontier* (1981), *Frontier* (1987) and *With the White People* (1990)—but relatively easy to see that this is so in the case of *The Law of the Land* (1987), which is the book for which Reynolds was probably best known before the rise in popularity of reconciliation in the mid-1990s.

52 Windschuttle assumes that the work that historians such as Reynolds have done on frontier conflict underpins Aboriginal claims to land rights (for

example, *Fabrication*, 28) but he provides no evidence for this. It might be noted that in any legal tribunal Aboriginal claimants to land are required to prove that they are original owners, not demonstrate that they were dispossessed of it by violent means or that they resisted this.

53 See my discussion of this in 'Historiography on the Australian Frontier', in Attwood and Foster (eds), *Frontier Conflict*, 177.

54 E.H. Carr, *What is History?* (1961), Penguin, Harmondsworth, 1964, 24; Peter Novick, *That Noble Dream: The 'Objectivity Question' and the American Historical Profession*, Cambridge University Press, New York, 1988, 458; Maier, *Unmasterable Past*, 71; Richard J. Evans, *Telling Lies about Hitler: The Holocaust, History and the David Irving Trial*, Verso, London, 2002, 40.

4 Genocide

1 Keith Windschuttle, *The Fabrication of Aboriginal History, Vol. 1: Van Diemen's Land, 1803–1847*, Macleay Press, Sydney, 2002, dustjacket, 4, 399.

2 In 1997 the report of Human Rights and Equal Opportunity Commission Inquiry into the removal of Aboriginal children, *Bringing Them Home*, argued that this constituted genocide. This was unfavourably received in many quarters and was central to an attack made on the report's findings by new conservatives. See for example Ron Brunton, *Betraying the Victims: The 'Stolen Generations' Report*, Institute of Public Affairs, Melbourne, 1998.

3 Mike Wallace, 'Culture War, History Front', in Edward T. Linenthal and Tom Engelhardt (eds), *History Wars: The Enola Gay and Other Battles for the American Past*, Metropolitan Books, New York, 1996, 175.

4 *Lateline*, ABC Television, 16 April 2001, <www.abc.net.au/lateline/s2777827.htm>; Nicholas Rothwell, 'Not all Black and White', *Australian*, 16–17 September 2000; Windschuttle, *Fabrication*, 9.

5 For a widely used definition of genocide, see the United Nations Convention on Prevention and Punishment of Genocide (1948).

6 It is also evident that Windschuttle's approach to genocide resembles a particular scholarly approach to the Nazi German destruction of European Jewry, which has been called 'intentionalist', emphasising as it does Hitler's goal to exterminate a group of people. This contrasts with a 'structuralist' approach that emphasises a long, gradual process of radicalisation rather than just Hitler's intent. The former has lost ground among scholars in recent years, but it still influences popular understandings of the Holocaust, which associate it with the gas chambers in particular. See Ian Kershaw, *The Nazi Dictatorship: Problems and Perspectives of Interpretation*, 4th edn, Arnold, London, 2000, Ch. 5.

7 Windschuttle, quoted by Rothwell, 'Not all Black', my emphasis.

8   Windschuttle, *Fabrication*, 1–2.

9   See Chapter 3, note 28 above.

10 Windschuttle, *Fabrication*, 2, my emphasis; Phillip Knightley, *Australia: A Biography of a Nation*, London, Jonathan Cape, 2000, flyleaf, 107.

11 Windschuttle was following in the footsteps of other Howard intellectuals who had beaten up this story in 2001. See, for example, Miranda Devine, 'Insult or a Hidden Code', *Daily Telegraph*, 21 March 2001. (Windschuttle first made these claims in April 2001: <www.sydneyline.com/National%20Press %20Club%20debate.htm>). Windschuttle fails to reference any of his argument regarding this matter, even though he regards this as a major weakness in the work of other historians (*Fabrication*, 132–33). For example, there seems to be no evidence to support Windschuttle's claim regarding Casey's 'accusation'.

12 Windschuttle, for example, assumes that the 'lightning bolt' is the National Museum of Australia's 'central construction'. More importantly, he assumes that the group responsible for selecting the design of the Museum *knew* that Raggatt's plans included the architectural reference to the Berlin Jewish Museum when it accepted these. However, Museum spokespersons have asserted that they were unaware of this reference at the time and would have been concerned had their attention been drawn to it (Peter Clack, 'Museum "Copy" Claims Rejected', *Canberra Times*, 15 April 2001; Dawn Casey, 'Vision for Museum Not Based in Mimicry', *Australian*, 23 April 2001; Christopher Pearson, 'Designs on History Derided', *Australian*, 26–27 July 2003). They have also put on the record that they were disconcerted when the implications of the design were drawn to their attention later (Susan Shineberg, 'Stepping into Controversy', *Chicago Tribune*, 15 May 2001). Windschuttle infers that Casey and the Museum's Council *must* have been aware of the nature of Raggatt's design at the time they accepted it because the author of a book the Museum published a few years *later* (for its opening in 2001), *Building History: The National Museum of Australia*, remarked that 'the form of the First Australians gallery . . . closely resembles the recently completed Jewish Museum in Berlin' (quoted in Windschuttle, 'How Not to Run a Museum', *Quadrant*, vol. 45, no. 9, 2001, 11). This inference is erroneous, I suggest. One might also note that journalist Anne Susskind, the author of *Building History*, interpreted the *interior* of the First Australians Gallery as a zigzag footprint that had 'a resonance with the Aboriginal Dreaming story in which the Rainbow Serpent made the land' (Anne Susskind, *Building History*, National Museum of Australia, Canberra, 2001, 23). Obviously, Windschuttle was more interested in focusing on the Museum's outside appearance rather than considering its inside essence.

13 Casey, quoted by Piers Ackerman, 'Museum is an Original Imitation', *Sunday Telegraph*, 8 April 2001; Windschuttle, *Fabrication*, 2.

14 Windschuttle, *Fabrication*, 2–3, my emphasis.

15 In fact, there are many more examples Windschuttle might have cited of overseas writers claiming Van Diemen's Land as a site of genocide. Henry Reynolds refers to these in his essay 'Genocide in Tasmania', in A. Dirk Moses (ed.), *Genocide and Settler Society: Frontier Violence and Stolen Indigenous Children in Australian History*, Berghahn Books, New York, 2004, 128.

16 Windschuttle, 'The Fabrication of Aboriginal History', *New Criterion*, vol. 20, no. 1, 2001, <www.newcriterion.com/archive/20/sept01/keith.htm>, 1–2, *Fabrication*, 2, 4, 11–12, 14.

17 Windschuttle does not make clear what Reynolds' argument is until much later in *The Fabrication*, though even then he misrepresents Reynolds' work on the subject (195, 296).

18 I have never argued that any of the Australian colonies pursued a policy of genocide on the frontiers of settlement, though I once raised the question of whether the concept might be useful in understanding later phases of colonisation ('The Stolen Generations and Genocide: Robert Manne's *In Denial: The Stolen Generations and the Right*', *Aboriginal History*, vol. 25, 2001, 170–71). I am sceptical about the value of 'genocide' as a conceptual tool for helping us to better understand settler responsibility for acts of colonisation that largely destroyed aboriginal peoples. I believe it is a problematic concept if its application is extended too far. Historians such as Dirk Moses have recommended that historians focus more on the processes, structures and contexts of colonisation in Australia, considering 'the gradual evolution of European attitudes and policies as they were pushed in an exterminatory direction by the confluence of their underlying assumptions, the demands of the colonial and international economy, their plans for the land, and the resistance to these plans by the indigenous Australians' ('An Antipodean Genocide: The Origins of the Genocidal Moment in the Colonisation of Australia', *Journal of Genocide Research*, vol. 2, no. 1, 2000, 92). However, I do not see how the concept of *genocide* is required for such an approach.

19 Windschuttle, *Fabrication*, 13; Lyndall Ryan, *The Aboriginal Tasmanians*, University of Queensland Press, St Lucia, 1981, 2–3, 259.

20 Ibid., 248, 255, 259; Windschuttle, *Fabrication*, 13, 195, my emphasis. Windschuttle has since tried to defend his claim regarding Ryan's argument, but the only evidence he has adduced is an opinion piece Ryan wrote for the *Australian* in December 2002, after his book was published, in which it was evident to those familiar with Ryan's *Aboriginal Tasmanians* that she had now formulated an argument she had not made in that 1981 study (Windschuttle, 'Why I'm a Bad Historian', *Australian*, 12 February 2003). In her article, Ryan wrote: 'it is possible to reach a plausible alternative conclusion [to Windschuttle regarding guerilla warfare and the Black War]. Indeed, this is

exactly what I did in my book *The Aboriginal Tasmanians* . . . This view asserts that the Tasmanian Aborigines did indeed constitute a threat to British settlers, that the Black War was "a conscious policy of genocide"' ('No Historian Enjoys a Monopoly Over the Truth', *Australian*, 17 December 2002). This strikes me as an odd argument. A prolonged undeclared war conducted by settlers (rather than government) does not constitute a *policy*. (In an article Ryan prepared several months later for an academic journal, she asserted that her book had 'four key points', none of which concern genocide: 'The Right Book for the Right Time?', *Labour History*, no. 85, 2003, <www.historycooperative.org/journals/lab/85/ryan.html>, 2–3.) More recently, Ryan has made it clear that she now characterises settler violence in a different way to how she treated it in either the first (1981) edition or the second (1996) edition of her book: she describes the acts of settlers (but *not* the policy of government) as genocidal ('The Little Matter of Genocide: The Black War in Tasmania Reconsidered', unpublished paper, 2004. I am indebted to Ryan for providing a copy of this paper to me and discussing this matter with me). In other words, Ryan has now articulated what Windschuttle would call an 'extirpation thesis', which he distinguishes from a 'genocide thesis', since the latter, in his opinion, requires the presence of a conscious policy (Windschuttle, '*Whitewash* Confirms the Fabrication of Aboriginal History', *Quadrant*, vol. 47, no. 10, 2003, 8).

21 Ryan, *Aboriginal Tasmanians*, 4, 88–99, 177–78, 257; Windschuttle, *Fabrication*, 194–95. Most recently, Windschuttle has again claimed that Ryan argued in *Aboriginal Tasmanians* that 'colonial authorities instigated "a conscious policy of genocide"' ('Foreword', in John Dawson, *Washout: On the Academic Response to The Fabrication of Aboriginal History*, Macleay Press, Sydney, 2004, viii), while John Dawson has claimed again and again that Ryan argued in her book that Van Diemen's Land was a 'conscious policy of genocide'. He also alleges that Ryan equated British colonisation with Nazi policy and the Holocaust, and that academic historians have claimed that 'the culture the British brought to Australia was akin to that of the Nazis' (Dawson, *Washout*, 7, 17, 46, 114, 157–60, 188, 216, 219, 240). Dawson beats up 'genocide' in many other references to it in his book: 42, 44, 53, 57, 65, 119, 122, 227, 231–32, 234.

22 Henry Reynolds, *An Indelible Stain? The Question of Genocide in Australia's History*, Viking, Melbourne, 2001, 50, 52, 59–66, 85. There is evidence to suggest that Windschuttle's treatment of Reynolds' work on Van Diemen's Land and the matter of genocide has been disingenuous. Windschuttle has asserted that Reynolds *once* argued that Van Diemen's Land was a case of genocide. In a paper published in *Frontier Conflict: The Australian Experience*, Windschuttle wrote: 'Whereas Lyndall Ryan was still claiming in 1996 that the

Tasmanian Aborigines were "victims of a conscious policy of genocide"'—that passage again—'Henry Reynolds now disagrees. In his latest book, *An Indelible Stain?*, he has conceded that what happened to the Aborigines in Tasmania did not amount to genocide' ('Doctored Evidence and Invented Incidents in Aboriginal Historiography', in Bain Attwood and S.G. Foster (eds), *Frontier Conflict: The Australian Experience*, National Museum of Australia, Canberra, 2003, 101). Reynolds heard Windschuttle make this claim when he gave this paper at a National Museum of Australia conference on frontier conflict in 2001. Reynolds pointed out that he had never made such an argument (videotape of the proceedings of conference, National Museum of Australia, 14 December 2001). Windschuttle nevertheless repeated his claim when he submitted his work for publication in *Frontier Conflict*. In the light of Reynolds' rejection of this, the editors of the book, Stephen Foster and myself, invited Windschuttle to provide evidence for his claim (S.G. Foster to Windschuttle, email, April 2002, and an edited version of Windschuttle's paper). He did not do so. In 2003, following the publication of *The Fabrication*, Windschuttle *altered* his story regarding Reynolds' work on genocide but did not acknowledge that he had done so. He wrote: 'Reynolds has always said that the government did not intend genocide against the Aborigines, hence there was no conscious *policy* at work'. Windschuttle then went on to argue: 'However, Reynolds's thesis is that it was the Tasmanian *settlers* who wanted to exterminate the Aborigines' ('*Whitewash* Confirms', 8, his emphasis). Yet, in *The Fabrication*, where Windschuttle discusses what he calls 'the genocide thesis' and 'the extirpation thesis' of 'orthodox' historians, his account suggests to readers that Reynolds has advanced both of these theses.

23 Academic historians specialising in Aboriginal or Australian history have pointed out that many government officials in the early to mid-nineteenth century expressed fears that Aboriginal people would suffer 'extermination' and 'extirpation' as a result of British colonisation. See, for example, Alan Atkinson and Marian Aveling (eds), *Australians 1838*, Fairfax, Syme & Weldon, Sydney, 1987, 367. However, these historians have not argued that the Australian frontier should be regarded as a case of 'conscious, wilful genocide'. Windschuttle slides between the language of the historical record of the past and that of some historians in the present when he alleges that academic historians have freely 'used terms such as "genocide", "extermination" and "exculpation"' (*Fabrication*, 2–3). It is true that some academic historians have begun to consider in a systematic manner whether the concept of genocide might be useful in the task of understanding the course of colonisation in Australia (see *Aboriginal History*, vol. 25, 2001, which has a special section: '"Genocide"? Australian Aboriginal History in International Perspective'; and Moses (ed.), *Genocide and Settler Society*), but this work has barely penetrated

the public realm and has only appeared since the renewal of historical controversy in 2000. Moreover, it seems that most specialist academic historians will conclude, as Henry Reynolds and Peter Read have done in recent times, and Bob Reece and Richard Broome did many years ago, that genocide is not a useful concept for the task of apprehending the general pattern of colonial violence on the frontier and that any examples of genocide on the frontiers of settlement were highly local ones in which stockmen and/or police forces were determined to destroy Aboriginal people but that they were not following a policy of the colonial state (Stephen Foster and I made this point in our introduction to Attwood and Foster (eds), *Frontier Conflict*, 10. We were referring to R.H.W. Reece, 'Aborigines in Australian Historiography', in John A. Moses (ed.), *Historical Disciplines and Culture in Australasia*, University of Queensland Press, St Lucia, 1979, 261; Reynolds, *An Indelible Stain?*, 120–21; and Peter Read, 'Review of *An Indelible Stain?*', *Aboriginal History*, vol. 25, 2001, 295–97. For Richard Broome's consideration, see his 'The Struggle for Australia: Aboriginal–European Warfare, 1770–1930', in Michael McKernan and Margaret Browne (eds), *Australia: Two Centuries of War and Peace*, Australian War Memorial/Allen & Unwin, Canberra, 1988, 116).

24 It is significant that Windschuttle does not try to provide any considered treatment of the matter of genocide in the remaining 400 or so pages of his book. Instead, he mostly returns to it in the form of asides, which repeat his earlier misrepresentation of the historical scholarship in the field of Aboriginal history. On at least one occasion he conflates arguments that historians *have* made in reference to frontier killings of Aboriginal people with arguments they have *not* made in respect of genocide. For example, he asks: 'How many Aborigines died violently at the hands of colonists in Van Diemen's Land? If the orthodox school and those who have repeated its claims about genocide are right, it must have been a great many'. Windschuttle implies that those who have argued for a high death toll from white settlers' violence have necessarily argued for genocide by claiming that Robert Hughes 'was certainly left with this impression'. But how can Hughes' suggested violence ratio of ten or perhaps even twenty Aboriginal deaths to one white death be said to have been derived from Ryan's ratio, which is 4:1 (as Windschuttle knows, since he refers to this a page later), or Reynolds' 'ratio', which suggests 250–400 Aborigines were killed versus 170 Europeans (which Windschuttle also notes)? (Windschuttle, *Fabrication*, 351–53, 362).

25 Ibid., 4, 27. It is noteworthy that Windschuttle promoted his subsequent book, *The White Australia Policy*, by asserting that academic historians have made 'a direct comparison' between racism in Australia and 'the "master race" nationalism of Nazi Germany', and that this comparison has become *de rigueur*. Here, too, the case he makes for this dramatic claim is built upon

evidence that is threadbare. It primarily consists of a chain of very loose infer-ences, as follows. Andrew Markus, the author of a general history, *Australian Race Relations*, has argued that this country was influenced by a new ideology of racism, especially between 1890 and 1945. 'He quotes the most influential theorist on the subject in the 1960s, Pierre van den Berghe, whose book *Race and Racism* (1967) sees racism as the principal ideological assumption of the white settler societies of this period . . . Van den Berghe labelled the settler societies "*Herrenvolk* democracies"'. 'The rest of Markus's book', Windschuttle alleges, 'is designed to demonstrate that Australia, too . . . was one of the *herrenvolk* democracies'. 'The German term "herrenvolk" means "master race"', Windschuttle explains. 'It punctuated many of the speeches of Adolf Hitler and was part of the theory behind the Nazi Holocaust of the Jews'. Windschuttle continues: 'This concept of a white master race, which van den Berghe claimed inspired the British settler societies, derived primarily from German social and philosophical theorists'. Windschuttle goes on to argue: '[These] historians took the racism that certainly existed in some parts of Europe and generalised it to all . . . The ultimate extension of this thesis was the claim examined here, that settler societies such as Australia subscribed to the form of racist theory that emerged within German nationalism and which eventually materialised as Nazism'. Windschuttle's argument depends on an inference that those who used the term '*herrenvolk* democracies' equated the racism of these settler societies with that of Nazi Germany, but he provides no evidence for this. A reading of both van den Berghe's book and Markus' book does not support Windschuttle's claim that these authors compared the expression of racism in settler societies such as the United States and Australia to the extreme racism of Nazi Germany, let alone its expression in the Nazi German genocide. Windschuttle's argument here amounts to a fantasy. He *wants* this to be the thesis of these other authors but, once again, it is actually his. He has again misrepresented the work of the scholars he attacks. It should be noted that both van den Berghe and Markus have rejected Windschuttle's interpretation of their work. See Windschuttle, *The White Australia Policy*, Macleay Press, Sydney, 2004, 2–3, 5, 34–36, 49–50, 'White Australia's Myths', *Australian*, 6 December 2004, *The White Australia Policy*, launch speech, Tattersalls Club, Sydney, 6 December 2004, <www.sydneyline.com/ WAP%20launch%20speech.htm>; van den Berghe, *Race and Racism: A Comparative Perspective*, Wiley, New York, 1967, especially 17–18, 77, 88, 101; Markus, *Australian Race Relations 1788–1993*, Allen & Unwin, Sydney, 1994, 17. I am grateful to Pierre van den Berghe and Andrew Markus for discussing this matter with me (personal communica-tions, 26 and 31 January 2005).

26 For another discussion of this, see Shayne Breen, 'Fabrication, Genocide and

Denial: The History Crusaders and Australia's Past', *History Australia*, vol. 1, no. 1, 2003, 80–81.

27 To repeat: the only evidence supporting this claim was one clause in one sentence in a newspaper article by Lyndall Ryan (see note 20 above) in which she had quoted Windschuttle misquoting her argument in *The Aboriginal Tasmanians*.

28 Bain Attwood, 'Old News From a Tabloid Historian', *Australian*, 6 January 2003; Windschuttle, 'Why I'm a Bad Historian', *Australian*, 12 February 2003; Windschuttle, 'White Settlement in Australia: Violent Conquest or Benign Colonisation? Keith Windschuttle, in debate with Pat Grimshaw', Melbourne Trades Hall, 5 March 2003, <www.sydneyline.com/RMIT%20debate%20with%20Grimshaw.htm>; Kate Legge, 'Aboriginal History Triggers Another War of Words', *Australian*, 28 August 2003; *Lateline*, 3 September 2003, <www.abc.net.au/lateline/content/2003/s938399.htm>; Windschuttle, '*Whitewash* Confirms the Fabrication of Aboriginal History', *Quadrant*, vol. 47, no. 10, 2003, 8, 12, 'The Fabrication of Aboriginal History', paper to New South Wales Higher School Certificate History Extension conference, 2 June 2004, <www.sydneyline.com/NSW%20HSC%20extension%202004.htm>; Pastoralists and Graziers Association of Western Australia, Convention Update Speaker Profile, 10 February 2004, <www.pgaofwa.org.au>; Windschuttle, 'Foreword', xi.

29 Paul Sheehan, 'Our History, Not Rewritten But Put Right', *Sydney Morning Herald*, 25 November 2002; Windschuttle, 'History as a Travesty of Truth', *Australian*, 9 December 2002; ABC Radio National, *PM*, 12 December 2002, <www.abc.net.au/pm/s7476130.htm>; Christopher Bantick, 'Historian Challenges the Orthodox View of Genocide in Tasmania', *Canberra Times*, 14 December 2002; Michael Duffy, 'PC Lessons and a Rewritten History', *Daily Telegraph*, 14 December 2002; Robert Manne, 'Pale Grey View of a Genocide', *Age*, 16 December 2002.

30 Miranda Devine, 'The Book Launch, Bluster and Backdowns', *Sydney Morning Herald*, 19 December 2002; Roger Sandall, 'Mr Windschuttle Versus the Professors', *Australian*, 23 December 2002; Andrew Bolt, 'Checking the Truth about Aboriginal Genocide', *Herald-Sun*, 23 December 2002.

31 Duffy, 'Once Again, Goal Posts Are Moved', *Daily Telegraph*, 21 December 2002; P.P. McGuinness, 'Tackling Fakery in the Halls of Academe', *Sydney Morning Herald*, 24 December 2002; Ron Brunton, 'Fabrication Fury But the Rest is History', *Courier-Mail*, 28 December 2002.

32 It is doubtful whether Windschuttle's work can be characterised as revisionist. On the question of genocide in Van Diemen's Land, it cannot be argued that he has revised the account of academic historians in the field of Aboriginal history, because (1) they have never advanced the interpretation that he and his supporters attribute to them, and (2) one of their number

(Reynolds) has already made the argument Windschuttle presents against the genocidal histories done by popular writers and overseas academic historians. On many other matters concerning the history of the Australian frontier, Windschuttle presents arguments that have already been made by other historians—including so-called 'orthodox historians'—as we will see.

33 'Tragedy and Truth in History Debate', *Australian*, 28–29 December 2002; Bernard Lane, 'History Breakers', and Deborah Cassrels, 'Evolution of Manne', *Australian*, 28–29 December 2002.

34 Duffy, '"Black armband" Furore has Restored the Right to Disagree', *Courier-Mail*, 7 June 2003; Bolt, 'Revenge of the Historians', *Sun-Herald*, 28 August 2003; Kate Legge, 'The History Wars', *Australian*, 30–31 August 2003; Neil McInnes, 'Requiem for a Genocide', *The National Interest*, Summer 2004, 177–78; Roger Kimball, Armavirumque blog site, extracted <www.sydney line.com/Home.htm>.

35 Geoffrey Blainey, 'Native Fiction', *New Criterion*, vol. 21, no. 8, 2003, <www.newcriterion.com/archive/21/apr03/blainey.htm>, 1, 5. A shorter version was published as an opinion, 'Undermining a Bloody Myth', *Australian*, 14 April 2003, and I have quoted from this here. Another professional historian has made the mistake of relying on Windschuttle's account of the academic historiography. See William D. Rubinstein, *Genocide: A History*, Pearson Longman, London, 2004, 71.

36 Sheehan, 'Our History'.

37 'No Winners in the Endless History Wars', *Australian*, 8 September 2003.

38 For a discussion of this in reference to what I have called the stolen generations narrative, see my '"Learning About the Truth": The Stolen Generations Narrative', in Bain Attwood and Fiona Magowan (eds), *Telling Stories: Indigenous History and Memory in Australia and New Zealand*, Allen & Unwin/Bridget Williams Books, Sydney, 2001, 194, 204, 257.

39 Peter Novick, 'Holocaust Memory in America', in James E. Young (ed.), *The Art of Memory: Holocaust Memorials in History*, Prestel-Verlag, New York, 1994, 159, 164, *The Holocaust in American Society*, Houghton Mifflin, Boston, 1999, 14, 234; Andreas Huyssen, 'Present Pasts: Media, Politics, Amnesia', in Arjun Appadurai (ed.), *Globalisation*, Duke University Press, Durham, 2001, 59–60, 63.

40 Manne, the son of German Jewish refugees whose parents perished in the Holocaust, has asserted that the Holocaust is the ground of his being and has remarked that it was a statement made by an administrator of Aboriginal Affairs, A.O. Neville, in the 1930s, the era which marked the rise of Nazism, that first 'plunged [him] into serious study' of this country's Aboriginal past: '"Are we going", Neville had asked, "to have a population of one million blacks in the Commonwealth or are we going to merge them into our white

community and eventually forget that there were any Aborigines in Australia?" Neville's rhetorical question struck me with the force of lightning. Was he really advocating a policy for the disappearance of the Aboriginal people? Was this not a clearly genocidal thought?' (A Manne for All Seasons, <www.media.anglican.com.au/au/tma/1999_05/manne.html>; 'The Journey of Manne', *Sunday Age*, 27 May 2001; see also Manne, 'Aboriginal Child Removal and the Question of Genocide, 1900–1940', in Moses [ed.], *Genocide and Settler Society*, 220).

41 Windschuttle, *Fabrication*, 9, 398–99, his emphasis.

42 It should go without saying that I am not arguing here that the racism in these countries was the same.

43 In 2003 Clendinnen wrote: 'Robert Manne, angered by Windschuttle's extravagant and provocative claim that in the story of the empire, Tasmania was probably the place where "the least indigenous blood of all was deliberately shed", riposted with an *extravagant* claim of his own: "Ever since the 1830s, civilised opinion has regarded Tasmania as the site of one of the greatest tragedies in the history of British colonialism" ['Aboriginal History: A Few Facts', *Age*, 25 August 2003]. If that is true, "civilised opinion" is, simply, wrong. British colonialism has contrived more than a few tragedies in its long history, many bloodier and more wilful tha[n] the piecemeal and partial destruction of the Tasmanians' ('Despatches from the History Wars', *Australian Financial Review*, 31 October 2003, my emphasis). Clendinnen is no doubt correct about the relative bloodiness and wilfulness but one might question whether 'piecemeal' and 'partial' are appropriate adjectives when nearly all a people were destroyed in Van Diemen's Land in the years following the act of British colonisation. Once more, it seems that consideration of the matter of genocide in the sense of mass killing has obstructed consideration of genocide in the sense of mass death.

44 Inga Clendinnen, 'First Contact', *Australian Review of Books*, vol. 6, no. 4, 2001, 7, 26; Geoffrey Bolton, in 'Roundtable on Tasmanian Aboriginal History: Fact or Fiction?', Queen Victoria Museum and Art Gallery, Launceston, 16 May 2003, DVD, transcribed by the author, my emphases. (I am indebted to Michael Powell and Hamish Maxwell-Stewart for providing me with a copy of this.)

45 Peter Novick and Miriam Bratu Hansen, among others, have made these arguments in reference to the preoccupation with the Jewish Holocaust in the United States. See Novick, *Holocaust*, 14–15; Hansen, '*Schindler's List* is not *Shoah*: Second Commandment, Popular Modernism, and Public Memory', in Yosefa Loshitzky (ed.), *Spielberg's Holocaust: Critical Perspectives on Schindler's List*, Indiana University Press, Bloomington, 1997, 98.

46 Alan Atkinson, 'Historians and Moral Disgust', in Attwood and Foster (eds), *Frontier Conflict*, 119.

47 See Larissa Behrendt, 'Genocide: The Distance Between Law and Life', *Aboriginal History*, vol. 25, 2001, 132.

48 Windschuttle has asserted that 'it is from findings [by academic historians] that [Aboriginal] activists draw comparisons between colonial Australia and Nazi Germany' ('My History Thesis Still Stands', *Australian*, 1 September 2003). He has not provided any evidence for this claim.

49 Jim Everett, in 'Roundtable on Tasmanian Aboriginal History' (in which he read a poem which he apparently wrote in the early 1980s); Michael Mansell, quoted in Elizabeth Feizkhah, 'Who Killed the Truth?', *Time*, 22 September 2003, <www.time.com/time/pacific/magazine/20030922/tasmania.html>.

5 War

1 Keith Windschuttle, 'The Myths of Frontier Massacres in Australian History, Part I', *Quadrant*, vol. 44, no. 10, 2000, 8–9; Windschuttle, cited in Nicholas Rothwell, 'Not All Black and White', *Australian*, 16–17 September 2000; Windschuttle, 'The Fabrication of Aboriginal History', paper to New South Wales Higher School Certificate History Extension conference, 2 June 2004, <www.sydneyline.com/NSW%20HSC%20extension%202004.htm>. See also Windschuttle, 'The Fabrication of Aboriginal History', *New Criterion*, vol. 20, no. 1, 2001, <www.newcriterion.com/archive/20/sept01/keith.htm>, 7; Windschuttle, 'Foreword', to John Dawson, *Washout: On the Academic Response to The Fabrication of Aboriginal History*, Macleay Press, Sydney, 2004, viii.

2 See, for example, Windschuttle, 'The Myths of Frontier Massacres in Australian History, Parts I–III', *Quadrant*, vol. 44, nos 10–12, 2000, 8–21, 17–24, 6–20, *The Fabrication of Aboriginal History, Vol. 1: Van Diemen's Land 1803–1847*, Macleay Press, Sydney, 2002, 9.

3 Ibid., 15, 26.

4 For a review of *The Fabrication*, Geoffrey Blainey took the trouble to ascertain that the late Lloyd Robson, one of his former colleagues at the University of Melbourne, did not mistake the incident at Risdon Cove for a mass killing ('Native Fiction', *The New Criterion*, vol. 21, no. 8, 2003, <www.newcriterion.com/archive/21/apr03/blainey, htm>, 3), but he did not extend this courtesy to Ryan and Reynolds. One might wonder why.

5 Windschuttle, *Fabrication*, 11–14; Lyndall Ryan, *The Aboriginal Tasmanians*, University of Queensland Press, St Lucia, 1981, 75; Lloyd Robson, *A History of Tasmania, Volume 1: Van Diemen's Land from the Earliest Times*, Oxford University Press, Melbourne, 1983, 45–46; Henry Reynolds, *Fate of a Free People*, Penguin, Melbourne, 1995, 76. It should be noted that Ryan does refer to the killings at one point as a massacre even though she actually calls and considers this event as a skirmish (*Aboriginal Tasmanians*, 75).

6   At a few points in *The Fabrication* Windschuttle does acknowledge that he has accepted Ryan's interpretation on some matter or other, but he does so only after he has drawn her scholarly reputation into question. See, for example, 48–49.

7   Ryan, *Aboriginal Tasmanians*, 75, 77; Windschuttle, *Fabrication*, 26–27. John Dawson has written: 'Ryan's position [in *The Aboriginal Tasmanians*] regarding the [Risdon Cove] incident was similar to Windschuttle's' (*Washout: On the Academic Response to The Fabrication of Aboriginal History*, Macleay Press, Sydney, 2004, 180). This chronology is rather odd. However, Dawson is not alone among new conservatives in making it seem as though historians, who wrote twenty or more years before Windschuttle began to advance much the same arguments, have somehow or other emulated *his* work. See, for example, Peter Coleman, 'Between Facts and Fudges', *Australian*, 24–26 December 2004.

8   Reynolds, *Fate*, 76; Windschuttle, *Fabrication*, 14–15.

9   James Bonwick, *The Last of the Tasmanians*, Sampson, Low, Son & Marston, London, 1870, 32–35, his emphasis (in the original, the passage quoted here forms part of three paragraphs); Windschuttle, *Fabrication*, 20, 25–26. It might also be argued that Windschuttle's approach to the myth of Risdon Cove bears some resemblance to the work of another historian, David Roberts, on the local settler tradition of the Bells Falls Gorge 'massacre'. Like Roberts, he surveys the contemporary historical sources to try to ascertain what actually happened, traces a tradition of settler stories, and interprets these as an example of the invention of a myth. The project of these two historians is, in the end, very different. For Roberts' approach, see the discussion in Chapter 9 below.

10 In the light of the fact that settler violence was not Ryan's focus, it could be argued that Windschuttle has exaggerated the significance of the weaknesses in her work in respect of this. Yet Ryan should have made clearer the basis of her assertions regarding the number of Aboriginal people killed. Windschuttle has demonstrated correctly that very few of the sources she cites contain information to support her interpretation regarding the number killed, and that this is a serious deficiency. Ryan might have pointed out to her readers that the nature of the historical record does not allow a historian to assemble the historical facts necessary to calculate the number of such killings, but that her reconstruction of the historical context of this frontier from the available historical sources suggests a level of white violence commensurate with the figures she has given. (In her response to Windschuttle's criticisms Ryan does not point this out. Indeed, some of her discussion of this matter has been rather unsatisfactory in my opinion. See her 'Who is the Fabricator?', in Robert Manne [ed.], *Whitewash: On Keith Windschuttle's Fabrication of*

Aboriginal History, Black Inc., Melbourne, 2003, 230–57). In *The Fabrication*, Windschuttle discusses a few paragraphs (92, 102) and half a dozen footnotes (100, 122) in Ryan's book at considerable length (135–43, 149–66). Recently, John Dawson has devoted most of a very long chapter to the same paltry material (*Washout*, Ch. 4 [113–60]). Windschuttle's criticisms of Ryan's footnotes had played an enormously important role in discrediting the interpretation she and other academic historians have advanced. Yet, it might be noted that Windschuttle has an unrealistic expectation of footnotes. He prefaces one of his attacks on the weaknesses in Ryan's footnotes by asserting: 'In traditional history teaching, the distinction was once clear: "the text persuades, the notes prove"' (132). He then has a footnote to two sources on footnoting: a book by Anthony Grafton and an article by Gertrude Himmelfarb. In fact what Grafton wrote draws into question Windschuttle's claims about historical method and its role in ensuring the integrity of historical scholarship, and so it deserves to be quoted at length: 'A hundred years ago, most historians would have made a simple distinction: *the text persuades, the notes prove . . .* Nowadays, by contrast, many historians would claim that their texts offer their most important proofs: proofs that take the form of statistical or hermeneutic analyses of evidence, only the sources of which are specified by notes. In each of these cases [I have been discussing] . . . many critics have responded much as a slow-footed fullback responds in a hard-fought soccer match to the evasive tactics of a fast-moving striker. *Just kick the legs out from under your opponents—show that they have misread, or misinterpreted, the documents—and you need not bother to refute their arguments.* Such criticisms vary radically in intellectual quality, scholarly rigor, and rhetorical tone. But most of them rest in part on a common and problematic assumption: that authors can, as manuals for dissertation writers say they should, exhaustively cite the evidence for every assertion in their texts. [At this point Grafton has a footnote to Himmelfarb's article, which he refers to as 'a provocative—and nostalgic—discussion of what footnotes can and cannot do.'] In fact, of course, *no one can ever exhaust the range of sources relevant to an important problem—much less quote all of them in a note.* In practice, moreover, every annotator rearranges materials to prove a point, interprets them in an individual way, and omits those that do not meet a necessarily personal standard of relevance. The very next person to review the same archival materials will probably line them up and sort them out quite differently. *A number of controversies about footnotes reveal some of the ways that polemicists have used—and misused—them: most often, perhaps, in order to make a charge of incompetence take the place of a counterargument'* (*The Footnote: A Curious History*, Harvard University Press, Cambridge, MA, 1997, 15–17, my emphases and paragraphing). It should also be noted here that

Windschuttle seems unable to accept that any historian who works on the same set of historical sources as he has done can legitimately construe the past in a different way to his. He assumes instead that the other historian(s) *must* be fabricating history. As Gary Ianziti points out, Windschuttle apparently believes that his case is proven if he can show that an alternative reading of the historical sources, namely his, is possible, yet by itself this only suggests that his interpretation might be *plausible*. For it to be persuasive, he would have to demonstrate that his account has greater probability of being true ('Windschuttle at War: The Politics of Historiography in Australia', in C. Bailey et al. (eds), *Proceedings Social Change in the 21st Century Conference*, Centre for Social Change Research, Queensland University of Technology, 2004, 7–8, <http://eprints.qut.edu.au/archive/00000636/>). In order to do this, historians usually have to build up a historical context, but Windschuttle does not do this. As a result, an alternative picture of the frontier is strikingly absent from his account.

11 Ryan, *Aboriginal Tasmanians*, 2, 6, Chs 4–10; Windschuttle, *Fabrication*, Ch. 5. A reading of these texts reveals that Windschuttle uses the term 'massacre' much more than Ryan does in describing the frontier conflict. Indeed, he devotes sections of this chapter to 'The Pitt Water Massacre', the 'Port Dalrymple Massacre', the 'Oyster Bay Massacre' and the 'Campbell Town Massacre', and discusses other incidents within this framework. Ryan calls only one of these a massacre. Robson, the other historian Windschuttle criticises here, discusses a few of these incidents. He only uses the term 'massacre' to refer to one of them but his account of this incident is sceptical: he seems unsure whether or not this is the best word to describe what happened (*History of Tasmania*, Chs 3 and 11, especially 217).

12 Reynolds, *The Other Side of the Frontier*, History Department, James Cook University, Townsville, 1981, 101, *Fate*, 77, 79, 96. Windschuttle knows that Reynolds has made this argument, as he refers to the last of the passages I have quoted here, though he fails to note its implications (*Fabrication*, 353–54, 354 note 11).

13 This tally does not include the occasions when the word appears in the work of the historians Windschuttle quotes.

14 Windschuttle, 'Myths', I, 9, 12, 14–15, 17, 20, II, 24, III, 8.

15 It is, perhaps, surprising that Windschuttle does not seem to grasp the metaphorical nature of such terms. In a report he wrote in 1970 of the police's quelling of a moratorium march in Sydney against the Vietnam War, he claimed that, 'from the pig point of view, it had been a massacre' ('The Pigs v the People', *Old Mole*, no. 6, 1970, 2).

16 Martin Krygier and Robert van Krieken have provided another explanation for this, compatible with the one I offer here. They argue that it can be

regarded as similar to the critical psychological problem the settlers originally faced. Paul Hasluck, they point out, remarked on this difficulty in an historical account published some 60 years ago: 'some degree of shame or the need to justify what had happened brought a tendency [among the colonisers] to defame the primitive defender of his soil as treacherous, black at heart, [and] murderous' (Hasluck, *Black Australians: A Study of Native Policy in Western Australia, 1829–1897* [1942], Melbourne University Press, Melbourne, 1970, 179; Martin Krygier and Robert van Krieken, 'The Character of the Nation', in Manne [ed.], *Whitewash*, 105).

17 Windschuttle, 'Myths', I, 17, III, 6, 8; Tim Rowse, 'Historians and the Humanitarian Critique of Australia's Colonisation', *Australian Historical Association Bulletin*, no. 96, 2003, 84.

18 Reynolds (comp.), *Aborigines and Settlers: The Australian Experience 1788–1939*, Cassell Australia, Melbourne, 1972, 1, *The Other Side*, 89, 101, *Frontier: Aborigines, Settlers and Land*, Allen & Unwin, Sydney, 1987, 9, *Why Weren't We Told? A Personal Search for the Truth About Our History*, Viking, Melbourne, 1999, 170; Richard Broome, 'The Struggle for Australia: Aboriginal–European Warfare 1770–1930', in Michael McKernan and Margaret Browne (eds), *Australia: Two Centuries of War and Peace*, Australian War Memorial/Allen & Unwin, Canberra, 1988, 115–16, 'Aboriginal Victims and Voyagers: Confronting Frontier Myths', *Journal of Australian Studies*, no. 42, 1994, 71–72, 74, and 'Massacres', in Graeme Davison, John Hirst and Stuart Macintyre (eds), *The Oxford Companion to Australian History*, Oxford University Press, Melbourne, 1998, 415; Mark McKenna, *Looking for Blackfellas' Point: An Australian History of Place*, University of New South Wales Press, Sydney, 2002, 37, 45; Windschuttle, 'Myths', II, 23, 'Fabrication', 3, *Fabrication*, 3.

19 Ibid., 416.

20 Tom Engelhardt, 'The Victors and the Vanquished', in Edward T. Linenthal and Tom Engelhardt (eds), *History Wars: The Enola Gay and Other Battles for the American Past*, Metropolitan Books, New York, 1996, 219; Ann Curthoys, 'National Narratives, War Commemoration and Racial Exclusion in a Settler Society: The Australian Case', in Timothy G. Ashplant et al. (eds), *The Politics of Memory: Commemorating War*, Transaction, New Brunswick, 2000, 129.

21 Reynolds, *The Other Side*, 165, *Fate*, 210–11; *Courier-Mail*, 18 November 1998.

22 Tom Griffiths, 'The Language of Conflict', in Bain Attwood and S.G. Foster (eds), *Frontier Conflict: The Australian Experience*, National Museum of Australia, Canberra, 2003, 147, 149 note 15.

23 Windschuttle, *Fabrication*, 84.

24 Griffiths, 'Language', 135, 143.

25 Windschuttle, *Fabrication*, dustjacket, 99, 102, 130, 196–98, 399. Windschuttle

also rules out Aboriginal warfare by arguing that Aborigines had to attack a military force and that they seldom did: 'The evidence about what happened on the Aborigines' side of the frontier in the 1820s shows it did not amount to warfare in any plausible meaning of the term. The overwhelming majority of the Aborigines' targets were not troops or police but the convict stockmen who worked as assigned servants' (99).

26 Ibid., 98, 196. At another point, Windschuttle objects: 'It is true that [Arthur] did on occasion use the term "warfare" to describe Aboriginal actions but it was always clear from the context that he never meant either traditional set-piece warfare or guerilla warfare' (98). Arthur might have had other forms of warfare in mind, but of course these do not count in Windschuttle's eyes.

27 Here, Windschuttle accepts a lower evidentiary standard than the one he requires for white killings of Aborigines. He writes, for example: 'In most cases there is enough evidence to show that it was Black Tom who was responsible' (ibid., 74). However, Naomi Parry has argued that Musquito's involvement in attacks on settlers 'lasted only seven months, and only a few of the attacks that occurred within that period can possibly be associated with Musquito'. She has also questioned the extent of Black Tom's role ('Many Deeds of Terror: Windschuttle and Musquito', *Labour History*, no. 85, 2003, <www.historycooperative.org/journals/lab/85/parry.html>, 2, 4).

28 Windschuttle, *Fabrication*, 66–68, 70, 74, 100, 129, 399, 404.

29 Windschuttle argues further: 'Tellingly, Robinson never recorded even one phrase in his discussions with Aborigines in which they express these ideas themselves' (ibid., 100). But it can be objected that this is telling in a way Windschuttle does not consider even though it is consistent with his portrait of Robinson: a man acting out a fantasy that *he* was the Aborigines' spokesman and saviour, and so putting Aboriginal people in a position of weakness in which they found it very difficult to express their own demands.

30 Ibid., 99–101, 103, my emphases. It should be noted, too, that Windschuttle insists that the evidence for Aboriginal political objectives discussed by his adversaries has to be expressed in the form of statements rather than actions, but when he advances an argument of his own he accepts actions as statements. He claims he can read motives into Aborigines' actions but refuses to allow that his historical adversaries can do this as well. And when Aboriginal people say what he wants them to say they are real Aborigines and it is they who are speaking and not whites (126–27).

31 Historians have primarily made an argument for Aboriginal resistance. Windschuttle implies that other historians have represented this as 'systematic'. This ignores the fact that, since the mid-1970s, historians such as Bob Reece have questioned whether Aboriginal resistance was ever 'a concerted effort'. In the 1980s, other historians such as Beverley Nance and Marie Fels explored

reasons other than resistance for Aboriginal attacks. Windschuttle's contention that Aboriginal attacks were often prompted by other factors than 'patriotism' and that they tended to be concentrated in particular areas has already been made by these historians (R.H.W. Reece, 'The Aborigines in Australian Historiography', in John A. Moses (ed.), *Historical Disciplines and Cultures in Australasia*, University of Queensland Press, St Lucia, 1979, 258; Beverley Nance, 'The Level of Violence: Europeans and Aborigines in Port Phillip 1835–50', *Historical Studies*, vol. 19, no. 77, 1981, 540–42, 549; Bob Reece, 'Inventing Aborigines', *Aboriginal History*, vol. 11, no. 1, 1987, 16; Marie Fels, *Good Men and True: The Aboriginal Police of the Port Phillip District 1837–53*, Melbourne University Press, 1988, Chs 6–8; Windschuttle, *Fabrication*, 65, 73, 102, 399). It should be noted that, in much of the first wave of academic historiography on frontier conflict, historians (such as Ryan) tended to be reductive in their treatment of the Aboriginal response to the colonial incursion on to their lands. As observed earlier, they overstated Aboriginal resistance and overlooked accommodation, and ignored the probability that the response of most Aboriginal peoples was characterised by movement backwards and forwards between these two poles. However, Windschuttle provides a very simplistic account of the reasons for Aboriginal attacks on settlers (which echoes the one many settlers gave). He claims Aborigines were motivated by revenge and plunder, principally the latter, which he argues was provoked by a desire for consumer goods (*Fabrication*, 99, 118, 120, 122, 128–30).

32 Windschuttle begins this by claiming that Reynolds has argued for commemoration of the Aboriginal war dead at the Australian War Memorial on the grounds that 'the guerilla war waged by Tasmanian Aborigines' was 'a struggle of momentous proportions' (*Fabrication*, 83–84). However, in the sources Windschuttle quotes, Reynolds does not make his argument in these terms (see for example Reynolds, 'A War to Remember', *Australian*, 1–2 April 1995). This means, once again, that one of Windschuttle's framing devices has misconstrued another historian's work and as a result readers have been misled.

33 For example, Windschuttle claims that 'Ryan describes the Aboriginal response from 1824 onwards as "guerilla activity"' (*Fabrication*, 65), citing p. 115 of her book as evidence, but all she says there is that 'Big River country was well suited for Aboriginal guerilla activity' (*The Aboriginal Tasmanians*). Indexes, it is often said, are a reliable guide to the preoccupations of a writer. 'Guerilla warfare' does not appear in any form in the indexes to Ryan's *Aboriginal Tasmanians* or Reynolds' *Fate of a Free People*. In Windschuttle's *Fabrication* he uses the term again and again and (appropriately, given that it is *his* thesis) 'guerilla warfare thesis' appears three times in his index (*Fabrication*, 65, 70, 83–84, 87, 98, 102–03, 114, 124, 126, 129, 353–54, 399, 404, 455, 462, 468).

34 Ibid., 65, 77, 83–84, 99, 102, 114, 118, 125–26, 353.
35 Ibid., 103, 399, 404. Windschuttle has repeated this story on other occasions
    since (for example, 'Fabrication of Aboriginal History'). Here Windschuttle
    is echoing an argument Reece made many years ago about a concept that
    historians such Reynolds and Ryan *have* used (resistance): 'Loaded with
    connotations of the anti-colonial movements of the period since the Second
    World War, particularly the struggles of the Vietnamese against the French
    and the Americans, "resistance" and "resistance fighter" have become part of
    the anti-colonial polemic. Brought into the arena of Aboriginal–European
    conflict in Australia . . . they can produce some gross distortions'. Reece gave
    examples of *popular* historical writing to evidence his point ('Inventing
    Aborigines', 16).
36 See, for example, A. Wyatt Tilby, *The English People Overseas, Vol. V:
    Australasia*, Constable and Co., London, 1912, 106. For contemporary histori-
    cal references see, for example, those discussed by Reynolds, 'Terra Nullius
    Reborn', in Manne (ed.), *Whitewash*, 125–26.
37 Has Windschuttle projected onto his so-called politically correct historians
    the very romantic politics of which he was once a part, and thereby lost sight
    of his earlier literary relationship to 'guerilla warfare' (even though this
    activity is evidently present in the slash-and-burn assault he makes on the
    work of 'orthodox' historians, primarily of his own generation of baby
    boomers)? Some evidence seems to suggest this. In the 1960s and into the
    1970s Windschuttle styled himself as a Marxist intellectual, whose political
    activity comprised writing and editing radical newspapers and journals, and
    lecturing. Between mid-1966 and early 1968 he was, first of all, news editor
    of *Honi Soit*, the University of Sydney student newspaper, and then, briefly,
    its editor. (When he resigned, the president of the Student Representative
    Council, Alan Cameron, described this as 'a petulant and childish reaction
    to a decision of the SRC'; Windschuttle riposted that Cameron had 'totally
    distorted the truth in an effort to justify himself' (*Honi Soit*, vol. 41, no. 5,
    1968).) A year or so later, Windschuttle founded a journal *Old Mole*, on the
    cover of which he emblazoned a passage attributed to Marx: 'We recognise
    our old friend, our old mole, who knows so well how to work underground,
    suddenly to appear: the Revolution'. During these years, the focus of much
    left-wing politics was American imperialism, in particular its role in the war
    in Vietnam. This entailed a celebration of the Viet Cong's 'guerilla warfare'.
    As the editor of *Old Mole*, Windschuttle published signed and unsigned
    articles urging 'student resistance' to American imperialism and support for
    the heroic Viet Cong's struggle for 'self-determination' (See, for example, *Old
    Mole*, no. 1, 1970, especially 'Don't Let the Bastards Grind You Down', 1, 'USA
    1970: 5,000,000 Students on Strike', 3; no. 2, 1970, especially 'The New

Militancy', 2, 'Poems of Vietnamese Partisans', 5; no. 5, 1970, especially 'Urban Guerillas in Uruguay', 6, Barry Cripps, 'Support the Revolution: There and Here', 7, 'Victory to the Heroic Vietnam Revolution' (poster), 5; no. 6, 1970, especially Hal Greenland, 'Viet Cong to Win', 4; no. 7, 1970, especially Warren Osmond, 'The Moratorium as Radicalism', 4–5). There is evidence to suggest that many of these reflected Windschuttle's point of view. In articles published under his own name, he referred critically to 'the bankrupt militarism of western society' and its 'war machine' (Windschuttle, 'Nowhere Men: Decline and Fall of the Beatles', *Old Mole*, no. 1, 1970, 10). In February 1971, an ASIO agent observing the Anti-War Centre in Sydney reported to his superiors a meeting which comprised a lecture by Windschuttle: 'WINDSCHUTTLE stated that the only way in which the present society is to be overcome is by violent revolution by the students'. The agent's 'comment' read: 'Much of WINDSCHUTTLE's talk was repetitive although I gained the impression that he was well versed in active revolutionary tactics'. The following month, this agent followed up with a report on Windschuttle's activities and background (ASIO reports, 9 and 25 February 1971, National Archives of Australia, Series A6119, item 3246, accessible at <http://naa12.naa.gov.au/scripts/Imagine.asp?B=4269838&I=1>, see pp. 6 and 8). Later in the 1970s, Windschuttle was a member of the collective that produced a journal called the *New Journalist*, and in the early 1980s he and Elizabeth Windschuttle compiled an anthology of its work, *Fixing the News*. At the beginning of the preface, this passage appears: 'Since 1972 the journal has maintained a constant guerilla campaign against the four media barons who determine what version of reality the Australian people will be allowed to see. So far, the barons have carried all before them, entrenching their power, extending their influence. But at the same time, a groundswell of articulate disbelief has burgeoned within the community, and signs of resistance have broken out within the industry itself. The guerillas may claim *some* victories' ([Keith Windschuttle] 'Preface', in Keith Windschuttle and Elizabeth Windschuttle (eds), *Fixing the News*, Cassell, Sydney, 1981, v, their emphasis). These sources seem to reveal that Windschuttle once imagined intellectuals such as himself as revolutionary figures waging campaigns against an oppressive order, whereas today it appears that he projects this 'romantic delusion' onto the 'orthodox school' of 'left-wing' historians that he has constructed, thereby losing sight of his own relationship to literary campaigns of 'guerilla warfare', which he continues to repeat or act out. To discover the truth about *The Fabrication* it seems that one must peer through the fog of Windschuttle's war.

38 Windschuttle, *Fabrication*, 364, 398.
39 Here, Windschuttle has more or less repeated an erroneous claim made by

Henry Reynolds, 'The Black War: A New Look at an Old Story', *Tasmanian Historical Research Association, Papers and Proceedings*, vol. 31, no. 4, 1984, 7.

40 Windschuttle, *Fabrication*, dustjacket, 4–5, '*Whitewash* Confirms the Fabrication of Aboriginal History', *Quadrant*, vol. 47, no. 10, 2003, 9. For example, Windschuttle has asserted, on the basis of a particular government record, that settlers 'had occupied only 3.1 per cent of land in Tasmania' by 1824 (and so alleges that historians have exaggerated the degree to which settlers had occupied land and thus were a cause of Aboriginal attacks). However, as James Boyce points out, Windschuttle's source actually reflects land ownership, not land occupation, because 'formal land title usually followed many years of other forms of increasingly intense white occupation and resource exploitation' (Windschuttle, *Fabrication*, 78–79, 88; Boyce, 'Fantasy Island', in Manne (ed.), *Whitewash*, 51, 54, 57).

41 Charles Rowley, *The Destruction of Aboriginal Society*, ANU Press, Canberra, 1970, 213, his emphasis.

42 See Windschuttle, *Fabrication*, especially Chs 5 and 10. Other historians have discussed this matter. See, for example, Lyndall Ryan, 'Waterloo Creek, Northern New South Wales, 1838', in Attwood and Foster (eds), *Frontier Conflict*, 36–43; Neville Green, 'Windschuttle's Debut', in Manne (ed.), *Whitewash*, 187–98.

43 Windschuttle, 'History, Truth and Tribalism', Lecture for Ashbrook Center, Ashland University, Ohio, 26 November 2001, and The Historical Society at University of Chicago, 28 November 2001, <www.sydneyline.com/History%20Truth%20and%20Tribalism.htm>, *Fabrication*, 359. It is ironic that the effect of Windschuttle's position is no different to that of 'postmodernists' he attacks: whereas his postmodernists assume that 'we can't know', he leads us to assume that 'there is nothing to know'.

44 Klaus Neumann, 'Among Historians', *Cultural Studies Review*, vol. 9, no. 2, 2003, 180.

45 Alan Atkinson, 'Historians and Moral Disgust', in Attwood and Foster (ed.), *Frontier Conflict*, 113.

46 As noted earlier, Windschuttle locates his work within what he claims is a distinctive intellectual tradition in Sydney, which he defines in terms of what 'it is for and against': 'In philosophy, it backs realism rather than idealism; objectivism rather than subjectivism; empirical induction rather than theoretical deduction; logic rather than rhetoric' ('About the Sydney Line', <www.sydneyline.com.About.htm>). Taking these terms in their popular rather than philosophical sense (and one should not take Windschuttle's turn to philosophy too seriously), it is interesting to note that his own writings are characterised by the presence of the very factors he claims to oppose: idealism, theory and rhetoric. Windschuttle also claims that the Sydney Line 'rejects

moral, cultural and cognitive relativism' (ibid.). In a philosophical sense, both idealism and relativism are apparent in *The Fabrication of Aboriginal History*. For example, he argues: 'To talk about the Tasmanian Aborigines acting with "humanity and compassion" is to invoke concepts they would have regarded with complete incomprehension. These terms come not from Aboriginal but from European culture. It was the European Enlightenment that founded the idea of the unity of humanity and the Christian religion that originated the notion of sharing the suffering of others' (406). Alan Atkinson has observed: 'It is certainly true that the words "humanity" and "compassion", with or without their precise parcel of connotations, did not exist in Tasmania before the arrival of the Europeans. But beyond that obvious point [Windschuttle's] argument descends into simple nonsense. We can, as a matter of common sense, talk of humanity and compassion among the Aborigines whenever those words seem to catch with reasonable accuracy feelings exhibited by recorded deeds. In the same way we are perfectly justified in stating that an infant loves its mother before it knows the words "love" and "mother". Windschuttle would have us believe that particular feelings cannot exist unless they have some exact expression in words—or even, maybe, unless they are intellectualised . . . He is a declared enemy of postmodern attitudes to language and reality. And yet this is postmodern relativism in its neatest form' ('Honey and Wax: A Review of Keith Windschuttle, *The Fabrication of Aboriginal History, Vol. 1*', *Journal of Australian Colonial History*, vol. 4, no. 2, 2002, 27).

47 Jane Cadzow, 'Who's Right, Now?', *Age Good Weekend Magazine*, 17 May 2003, 24; *Lateline*, 3 September 2003, <www.abc.net.au/lateline/content/2003/s938399.htm>; History Wars Forum, State Library of Victoria, broadcast *Late Night Live*, ABC Radio National, Part 1, 3 September 2003, recording transcribed by author.

48 Some points made by an American historian, Thomas L. Haskell, are relevant here: 'My impression . . . is that among the influential members of the historical profession the term objectivity has long since lost whatever connection it may once have had with passionlessness, indifference, and neutrality . . . The very possibility of historical scholarship as an enterprise distinct from propaganda [undoubtedly] requires of its practitioners that vital minimum of ascetic self-discipline that enables a person to do such things as abandon wishful thinking, assimilate bad news, [and] discard pleasing interpretations that cannot pass elementary tests of evidence and logic . . . All of these mental acts . . . require *detachment*, an undeniably ascetic capacity to achieve some distance from one's own spontaneous perceptions and convictions . . . to develop . . . a view of the world in which one's own self stands not at the center, but appears merely as one object among many . . . Fairness and honesty are

qualities we can rightfully demand of human beings, and those qualities require a very substantial measure of self-overcoming . . . The tendency of past generations [however] to associate objectivity with "selflessness", and to think of truth-seeking as a matter of emptying oneself of passion and preconceptions, so as to become a perfectly passive and receptive mirror of external reality, has, for good reason, become notorious . . . [I]n valuing . . . the elementary capacity for self-overcoming, we need not aspire to the unrealistic and undesirable extreme of extinguishing the self . . . Likewise, in making detachment a vital criterion of objective thinking, we need not make the still greater error of confusing objectivity with neutrality . . . What we demand of [historians] is self-control, not self-immolation . . . The demand is for detachment and fairness, not disengagement from life' ('Objectivity is Not Neutrality: Rhetoric vs Practice in Peter Novick's *That Noble Dream*', *History and Theory*, vol. 29, no. 2, 1990, 131–34, 139, his emphasis). For all his insistence on 'passionlessness', Windschuttle fails to proceed with a substantial measure of self-overcoming in his work. Instead, as Alan Atkinson has observed (and as we noted earlier), his self is writ large. Presumably, Windschuttle knows this but assumes that the only way he can handle his self is by adopting an ideal of extinguishing passion rather than working through this practically so that he achieves a degree of detachment. As we have remarked elsewhere, for Windschuttle it often seems to be a case of all or nothing.

49 Raimond Gaita, 'Guilt, Shame and Collective Responsibility', in Michelle Grattan (ed.), *Essays on Australian Reconciliation*, Black Inc., Melbourne, 2000, 276; Windschuttle, *Fabrication*, 143–44; Peter Coleman, 'The Windschuttle Thesis', *Quadrant*, vol. 46, no. 12, 2002, 81; Atkinson, 'Honey', 21; Stuart Macintyre and Anna Clark, *The History Wars*, Melbourne University Press, Melbourne, 2003, 170; Robert Manne, 'Introduction', Krygier and van Krieken, 'Character', and Reynolds, 'Terra Nullius', in Manne (ed.), *Whitewash*, 11, 88, 131, 133.

50 Windschuttle, 'Exposing Academic Deception of Past Wrongs', *Sydney Morning Herald*, 19 September 2000; Mark Finnane, 'Counting the Cost of the Nun's Picnic', and A. Dirk Moses, 'Revisionism and Denial', in Manne (ed.), *Whitewash*, 304, 306, 362. Finnane has also argued that Windschuttle's figures for Aboriginal deaths do not support his argument for a low level of settler violence (see Finnane, 'Counting the Cost').

51 Windschuttle accuses Robinson, the principal humanitarian figure he considers in *The Fabrication*, of the same offences he charges historians with committing. Robinson exaggerates, invents, concocts, fabricates, tricks, defrauds and deceives, and sacrifices truth for drama. But most of all, Windschuttle is convinced that Robinson is an imposter (201, 209, 215, 221–22, 230, 234, 242, 247, 267, 274). Ironically, a reader of Windschuttle's

Fabrication could readily conclude that he has projected the characteristics of his work onto that of humanitarians such as Robinson and historians such as Reynolds.

52 See Reynolds, *This Whispering in Our Hearts*, Allen & Unwin, Sydney, 1998, xiv (and Windschuttle, 'Myths', III, 6, where he notes this). See also Reece, 'The Aborigines', 272.

53 Windschuttle, 'Myths', III, 10, *Fabrication*, 217–19, 415, 'The Historian as Prophet and Redeemer', *Quadrant*, vol. 46, no. 12, 2002, 17–18.

54 See Raymond Evans and Bill Thorpe, 'Indigenocide and the Massacre of Aboriginal History', *Overland*, no. 163, 2001, 29.

55 See Mark McKenna, 'Reflections on *Looking for Blackfellas' Point*', *Aboriginal History*, vol. 27, 2003, 134.

6 Law

1 This is not only true of self-consciously patriotic or jingoistic historians. See my discussion of one of Henry Reynolds' books: '*The Law of the Land* or the Law of the Land? History, Law and Narrative in a Settler Society', *History Compass*, vol. 2, 2004, 1–27.

2 Keith Windschuttle, *The Fabrication of Aboriginal History, Vol. 1: Van Diemen's Land, 1803–1847*, Macleay Press, Sydney, 2002, 195, 196–97 note 89, 296, 307–08, 322, 326, 341, 350, 361.

3 Ibid., 183–84, 190, 300, 316, 360.

4 Ibid., 184, 186, his emphasis. See, for example, Jean Woolmington (comp.), *Aborigines in Colonial Society*, Cassell Australia, Melbourne, 1973, Ch. 1; R.H.W. Reece, *Aborigines and Colonists: Aborigines and Colonial Society in New South Wales in the 1830s and 1840s*, Sydney University Press, Sydney, 1974, 104; Richard Broome, *Aboriginal Australians: Black Responses to White Dominance*, Allen & Unwin, Sydney, 1982, 26–27; Henry Reynolds, *Frontier: Aborigines, Settlers and Land*, Allen & Unwin, Sydney, 1987, 83–96.

5 Windschuttle, *Fabrication*, 32, 297–98, 361, 399, 412; Alan Atkinson, 'Honey and Wax: A Review of Keith Windschuttle, *The Fabrication of Aboriginal History, Vol. 1*', *Journal of Australian Colonial History*, vol. 4, no. 2, 2002, 23. For examples of this 'orthodox' historiography, see Reece, *Aborigines*, Chs 2–5; Lyndall Ryan, 'Aboriginal Policy in Australia—1838—a Watershed?', *Push From the Bush*, no. 8, 1980, 14–22; S.G. Foster, 'Aboriginal Rights and Official Morality', *Push From the Bush*, no. 11, 1981, 68–98; Alan Atkinson and Marian Aveling (eds), *Australians 1838*, Fairfax, Syme & Weldon, Sydney, 1987, 301–10, 356–67, 392–97; Reynolds, *Frontier*, Ch. 4; A.G.L. Shaw, 'British Policy towards the Australian Aborigines, 1830–1850', *Australian Historical Studies*, vol. 25, no. 99, 1992, 265–85; Mark McKenna, *Looking for Blackfellas' Point:*

An Australian History of Place, University of New South Wales Press, Sydney, 2002, Ch. 2.

6 Windschuttle, *Fabrication*, 187–88, 298–99. Cf. A.G.L. Shaw, *Sir George Arthur, Bart 1784–1854*, Melbourne University Press, Melbourne, 1980, 17, 22, 50–52; Henry Reynolds, *Fate of a Free People*, Penguin, Melbourne, 1995, 90–92, 121–23, 130, *An Indelible Stain? The Question of Genocide in Australia's History*, Viking, Melbourne, 2001, 60–63, 74. Reynolds also discusses humanitarianism in his *Frontier, The Law of the Land*, Penguin, Melbourne, 1987, and *This Whispering in Our Hearts*, Allen & Unwin, Sydney, 1998.

7 Windschuttle does not acknowledge that Gascoigne, who is primarily a historian of (high) intellectual thought, does not really consider popular opinion on the frontiers of settlement, let alone other expressions of racism (see Gascoigne, *The Enlightenment and the Origins of European Australia*, Cambridge University Press, Melbourne, 2002, Ch. 8, especially 152).

8 Windschuttle, *Fabrication*, 119, 297, 300, my emphases. As his *White Australia Policy* also reveals, Windschuttle confines a good deal of his account of racism in Australia to the realm of ideas among intellectuals and the like (*The White Australia Policy*, Macleay Press, Sydney, 2004).

9 Windschuttle, *Fabrication*, 298, 318, 342.

10 Atkinson, 'Honey', 25; Martin Krygier and Robert van Krieken, 'The Character of the Nation', in Robert Manne (ed.), *Whitewash: On Keith Windschuttle's Fabrication of Aboriginal History*, Black Inc., Melbourne, 2003, 100–02, their emphasis.

11 Windschuttle, *Fabrication*, 119, 190, 349, my emphasis; James Boyce, 'Fantasy Island', in Manne (ed.), *Whitewash*, 34–35.

12 See, for example, M.B. and C.B. Schedvin, 'The Nomadic Tribes of Urban Britain: A Prelude to Botany Bay', *Historical Studies*, vol. 18, no. 71, 1978, 254–76.

13 Instead, Windschuttle devotes a long discussion to the available opinions of those he largely regards as 'farmers, pastoralists and professional men' (*Fabrication*, 327). In researching this book, I thought I should check at least one set of unpublished sources that Windschuttle had used in the Tasmanian State Archives, and I chose this example. (I also checked printed sources.) In his book, Windschuttle devotes a long discussion to the answers of a questionnaire the government committee on Aborigines distributed in 1830 to settlers. It relates to his argument that accounts of the killings at Risdon Cove amount to a myth (i.e. a falsehood). He claims that the '*most common answer*' given to the question, 'To what causes would you attribute the rise and progress of the hostility displayed by the Natives?', was one that 'blame[d] the hostilities on the shooting of Aborigines at Risdon Cove in 1804' (ibid., 334, my emphasis). Here is my interpretation of this source: Of the fourteen

settlers who answered this questionnaire only one (Edward Franks) categorically claimed that Risdon Cove was to blame for the later hostilities. A second, James Scott, noted that he had 'always understood' that the 'first rise of hostilities between the Europeans and the Natives . . . was attributed to the officer who had the command at Risdon Cove in 1804' but he then went on to say: 'The animosity has been kept up every year since, by various wanton acts of Bushrangers, Sealers, Stock keepers, and others'. A third, John Hudspeth, claimed that the hostility of Aborigines was 'co-eval with the first settlement', but he did not actually refer to white aggression at Risdon Cove, as Windschuttle claims. A fourth, Thomas Anstey, stated: 'I have heard, and read, much, of the Natives having been wantonly subjected to a murderous platoon firing, in the early days of the Colony'; however, it seems he did not necessarily accept that this event had occurred, since he continues: 'but of this I know nothing beyond common report'. A fifth, William Gray, began: 'I only know by hearsay that the cause of such a hostile feeling on the part of the natives originated in some premature and ill judged severity practised upon them by the white people immediately after the first settlement was formed'. Windschuttle only quotes part of this passage. He omits the beginning and thus disguises the fact that Gray, too, does not seem to have embraced this 'myth'; more importantly, he does not quote the rest of this sentence in Gray's response, which reads: 'and that its progress has been the result of many brutal, & unfeeling acts of aggression on the part of Stockmen and Sealers who have had opportunities of communicating with them'. Legitimate differences in interpretation aside, it seems apparent that Windschuttle's treatment of these sources is quite unsatisfactory (ibid.; Answers by settlers to the questionnaire of the Aborigines Committee, 1830, Archives Office of Tasmania, CSO 1/323/7578, 310, 316, 331, 341, 347–48).

14 Windschuttle, *Fabrication*, 192; Boyce, 'Fantasy', 24, 26, 33–34; Krygier and van Krieken, 'Character', 92; Atkinson, 'Honey', 33.
15 Windschuttle, *Fabrication*, 348–49, my emphases.
16 Boyce, 'Fantasy', 33. See, for example, Broome, *Aboriginal Australians*, 38–42.
17 Windschuttle, *Fabrication*, 118, 183, 189–90, 309, 323.
18 Ibid., 183, 186, 194; McKenna, *Blackfellas' Point*, 54, 57–58; Atkinson, 'Historians and Moral Disgust', in Bain Attwood and S.G. Foster (eds), *Frontier Conflict: The Australian Experience*, National Museum of Australia, Canberra, 2003, 115.
19 See M.F. Christie, *Aborigines in Colonial Victoria, 1835–1886*, Sydney University Press, Sydney, 1979, Ch. 5; Foster, 'Aboriginal Rights'; Shaw, 'British Policy'; McKenna, *Blackfellas' Point*, 53–55.
20 George Arthur, Proclamation, 15 April 1828, Copies of All Correspondence . . . On the Subject of Military Operations', *British House of*

Commons Sessional Papers, 1831, vol. 19, no. 259, 194–96; Windschuttle, *Fabrication*, 149–50.

21 In his earlier work Windschuttle asserted: 'This was enshrined in one cele-brated incident, the Myall Creek Massacre [trial] of 1838 . . . Modern historians try to argue this event away by saying it was the exception rather than the rule' ('The Fabrication of Aboriginal History', *New Criterion*, vol. 20, no. 1, 2001, <www.newcriterion.com/archive/20/sept01/keith.htm>, 7). But the outcome of the Myall Creek trial *was* exceptional, as Andrew Markus has pointed out. While it can be regarded as an example of the impartial admin-istration of the law, closer consideration of the two Myall Creek trials and the controversy they provoked also reveals that many colonists were unwilling to treat the murder of Aboriginal people as a crime. Most importantly, there is no evidence that the outcome of the second trial created a precedent. On the contrary, there are only four known cases in which whites were executed for the murder of Aborigines during the period of frontier conflict; and only ten whites are known to have been executed for killing Aborigines in the nine-teenth century, and seven of these were those men hung for the same deed at Myall Creek. Markus acknowledges that other executions might have escaped the attention of historians, but considers this to be unlikely given that events like the hanging of white men for the murder of Aboriginal people tended to be remembered well by settler communities (*Australian Race Relations, 1788–1993*, Allen & Unwin, Sydney, 1994, 46–49). It should also be noted that the Myall Creek trials seem to have had the opposite effect to that intended by government, driving much of the settler violence underground (Reece, *Aborigines and Colonists*, 191–92).

22 See Boyce, 'Fantasy', 36.

23 See Mark Finnane and Jonathan Richards, '"You'll Get Nothing Out of It"? The Inquest, Police and Aboriginal Deaths in Colonial Queensland', *Australian Historical Studies*, vol. 35, no. 123, 2004, 104 note 63.

24 Windschuttle, *Fabrication*, 134, 190–91. See Alex C. Castles, *An Australian Legal History*, Law Book Company, Sydney, 1982, 517, 519–20; Bruce Kercher, *An Unruly Child: A History of Law in Australia*, Allen & Unwin, Sydney, 1995, 5–9.

25 Windschuttle, *Fabrication*, 192.

26 See most of the references in note 4 above. For a more recent discussion of humanitarianism, which takes a somewhat different approach, see Hannah Robert, 'Colonizing Concepts of Aboriginal Rights in Land in Port Phillip and South Australia in the 1830s', MA thesis, University of Melbourne, 2002.

27 In *The Fabrication*, one can also note, Windschuttle idealises 'Evangelical Christianity', 'Enlightenment humanism' and 'the rule of law' and treats their antagonism to violence in much the same way as he idealises 'the Enlightenment'

in the fight he creates with 'postmodernism' in *The Killing of History*, and for much the same reason: to settle down a threat he has created in the first place. Daniel Gordon has observed: 'Just as postmodernists have transformed the Enlightenment into the scapegoat of their own theories, Windschuttle elevates it to the status of an unproblematic inspiration . . . [W]hat he upholds is really a simple form of common-sense philosophy that has emerged only in angry reaction to the extremities of postmodernism. [It is] a philosophy that has no roots in the Enlightenment at all' ('Capital Punishment for Murderous Theorists?', *History and Theory*, vol. 38, no. 3, 1999, 379).

7 Culture

1   See Johannes Fabian, *Time and the Other: How Anthropology Makes its Object*, Columbia University Press, New York, 1983.
2   Dipesh Chakrabarty, *Provincialising Europe: Postcolonial Thought and Historical Difference*, Princeton University Press, Princeton, 2000, 7–8, his emphasis.
3   See R.L. Meek, *Social Science and the Ignoble Savage*, Cambridge University Press, New York, 1976; Robert Dixon, *The Course of Empire: Neo-Classical Culture in New South Wales 1788–1860*, Oxford University Press, Melbourne, 1986; D.L. Spadafora, *The Idea of Progress in Eighteenth-Century Britain*, Yale University Press, New Haven, 1990; Barbara Arneil, *John Locke and America: The Defence of English Colonialism*, Clarendon Press, Oxford, 1996.
4   John West, *The History of Tasmania* (1852), edited by A.G.L. Shaw, Angus & Robertson, Sydney, 1971, 330–31.
5   Jeremy Beckett, 'The Past in the Present; the Present in the Past: Constructing a National Aboriginality', in Jeremy R. Beckett (ed.), *Past and Present: The Construction of Aboriginality*, Aboriginal Studies Press, Canberra, 1988, 196. See Russell McGregor, *Imagined Destinies: Aboriginal Australians and the Doomed Race Theory, 1880–1939*, Melbourne University Press, Melbourne, 1997.
6   Geoffrey Blainey, *Our Side of the Country: The Story of Victoria*, Methuen Haynes, Sydney, 1984, 28, 'Mabo: What Aboriginals Lost', *Age*, 31 July 1993, 'Land that Bypassed a Revolution', *Age*, 21 August 1993, 'Sitting in Judgment on History', *Australian Business Monthly*, vol. 13, no. 10, 1993, 44, 'Drawing Up a Balance Sheet of Our History', *Quadrant*, vol. 37, nos 7–8, 1993, 14–15, *A Shorter History of Australia*, William Heinemann, Melbourne, 1994, 22, 46–47. For a discussion of some aspects of Blainey's writings on this matter, see Tim Rowse, 'Triumph of the Colonists', in Deborah Gare et al. (eds), *The Fuss that Never Ended: The Life and Work of Geoffrey Blainey*, Melbourne University Press, Melbourne, 2003, 39–52.

7 Keith Windschuttle, quoted by David Myton, 'Windschuttle's Way', *Campus Review*, vol. 12, no. 2, 2002, 11; Windschuttle, *The Fabrication of Aboriginal History, Vol. 1: Van Diemen's Land, 1803–1847*, Macleay Press, Sydney, 2002, 115, 386, 399.

8 Ibid., 128, 369–70, 377–82, 386, 398.

9 See Tim Murray, 'Aboriginal (Pre)History and Australian Archaeology: The Discourse of Australian Prehistoric Archaeology', and Gillian Cowlishaw, 'Studying Aborigines: Changing Canons in Anthropology and History', in Bain Attwood and John Arnold (eds), *Power, Knowledge and Aborigines*, La Trobe University Press, Melbourne, 1992, 1–19 and 20–31.

10 Windschuttle, 'Doctored Evidence and Invented Incidents in Aboriginal Historiography', in Bain Attwood and S.G. Foster (eds), *Frontier Conflict: The Australian Experience*, National Museum of Australia, Canberra, 2003, 106–07.

11 For a brief history of anthropology in Australia, see D.J. Mulvaney, 'Australasian Anthropology and ANZASS: "Strictly Scientific and Critical"', in Roy Macleod (ed.), *The Commonwealth of Science*, Oxford University Press, Melbourne, 1988, 196–221.

12 Windschuttle refers to the work of an American writer who has done little if any serious research in the area: Robert B. Edgerton, *Sick Societies: Challenging the Myth of Primitive Societies*, The Free Press, New York, 1992 (*Fabrication*, 382). (The Free Press published the American edition of Windschuttle's *Killing of History* in 1997.) As the publisher at Macleay Press, Windschuttle contracted a similarly swingeing attack on indigenous societies by Roger Sandall (Sandall, 'There is No Going Back for Aborigines', *Age*, 6 June 2001), which was eventually published in the United States instead: *The Culture Cult: Designer Tribalism and Other Essays*, Westview Press, Boulder, CO, 2001.

13 H. Ling Roth, *The Aborigines of Tasmania*, 2nd edn, F. King & Sons, Halifax, 1899; *Australian Dictionary of Biography*, vol. 11, 1988, 461–62; Windschuttle, *Fabrication*, 377 note 87; Tim Murray and Christine Williamson, 'Archaeology and History', in Robert Manne (ed.), *Whitewash: On Keith Windschuttle's Fabrication of Aboriginal History*, Black Inc., Melbourne, 2003, 312–14; Inga Clendinnen, 'Dispatches From the History Wars', *Australian Financial Review*, 31 October 2003. For Murray making this argument earlier, see, for example, his 'Aboriginal (Pre)History', 18–19.

14 For a lengthy discussion of this matter, which draws on her own research and that of several archaeologists (published prior to Windschuttle's *Fabrication*), see Rebe Taylor, '"Caught with the Line After Got with the White People"', and 'A Fireless People', *Aboriginal History*, forthcoming. I am indebted to Taylor for providing me with drafts of these articles.

15 Windschuttle, *Fabrication*, 378–79 note 91; Murray and Williamson, 'Archaeology', 312, 314.

16 Geoffrey Blainey, *Triumph of the Nomads: A History of Ancient Australia* (1975), Sun Books, Melbourne, 1976, 106–15, *A Land Half Won* (1980), Sun Books, Melbourne, 1983, 88–90, 367; Henry Reynolds, 'Blainey and Aboriginal History', in Andrew Markus and M.C. Ricklefs (eds), *Surrender Australia? Essays in the Study and Uses of History*, Allen & Unwin, Sydney, 1985, 85–87; Windschuttle, *Fabrication*, 372 note 65, 382 note 105.

17 Murray and Williamson, 'Archaeology', 316, 319, 323, 328.

18 Julie Nimmo, quoted Bernard Lane, 'British Arrival a Benign "Picnic"', *Australian*, 10 December 2002; Alan Atkinson, 'Honey and Wax: A Review of Keith Windschuttle, *The Fabrication of Aboriginal History, Vol. 1*', *Journal of Australian Colonial History*, vol. 4, no. 2, 2002, 21, his emphasis; Guy Rundle, 'Wounds Above the Heart', *Arena Magazine*, no. 67, 2003, 15–16. In his *White Australia Policy*, Windschuttle repeats, at greater length, his historicist theory. He reduces racism to just one of the ways it has been defined—biological racism—and claims that what other writers have seen as an important form of racism—cultural differentialism, of which historicism has been an especially significant part—is so radically different that it does not constitute anything like racism. He seems to believe that it is an unimportant historical fact that generations and generations of peoples claimed by historicist theories to be in an earlier 'stage of history' or 'historical development' were denied human and other rights and suffered as a result. Windschuttle seems to suggest that the suffering of those long dead does not really matter given that their descendants were finally granted equal rights. Apparently this means that the denial of their rights cannot be described as an example of racism (Macleay Press, Sydney, 2004, 5–6, 28, 43–50, 67–74).

19 Windschuttle, *Fabrication*, 375, 379, 386, 398.

20 Henry Reynolds (comp.), *Aborigines and Settlers: The Australian Experience*, Cassell Australia, Melbourne, 1972, 71. This said, Reynolds overlooked the significance of disease when he revised this collection in the late 1980s, omitting the chapter on disease. As I noted in a review of *Dispossession* (Allen & Unwin, Sydney, 1989), there was 'a narrowing in Reynolds' conception of the nature of the relationships between the colonisers and the colonised . . . As a result much is necessarily omitted . . . [T]he role of disease is neglected ('Review of *Dispossession*', *Aboriginal History*, vol. 15, no. 2, 1991, 169–70).

21 Noel Butlin, *Economics and the Dreamtime: A Hypothetical History*, Cambridge University Press, Melbourne, 1993, Ch. 26; Judy Campbell, *Invisible Invaders: Smallpox and Other Diseases in Aboriginal Australia, 1780–1880*, Melbourne University Press, Melbourne, 2002, Chs 1 and 2; Windschuttle, *Fabrication*, 372–73, 398.

22 At one point Windschuttle chooses to quote an early work of Henry Reynolds where his argument depended on the research of another historian (Lyndall

Ryan) rather than a later book where Reynolds advances a different argument that is based on his own research (*Fabrication*, 372; cf. Reynolds, *Fate of a Free People*, Penguin, Melbourne, 1995, 4, 142). This pales into insignificance compared with the following examples of misrepresentation, which necessarily require a rather tedious account: In his chapter on the death toll in Van Diemen's Land, Windschuttle asserts: 'Henry Reynolds . . . implies the total [killed] was more than a thousand'. To support this claim, Windschuttle quotes a passage from Reynolds' *An Indelible Stain?*, part of which reads: 'There is hard evidence of a decline from perhaps 1500 indigenous Tasmanians at the beginning of the Black War in 1824, to about 350 in 1831 . . . [M]any Aborigines must have been killed by British troops, official paramilitary roving parties or armed settlers encouraged by the government to defend themselves. Many others may have succumbed to the extreme rigours of guerilla war and the pressure exerted by the military campaign waged at the direction of Governor Arthur'. Windschuttle then comments: 'While Reynolds here avoids putting a precise figure on it himself, the implication of this statement is that between 1824 when there were 1500 and 1831 when only 350 were left, some 1150 Aborigines were shot dead by armed parties of troops and settlers or else succumbed to exposure and hunger during the military campaign'. This seems a reasonable inference until one checks Reynolds' book and discovers that Windschuttle has taken Reynolds' argument out of its context and so misrepresented it by omitting the sentence that precedes the passage in *An Indelible Stain?* that he has quoted. When one reads Reynolds' passage in full, one realises that he is conducting a general discussion about 'the demographic disaster' that befell Aboriginal people rather than making a particular argument about the number of Aborigines killed. Next, Windschuttle provides, in a footnote, vital information, namely that in Reynolds' *Fate of a Free People* he had suggested the total of Aboriginal people killed was only between 250 and 400, yet, having noted this, he proceeds to claim that Reynolds supports a higher number of Aboriginal deaths by killing in *An Indelible Stain?* even though he clearly does not do so. After this, Windschuttle, using the figure for deaths by killing that he has attributed to Reynolds on the basis of his misreading or misrepresentation of Reynolds' *An Indelible Stain?* (1150) rather than the one Reynolds himself offers in the *Fate* (between 250 and 400), claims that Ryan's and Reynolds' numbers for Aborigines killed are more or less the same proportion of their estimates of precolonial Aboriginal population (between 16 and 17 per cent, and 16 and 24 per cent). But here Windschuttle has cited Ryan's total of 'killings' *alone* and Reynolds' total for killings *and* exposure and hunger. Several pages later Windschuttle again misrepresents Reynolds. Using the figure of Aboriginal deaths by killing that he has incorrectly attributed to

Reynolds, he asserts that Reynolds has claimed that 'whites killed . . . six times more blacks'. Yet, Reynolds wrote in the *Fate*: 'There is no doubt that in the earliest years of settlement from 1804–24 the Europeans took more lives than the Aborigines. But in the period of the Black War—from 1824 to 1831—the mortality rate on each side was more even: perhaps somewhere between 150 and 250 [Aboriginal] Tasmanians were killed in conflict with the Europeans after 1824 . . . while they killed about 170 Europeans'. Two pages later, Windschuttle notes that Reynolds had taken Ryan to task in the *Fate* by arguing that Ryan's estimate of killings 'may have been wide of the mark' and 'No one had any idea of the real figure' but that in *An Indelible Stain?* 'Reynolds seems to have forgotten his own comments and now made estimates of the same kind he criticised in Ryan's work . . . claim[ing] there is "hard evidence" that the Aboriginal population declined from 1500 in 1824 to 350 in 1831'. As we have seen, Reynolds made no such claim in *An Indelible Stain?* in respect of killings: he was referring to those killed *and* those who succumbed to hunger and exposure; Ryan to those killed alone. At the end of this particular discussion, Windschuttle adds: 'A later section of this chapter looks at the credibility of [Reynolds'] . . . estimates of the Aboriginal [precolonial] population'. There, Windschuttle claims that Reynolds changes his figures in the same book, dropping it from 5000–7000 on one page to 4000 on another, and so he alleges that 'Reynolds has no consistent view about the size of the Aboriginal population'. Here, it seems that Windschuttle has misread Reynolds once again. At the beginning of his *Fate*, Reynolds comments: 'Having lived in isolation for ten thousand years, the 5–7000 Islanders were visited by numerous expeditions . . . for varying periods between 1772 and 1802'. Later, he says: 'In 1830 alone over 2000 whites arrived, a figure representing perhaps half the total indigenous population at the time of settlement'—that is, roughly 4000–5000. It seems reasonable to assume that in the first of these two passages Reynolds is suggesting that in *1772* the population was 5000–7000 but that in the second passage, having referred elsewhere to the introduction of diseases by the earliest European colonists, he puts the population by *the early nineteenth century*, when permanent settlement began, at c. 4000–5000 rather than 5000–7000. There is, therefore, no necessary inconsistency in Reynolds' statements about the size of the Aboriginal population, and thus no grounds for Windschuttle casting aspersions on his credibility (Reynolds, *Fate*, 3–4, 52, 81–82, *An Indelible Stain? The Question of Genocide in Australia's History*, Viking, Melbourne, 2001, 71; Windschuttle, *Fabrication*, 352–53, 356, 358–59, 366). Windschuttle repeats one of these erroneous claims in his 'Historical Error versus Historical Invention: A Reply to Stuart Macintyre and Patricia Grimshaw on *The Fabrication of Aboriginal History*', *Australian Historical Studies*, vol. 36, no. 124, 2004, 381.

23 Windschuttle, *Fabrication*, 375, 382 note 105.

24 Lyndall Ryan, *The Aboriginal Tasmanians*, University of Queensland Press, St Lucia, 1981, 175–76; James Boyce, 'Fantasy Island', in Manne (ed.), *Whitewash*, 42–44, '"Better to be Mistaken than to Deceive": The Fabrication of Aboriginal History and the Van Diemonian Record', *Island*, no. 96, 2004, 13. Judy Campbell accepts their assessment regarding venereal disease (*Invisible Invaders*, 19).

25 See Raymond Evans and Bill Thorpe, 'Indigenocide and the Massacre of Aboriginal History', *Overland*, no. 163, 2001, 28.

26 Windschuttle, *Fabrication*, 398–99.

27 Ibid., 110–11, 399, 418; Windschuttle, 'Historical Error', 375.

28 Windschuttle, *Fabrication*, 184–86.

29 Other scholars, such as Merete Borch, have since questioned whether this was so. See her 'Rethinking the Origins of *Terra Nullius*', *Australian Historical Studies*, vol. 32, no. 117, 2001, 222–39.

30 Alan Frost, 'New South Wales as *Terra Nullius*: The British Denial of Aboriginal Land Rights', *Historical Studies*, vol. 19, no. 77, 1981, 513–23 (which was reprinted in Susan Janson and Stuart Macintyre (eds), *Through White Eyes*, Allen & Unwin, Sydney, 1990, 65–76, and republished, in a slightly revised form, as 'Our Original Aggression: New South Wales as *Terra Nullius*', in Frost, *Botany Bay Mirages: Illusions of Australia's Convict Beginnings*, Melbourne University Press, Melbourne, 1994, 176–89). For a discussion of the manner in which both Frost and Henry Reynolds have approached this matter, see my '*The Law of the Land* or the Law of the Land? History, Law and Narrative in a Settler Society', *History Compass*, vol. 2, 2004, 1–27.

31 Windschuttle, *Fabrication*, 103–12, 114.

32 Henry Reynolds, *The Other Side of the Frontier*, History Department, James Cook University, Townsville, 1981, 52–54, 56–57; Windschuttle, *Fabrication*, 107–08, 111.

33 Les Hiatt, 'The Tasmanian Aborigines', *Quadrant*, vol. 47, no. 4, 2003, 5. For Hiatt's work on this subject see, for example, his *Arguments About Aborigines: Australia and the Evolution of Social Anthropology*, Cambridge University Press, Cambridge, 1996, Ch. 2.

34 Windschuttle, *Fabrication*, 110, 112, 419; Reynolds, 'Terra Nullius Reborn', in Manne (ed.), *Whitewash*, 112; Windschuttle, '*Whitewash* Confirms the Fabrication of Aboriginal History', *Quadrant*, vol. 47, no. 10, 2003, 13. I am sceptical of the approach adopted by both Windschuttle and Reynolds here. They seem to assume that compilations of Aboriginal words (rather than language) would have captured the ways in which Aborigines conceptualised their relationship to land. Modern linguists would treat this sceptically, as Reynolds more or less acknowledges himself ('Terra Nullius', 110).

35 For an example, see Bain Attwood and Andrew Markus, *The Struggle for Aboriginal Rights: A Documentary History*, Allen & Unwin, Sydney, 1999, 32, 41–43. The Canadian legal scholar Jeremy Webber has made this important point: 'the need to express indigenous interests as "rights" may only arise once indigenous societies are confronted with colonisation. Before then, the interests may well still exist . . . The need to characterise the interests as rights becomes relevant only when they are subjected to the threats posed by colonisation and one is forced to find some means of protection that is comprehensible to and efficacious within a non-indigenous system of law . . . It is generally the case that the articulation of rights is prompted by some threat or perceived challenge . . . It is not at all unfamiliar to see fundamental interests recognised as rights, once subjected to threat. That progression lies at the origin of virtually all common-law and equitable rights . . . The fact that the right emerges only in response to challenge does not diminish its force in the slightest' ('Beyond Regret: Mabo's Implications for Australia's Constitutionalism', in Duncan Ivison et al. (eds), *Political Theory and the Rights of Indigenous Peoples*, Cambridge University Press, Cambridge, 2000, 64–65).

36 Windschuttle, *Fabrication*, 104. According to Windschuttle, none of these colonists ever directly quoted an Aboriginal man or woman objecting to his dispossession. This means, he claims, that they had no sense of property rights (104–05). He overlooks other ways of explaining such a silence in the historical record, one of which I more or less noted earlier: white paternalism (which Windschuttle disparages) commonly led colonists to presume that Aboriginal people could not represent themselves and that they had to perform this task on their behalf instead.

37 Charles S. Maier, *The Unmasterable Past: History, Holocaust, and German National Identity*, Harvard University Press, Cambridge, MA, 1988, 12.

38 Ibid., 54, 64.

39 See my 'Historiography on the Australian Frontier', in Attwood and Foster (eds), *Frontier Conflict*, 182.

40 In reading Windschuttle's writings I have found it difficult to establish how much he has been taken in by his own construction of the historiography and the history in this field. As a result, I am not sure to what degree he can be held responsible for the nature of his work. It seems to me that the responsibility of some of his new conservative supporters is greater, because they seem to have had a clear sense of the problematic nature of his work and yet have chosen to remain silent.

8 History

1   In the final part of this book, as in the rest of it, this question will be considered largely in reference to the frontier era, though much of what I argue holds true and probably truer for some of the later epochs.

2   For a critical account of the rise of memory, see Kirwin Lee Klein, 'On the Emergence of *Memory* in Historical Discourse', *Representations*, no. 69, 2000, 127–50.

3   For estimates of precolonial population, see D.J. Mulvaney and J. Peter White (eds), *Australians to 1788*, Fairfax, Syme & Weldon, Sydney, 1987, Ch. 6, and Noel Butlin, *Economics and the Dreamtime: A Hypothetical History*, Cambridge University Press, Melbourne, 1993, 98–99, 138–39.

4   Richard White, 'Indian Peoples and the Natural World: Asking the Right Questions', in Donald L. Fixico (ed.), *Rethinking American Indian History*, University of New Mexico Press, Albuquerque, 1997, 93.

5   The argument made here probably does not hold so true of the frontier in Queensland. Whereas in other Australian colonies the frontier era occurred at a time when government was under imperial control, and so settler violence was under its critical oversight to some degree, in Queensland it took place under 'responsible government' that was dominated by white settlers. In the case of Western Australia, the imperial government reserved its powers in Aboriginal affairs until late in the nineteenth century.

6   Dipesh Chakrabarty, *Provincialising Europe: Postcolonial Thought and Historical Difference*, Princeton University Press, Princeton, 2000, 100–01. For a discussion of subaltern history, see Vinayak Chaturvedi (ed.), *Mapping Subaltern Studies and the Postcolonial*, Verso, London, 2000.

7   This approach is apparent most recently in the writings of the critics of 'revisionist' historians. For example, James Boyce attributes the flaws in Keith Windschuttle's account of the Van Diemonian frontier to a lack of research generally, and to selective use of historical sources. He suggests that Windschuttle's interpretation would have been different had he researched 'crucial and readily accessible primary source material' such as private or unofficial documents. Yet Boyce is unable to demonstrate that this work would have provided factual evidence of settler killings of Aborigines ('Fantasy Island', in Robert Manne (ed.), *Whitewash: On Keith Windschuttle's Fabrication of Aboriginal History*, Black Inc., Melbourne, 2003, 17, 20, 23, 25, 27–29, 46).

8   Reynolds expanded the sources historians had conventionally used but not the manner in which he used them, reading them for information much more than for meaning. His numerous insights were largely derived from reading

latter-day anthropological studies of Aboriginal communities rather than interpreting the contemporary historical sources of the frontier.

9 Henry Reynolds, *The Other Side of the Frontier*, History Department, James Cook University, Townsville, 1981, 163.

10 It is by no means insignificant that much of Reynolds' research, at least initially, was on the frontier in Queensland. See note 5 above.

11 Tom Griffiths, 'The Language of Conflict', in Bain Attwood and S.G. Foster (eds), *Frontier Conflict: The Australian Experience*, National Museum of Australia, Canberra, 2003, 138–39, 146.

12 Michel de Certeau, *Heterologies: Discourse on the Other*, trans. Brian Massumi, Manchester University Press, Manchester, 1986, 4.

13 Mark Salber Phillips, 'Distance and Historical Representation', *History Workshop Journal*, no. 57, 2004, 125.

14 Reynolds, *The Other Side*, 2–3. Reynolds discusses this further in *Why Weren't We Told? A Personal Search for the Truth About Our History*, Viking, Melbourne, 1999, especially 3, 38–41, 52, 83, 89.

15 Reynolds, *The Other Side*, 3, *Why*, 97, 99–101. It should be noted that Reynolds defines oral history in a rather loose and idiosyncratic way.

16 Reynolds, *The Other Side*, 1, my emphases, *Frontier: Aborigines, Settlers and Land*, Allen & Unwin, Sydney, 1987, ix, my emphasis, *Why*, 3, 124, my emphasis; Alan Atkinson, 'Do Good Historians Have Feelings?', in Stuart Macintyre (ed.), *The Historian's Conscience: Australian Historians on the Ethics of History*, Melbourne University Press, Melbourne, 2004, 24–25. 'Revisionist' critics have seized upon these references to the political for their political campaign against the 'politicisation of history'. See, for example, Keith Windschuttle, *The Fabrication of Aboriginal History, Vol. 1: Van Diemen's Land, 1803–1847*, Macleay Press, Sydney, 2002, 6.

17 Peter Novick, *That Noble Dream: The 'Objectivity Question' and the American Historical Profession*, Cambridge University Press, New York, 1988, 2.

18 Gillian Cowlishaw, 'Studying Aborigines: Changing Canons in Anthropology and History', in Bain Attwood and John Arnold (eds), *Power, Knowledge and Aborigines*, La Trobe University Press, Melbourne, 1992, 26–27; Patrick Wolfe, 'Nation and MiscegeNation: Discursive Continuity in the Post-Mabo Era', *Social Analysis*, no. 36, 1994, 96; Klaus Neumann, 'Remembering Victims and Perpetrators', *UTS Review*, vol. 4, no. 1, 1998, 8, 10, 12, 15.

9 Memory

1 Bruce A. Sommer, 'The Bowman Incident', in Luise Hercus and Peter Sutton (eds), *This is What Happened: Historical Narratives by Aborigines*, Australian Institute of Aboriginal Studies, Canberra, 1986, Ch. 23; Deborah Bird Rose,

'Oral Histories and Knowledge', in Bain Attwood and S.G. Foster (eds), *Frontier Conflict: The Australian Experience*, National Museum of Australia, Canberra, 2003, 124.

2   See Tom Griffiths, *Hunters and Collectors: The Antiquarian Imagination in Australia*, Cambridge University Press, Melbourne, 1996, Ch. 5. Robert Foster, Rick Hosking and Amanda Nettelbeck, *Fatal Collisions: The South Australian Frontier and the Violence of Memory*, Wakefield Press, Adelaide, 2001 is the most thorough discussion available of the ways in which settler violence has been turned into myth or legend by settlers or settler communities.

3   See David Roberts, 'Bells Falls Massacre and Bathurst's History of Violence: Local Tradition and Australian Historiography', *Australian Historical Studies*, vol. 26, no. 105, 1995, 615–33, and 'The Bells Falls Massacre and Oral Tradition', in Attwood and Foster (eds), *Frontier Conflict*, 150–57.

4   See Mary Binks, 'Violence at Risdon Cove', *Mercury* (Launceston), 12 September 1988; Greg Lehman, 'Our Story of Risdon Cove', *Pugganna News*, no. 34, 1992, 44–45; 'Risdon Cove Massacre Commemoration', *Pugganna News*, no. 35, 1992, 33–35; John Briggs, 'Day of Honour Marks Dark History', *Mercury* (Hobart), 4 May 2004. See also Greg Lehman, 'Telling Us True', in Robert Manne (ed.), *Whitewash: On Keith Windschuttle's Fabrication of Aboriginal History*, Black Inc., Melbourne, 2003, 174–84.

5   See Paul Thompson, *The Voice of the Past: Oral History*, Oxford University Press, Oxford, 1978, 66, 71, 88–90; David Henige, *Oral Historiography*, Longman, London, 1982, 111; John Murphy, 'The Voice of Memory: History, Autobiography and Oral Memory', *Historical Studies*, vol. 22, no. 87, 1986, 158; Paula Hamilton, 'Oral History', in Graeme Davison, John Hirst and Stuart Macintyre (eds), *The Oxford Companion to Australian History*, Oxford University Press, Melbourne, 1998, 481–83.

6   C.D. Rowley, *The Destruction of Aboriginal Society*, Australian National University Press, Canberra, 1970; Henry Reynolds (comp.), *Aborigines and Settlers: The Australian Experience*, Cassell Australia, Melbourne, 1972; R.H.W. Reece, *Aborigines and Colonists: Aborigines and Colonial Society in New South Wales in the 1830s and 1840s*, Sydney University Press, Sydney, 1974; Raymond Evans et al., *Exclusion, Exploitation and Extermination: Race Relations in Colonial Queensland*, ANZ Book Co., Sydney, 1975; M.F. Christie, *Aborigines in Colonial Victoria 1835–1886*, Sydney University Press, Sydney, 1979; Lyndall Ryan, *The Aboriginal Tasmanians*, University of Queensland Press, St Lucia, 1981; Noel Loos, *Invasion and Resistance: Aboriginal–European Relations on the North Queensland Frontier 1861–1897*, Australian National University Press, Canberra, 1982.

7   See Bruce Shaw, *My Country of the Pelican Dreaming: The Life of an Australian Aborigine of the Gadjerong, Grant Njabidj, 1904–1977*, Australian Institute of

Aboriginal Studies, Canberra, 1981; John Cribbin, *The Killing Times: The Coniston Massacre*, Fontana/Collins, Sydney, 1984; Howard and Frances Morphy, 'The "Myths" of Ngalakan History: Ideology and Images of the Past in Northern Australia', *Man* (n.s.), vol. 19, no. 3, 1985, 459–78; Hercus and Sutton (eds), *This is What Happened*; Ann McGrath, *'Born in the Cattle': Aborigines in Cattle Country*, Allen & Unwin, Sydney, 1987; Peter and Jay Read (eds), *Long Time, Olden Time: Aboriginal Accounts of Northern Territory History*, Institute for Aboriginal Development Publications, Alice Springs, 1991; Deborah Bird Rose, *Hidden Histories: Black Stories from Victoria River Downs, Humbert River and Wave Hill Stations*, Aboriginal Studies Press, Canberra, 1991; Grace and Harold Koch (comps), *Kaytetye Country: An Aboriginal History of the Barrow Creek Area*, Institute for Aboriginal Development, Alice Springs, 1993. The stories for *This is What Happened* were recorded between the mid-1960s and the mid-1970s, and the interviews for *Long Time* were conducted in the late 1970s.

8   Trevor Lummis, *Listening to History: The Authenticity of Oral Evidence*, Hutchinson, London, 1987, 120; Henige, *Oral Historiography*, 110; Thompson, *Voice of the Past*, 132.

9   Peter Novick, *The Holocaust in American Life*, Houghton Mifflin, Boston, 1999, 3–4, his emphasis.

10 Luisa Passerini 'Work Ideology and Consciousness under Italian Fascism', *History Workshop Journal*, no. 8, 1979, 82–108; Alessandro Portelli, 'The Peculiarities of Oral History', *History Workshop Journal*, no. 12, 1981, 96–107.

11 Dipesh Chakrabarty, 'Reconciliation and its Historiography: Some Preliminary Thoughts', *UTS Review*, vol. 7, no. 1, 2001, 10; Bill Schwarz, '"Already the Past": Memory and Historical Time', in Katharine Hodgkin and Susannah Radstone (eds), *Regimes of Memory*, Routledge, London, 2003, 141–42.

12 See, for example, Heather Goodall, 'Colonialism and Catastrophe: Contested Memories of Nuclear Testing and Measles Epidemics at Ernabella', in Kate Darian Smith and Paula Hamilton (eds), *Memory and History in Twentieth-Century Australia*, Oxford University Press, Melbourne, 1994, 55–76.

13 Morphy and Morphy, '"Myths"', 459, 462; Jeremy Beckett, 'Walter Newton's History of the World—or Australia', *American Ethnologist*, vol. 20, no. 4, 1993, 675.

14 But see also Robert Foster, 'The Legend of James Brown', *Australian Historical Studies*, vol. 29, no. 111, 1998, 210–29.

15 See Roberts, 'Bells Falls', 628–33, and 'The Bells Falls Massacre', 153–54. Keith Windschuttle used and abused Roberts' work to discredit an exhibit in the National Museum of Australia ('How Not to Run a Museum', *Quadrant*, vol. 45, no. 9, 2001, 19). For Roberts' criticisms of Windschuttle's claims, see

his 'The Bells Falls Massacre', especially 150, 156. For a further discussion of the exhibit in question, see my 'Bells Falls Gorge and the National Museum of Australia', forthcoming.

16 Eric Hobsbawm, 'Introduction', in Eric Hobsbawm and Terence Ranger (eds), *The Invention of Tradition*, Cambridge University Press, Cambridge, 1983, 1–5, 8, 10; J.G.A. Pocock, 'The Treaty Between Histories', in Andrew Sharp and Paul McHugh (eds), *Histories, Power and Loss: Uses of the Past—A New Zealand Commentary*, Bridget Williams Books, Wellington, 2001, 75.

17 See, for example, Deborah Bird Rose, *Reports from a Wild Country: Ethics for Decolonisation*, University of New South Wales Press, Sydney, 2004. It should be noted, though, that Rose does not frame her work in terms of any theory of trauma.

18 Griffiths, 'The Language of Conflict', in Bain Attwood and S.G. Foster (eds), *Frontier Conflict*, 143; personal communication, 27 April 2004. Earlier in this essay, Griffiths refers to Bernard Smith's argument that Australian settler culture is haunted by the violence and dispossession done to Aboriginal people. It is 'a nightmare to be thrust out of mind', Smith writes. 'Yet like the traumatic experiences of childhood it continues to haunt our dreams' (see Griffiths, 'Language of Conflict', 138).

19 It should be noted that there are many definitions and descriptions of trauma. See Cathy Caruth (ed.), *Trauma: Explorations in Memory*, Johns Hopkins University Press, Baltimore, 1995.

20 Caruth, 'Introduction', and 'Recapturing the Past', in ibid., 4–9, 151–56; Michael Rothberg, *Traumatic Realities: The Demands of Holocaust Representation*, University of Minnesota Press, Minneapolis, 2000, 62; Katharine Hodgkin and Susannah Radstone, 'Remembering Suffering: Trauma and History', in Katharine Hodgkin and Susannah Radstone (eds), *Contested Pasts: The Politics of Memory*, Routledge, London, 2003, 100.

21 Esther Faye, 'Impossible Memories and the History of Trauma', in Jill Bennett and Rosanne Kennedy (eds), *World Memory: Personal Trajectories in Global Time*, Palgrave, New York, 2003, 164.

22 Caruth, 'Introduction', 5.

23 Paula Hamilton, 'Sale of the Century? Memory and Historical Consciousness in Australia', in Hodgkin and Radstone (eds), *Contested Pasts*, 145; Bird Rose, 'Oral Histories and Knowledge', in Attwood and Foster (eds), *Frontier Conflict*, 121.

24 Klaus Neumann, 'Among Historians', *Cultural Studies Review*, vol. 9, no. 2, 2003, 182, 189.

25 In the following section, I am drawing on this work by Dominick LaCapra: *Soundings in Critical Theory*, Cornell University Press, Ithaca, 1989, Ch. 1; *History and Memory After Auschwitz*, Cornell University Press, Ithaca, 1998,

Chs 1 and 6; *Writing History, Writing Trauma*, Johns Hopkins University Press, Baltimore, 2001, Preface and Ch. 1.

26 LaCapra, 'Trauma, Absence, Loss', *Critical Inquiry*, vol. 25, no. 4, 1999, 722–23.

27 LaCapra, 'Holocaust Testimonies', in Moishe Postone and Eric Santner (eds), *Catatrosphe and Meaning: The Holocaust and the Twentieth Century*, Univeristy of Chicago Press, Chicago, 2003, 223; Ross Gibson, *Seven Versions of an Australian Badland*, University of Queensland Press, St Lucia, 2002.

10 Truth and recognition

1   Arguably, the degree of this burden differs between settler Australians, depending upon the time and terms upon which they or their forebears came here, as does the degree to which they have benefited from the historical destruction and dispossession of Aboriginal people.

2   Too much has been asked and expected of legal mechanisms, at least of the kinds found in courts conducted along traditional Anglo-Australian lines.

3   Council for Aboriginal Rights (CAR), *Walking Together: The First Steps*, <www.austlii.edu.au/other/IndigLRes/car/1994/1/2>; CAR, *Addressing the Key Issues for Reconciliation*, <www.austlii.edu.au/other/IndigLRes/car/1993/9/2>.

4   CAR, *Sharing History*, <www.austlii.edu.au/other/IndigLRes/car/1993/4>; CAR, *Walking Together*; CAR, Addressing the Key Issues; CAR, Reconciliation: Australia's Challenge: Final Report of the Council for Aboriginal Reconciliation to the Prime Minister and the Commonwealth Parliament, <www.austlii.edu.au/other/IndigLRes/car/2000/16>.

5   Michael Ignatieff, *The Warrior's Honor: Ethnic War and the Modern Conscience*, Vintage, London, 1999, 173–74, 185; Dipesh Chakrabarty, 'Reconciliation and its Historiography: Some Preliminary Thoughts', *UTS Review*, vol. 7, no. 1, 2001, 11. See also Heribert Adam and Kanya Adam, 'The Politics of Memory in Divided Societies', in Wilmot James and Linda van de Vijwer (eds), *After the TRC: Reflections on Truth and Reconciliation in South Africa*, Ohio University Press, Athens, Ohio, 2000, 44.

6   Richard Mulgan, 'Citizenship and Legitimacy in Postcolonial Australia', in Nicolas Peterson and Will Sanders (eds), *Citizenship and Indigenous Australians: Changing Conceptions and Possibilities*, Cambridge University Press, Melbourne, 1998, 184–85.

7   See my 'The Past as Future: Aborigines, Australia and the (Dis)Course of History', in Bain Attwood (ed.), *In the Age of Mabo: History, Aborigines and Australia*, Allen & Unwin, Sydney, 1996, xxxviii, for another discussion of this.

8   Dipesh Chakrabarty, *Provincialising Europe: Postcolonial Thought and Historical Difference*, Princeton University Press, Princeton, 2000, 98, 101.

9   Ibid., 99.

10 Ibid., 107.

11 My suggestions here do not refer to legal ones. I do not know how the challenge posed by 'subaltern pasts' can be handled in courts. This said, it should be noted that in some instances the legal system has been adapted to allow forms of historical narrative without fracturing the structure of Anglo-Australian law.

12 Deborah Bird Rose, 'Oral Histories and Knowledge', in Bain Attwood and S.G. Foster (eds), *Frontier Conflict: The Australian Experience*, National Museum of Australia, Canberra, 2003, 124–25.

13 CAR, *Addressing the Key Issues*; Heather Goodall, 'Too Early or Not Soon Enough? Reflections on Sharing Histories as Process', *Australian Historical Studies*, vol. 33, no. 118, 2002, 12.

14 Mulgan, 'Citizenship and Legitimacy', 193.

15 In this final section, my suggestion owes something to the argument advanced by Richard Mulgan in the aforementioned essay.

16 New conservatives have repeatedly attacked what they have called 'the Aboriginal rights agenda'. They imply that there was a political movement that assumed that rights were the solution to Aboriginal problems. This is a historical misrepresentation. In the course of the research I conducted on campaigns for Aboriginal rights from the 1870s and the 1970s, it was clear to me that the goal of Aboriginal rights was seldom advocated by activists as an end in itself but rather as a means to an end. For example, the call for land rights in the 1960s and 1970s not only entailed a demand for the right to land but also a demand for compensation to provide capital to develop that land and provide other resources for Aboriginal people. See my *Rights for Aborigines*, Allen & Unwin, Sydney, 2003, especially Parts IV and V.

17 Mark McKenna, *This Country: A Reconciled Republic?*, University of New South Wales Press, Sydney, 2004, 111.

18 See, for example, *Council for Aboriginal Reconciliation and Constitutional Centenary Foundation, The Position of Indigenous People in National Constitutions*, Commonwealth Printer, Canberra, [1993].

19 For a discussion of the demands for constitutional change, see McKenna, *This Country*, especially Chs 1, 4 and 5.

20 Jeremy Webber, 'Beyond Regret: Mabo's Implications for Australia's Constitutionalism', in Duncan Ivison et al. (eds), *Political Theory and the Rights of Indigenous Peoples*, Cambridge University Press, Cambridge, 2000, 81–83, 87.

21 In a recent essay, Deborah Bird Rose has outlined an ethical basis for such recuperative work. See her *Reports from a Wild Country: Ethics for Decolonisation*, University of New South Wales Press, Sydney, 2004, Ch. 1.

22 Stephen Muecke, *No Road (Bitumen all the Way)*, Fremantle Arts Centre Press, Fremantle, 1997, 227; Rose, *Reports*, 28–29.

23 Henry Reynolds (comp.), *Aborigines and Settlers: The Australian Experience 1788–1939*, Cassell Australia, Melbourne, 1972, 1; Dominick LaCapra, 'Trauma, Absence, Loss', *Critical Inquiry*, vol. 25, no. 4, 1999, 713; Stephan Feuchtwang, 'Loss: Transmissions, Recognitions, Authorisations', in Katharine Hodgkin and Susannah Radstone (eds), *Regimes of Memory*, Routledge, London, 2003, 78.

24 There is already an annual National Sorry Day on 26 May, but it has no status as a national (holi-)day. In 1938 Aboriginal organisations held a national Day of Mourning in Sydney, and it has been marked by some Aboriginal people in subsequent years. See Jack Horner and Marcia Langton, 'The Day of Mourning', in Bill Gammage and Peter Spearritt (eds), *Australians 1938*, Fairfax, Syme & Weldon, Sydney, 1987, 29–35, and Attwood, *Rights for Aborigines*, 54–55, 69–74, 195–96, 335–39.

25 Webber, 'Beyond Regret', 79.

● INDEX

ABC (Australian Broadcasting
    Commission), 17, 87–88, 96
Aboriginal art, 23–24, 26, 53, 159
Aboriginal history
    audience, 45
    by Aboriginal people, 4, 17, 170–73,
        175–76
    by settler Australians, 17–19, 39–42, 93,
        110–11
    complexity of field, 51–53, 58–59, 65,
        83
    custodianship or control, 45–46, 48
    development, 17, 22–25, 42–48, 80
    disciplines, 44, 50, 57–58
    perspective, 43, 157–58
    see also historical revision; historicism
Aboriginal History (journal), 42–44
Aboriginal identity, 44–45, 116, 190
Aboriginal people
    agency, 43–44
    dispossession and destruction, 25, 28,
        39–40, 94, 105, 122–23, 144–46, 151,
        159, 185, 222, 227, 255–56
    legal status, 133
    population, 20, 141, 143, 145, 159, 248,
        251
    relations among and between groups, 44,
        114, 140–41, 143–44
    renaissance, 44
    see also Aboriginal history, by Aboriginal
        people
Aboriginal policy, 25–27, see also
    assimilation; self-determination
Aboriginal resistance, 39, 110–11, 114–16,
    148–49, 151, 233–35
Aboriginal rights, 20, 25–26, 34, 190–94,
    257
Aboriginality, 20, 30
    Aboriginal representations, 46

appropriation and promotion by
    government, 24–26
settler representations, 15–16, 18, 21–25,
    45, 136–44, 146–48
traditional culture, 23–25
African Americans, 37, 198
Anderson, Benedict, 13
Anderson, John, 75–76, 215
anthropologists, 17, 40, 42, 45–46, 48–49, 58,
    141–42, 149–50, 169, 173, 175, 177, 205
anthropology, 16, 18, 23, 43–44, 136, 141,
    245, 252
anti-racism, 20, 25–26, 40
ANZAC (Australia and New Zealand Army
    Corps) Day, 114, 195
apology, 32–33
archaeologists, 17, 42, 44, 46, 48–49, 142–43,
    201, 245
archaeology, 18, 23, 136, 141
    deep past, 23, 30
Arthur, Sir George, 94, 101, 115, 127,
    129–30, 132–33, 233, 247
ASIO (Australian Security Intelligence
    Organisation), 236
assimilation, 20–22, 26, 34, 93
Atkinson, Alan, 69, 104–05, 120–21, 127,
    129–30, 132, 143, 168, 200, 212, 238–39
ATSIC (Aboriginal and Torres Strait Islander
    Commission), 34
Attwood, Bain, 40, 42, 92, 217, 220–23, 226,
    246, 249, 255, 257
Australia
    Asia–Pacific region, in reference to
        Australia's place, 21–22, 27–28
    Britishness, 14–15, 21–23, 27–28, 30, 33,
        103
    colonisation, 14–15, 18–19, 39–40, 203
    Constitution, 192–93, 257, see also
        referendums for constitutional change

Australia *continued*
    new nationalism, 22–25
    settler national identity, 14–16, 20–25,
        27–34, 113, 116, 123, 186, 190, *see also*
        national identity
Australian (newspaper), 2, 61–62, 96, 98–99,
    209, 220–21, 226
Australian history
    bicentenary, 19, 23, 31
    chronologies, 14, 18, 32
    controversies and disputation, 2–7,
        61–62, 198–99, 210
    falsification, 31
    new Australian history, 18–19, 25, 27, 29
    pioneering, 14–15, 19, 31–31, 191, 200
    radical, 18–19
    unsettlement, 19, 25, 29–32
    see also nation states and history, moral
        legitimacy
Australian Institute of Aboriginal and Torres
    Strait Islander Studies, 42
Australian Labor Party, 21, *see also* Labor
    governments
Australian War Memorial, 114, 195, 234
Australians, white, 3, 49, 73, *see also*
    Australian history

Bantick, Christopher, 97
Barwick, Diane, 40, 42
Beckett, Jeremy, 175
Bells Falls Gorge, 171, 175–76, 229, 254–55
Berendt, Larissa, 228
Berndt, Ronald and Catherine, 201, 205
Bhabha, Homi, 51
'black armband history', 33–34, 38, 63
Black Jack, 115–16
Black Tom, 115–16, 233
Blainey, Geoffrey, 23, 31–34, 60, 63–64, 67, 75,
    99, 114, 139, 143, 146, 203, 210, 228, 244
Bolt, Andrew, 60, 97–98
Bolton, Geoffrey, 104, 201
Bonwick, James, 109–10
Boyce, James, 131, 237, 251
Brett, Judith, 21
Broome, Richard, 40, 200, 223
Brunton, Ron, 60, 97, 218
Butlin, Noel, 41, 201

Cadzow, Jane, 3, 70, 78, 121, 212, 215
Campbell, Judy, 41, 249
Canada, 1, 14, 191
Carr, E.H., 83
Carter, David, 29, 53–55
Caruth, Cathy, 178, 255
Casey, Dawn, 90–91, 219

Chakrabarty, Dipesh, 50, 55, 137, 160–61,
    185–88
Christianity, *see* humanitarianism;
    missionaries
Christie, Michael, 39, 161
Clark, Anna, 5–6, 209–10
Clark, Manning, 64, 210
Clendinnen, Inga, 53–54, 69, 103–04, 227
Coleman, Peter, 60–61, 209, 229
Cook, Captain James, stories, 18, 47–48, 147,
    171, 175
Council for Aboriginal Reconciliation,
    184–86, 189–90
Cowlishaw, Gillian, 169
Critchett, Jan, 41
culture, 12, 23, 26, 27, 53, 64 *see also*
    Aboriginality; Australia, Britishness;
    public intellectuals
'culture wars', 34, 61, 71, 136
Curran, James, 22, 28
Curthoys, Ann, 201

Davison, Graeme, 69, 77, 213
Dawson, John, 199–200, 221, 229–30
Deane, Sir William, 90–91, 114
decolonisation, 20–21, 137
DeLong, Bradford, 72, 213
Demidenko, Helen, 4, 51, 199, 207
democracy, 13, 38, 59, 158, 179, 186–89,
    see also history, democratisation
denialism, 4, 151–52
Devine, Miranda, 60, 97, 214, 219
disease, 39, 114, 144–45, 246–49
Duffy, Michael, 60, 97–98

Edgerton, Robert B., 245
egalitarianism, 74
Elder, Bruce, 52, 57, 176
Enlightenment, 126–27, 135, 138, 146, 238,
    243–44
Enola Gay affair, 60, 208, 210
Evans, Raymond, 39
Evans, Richard, 58, 83
Everett, Jim, 105, 228
evolution, theory of, 139–42

Fels, Marie, 41, 43, 233–34
film and television, 11, 53, 55, 57
Finnane, Mark, 122, 239
footnotes, 219, 229–31
Foster, Robert, 253, 254
Foster, S.G., 42, 201, 222–23
Fox-Genovese, Elizabeth, 213
Free Press (publisher), 75, 245
frontier conflict, 18–19, 39–40, 42–43,

47–48, 55–58, 107–08, 110–12, 114–19,
125, 128–34, 160, 169–71, 237, 241–43,
251, 253, *see also* 'massacre history';
massacres; wars
frontier cooperation, 40–42, 185–86, 234
Frost, Alan, 147–48, 249

Gaita, Raimond, 54, 122
Gascoigne, John, 128, 241
genocide, 87–108, 110, 112, 125, 135, 195,
213, 218–26
Gibson, Ross, 182
globalisation, 22, 100–03
Goldhagen, Daniel, 60, 209
Goodall, Heather, 52, 189
Gordon, Daniel, 71–72, 244
Grassby, Al, 52, 176
Green, Neville, 57–58, 237
Griffiths, Tom, 69, 114, 164, 177, 255
'guerilla warfare', 116–17, 214, 233–36
guilt, *see* shame

Hamilton, Paula, 179
Haskell, Thomas L., 238–39
Hasluck, Paul, 205, 232
Healy, Chris, 201
Henderson, Gerard, 60, 209
Hercus, Luise, 52, 173
heritage, 23–24
Hiatt, Les, 149–50, 249
Hill, Marji, 52, 176
historians, academic/professional, 2–5
integrity, 2, 5–6, 97
qualifications, credentials and/or
credentialism, 65, 213–14
historical authority, 3, 5–6, 14, 36–37, 39–40,
45–46, 49, 54–58, 115, 157, 167–68,
170, 172
historical knowledge, 3, 36–37, 39, 44,
49–51, 54–58, 158, 161–69, 174–75,
179–80, 184–90
historical narratives, 13, 29–30, 57, *see also*
narratives
historical realism, 46, 118, 161–63, 175
historical revision, 40–42, 206
historical 'revisionists', 198, 209, 225–26
Historical Society (organisation), 213
historicism, 15–16, 22–23, 105, 136–43,
186–88
Historikerstreit, 60, 151, 200, 208
history
antiquarian, 118
critical, 36–37
democratisation, 6, 36–37, 54, 58–59, 65,
74, 83, 172, 187

distance, 46–47, 49, 121–22, 164–69,
176–78, 181–82, 189–90
ethical questions, 6, 48, 158, 179
family, 45–46
local, 201
methodology, 118–21, 160, 162, 229–31
monumental, 36
morality, 54–55, 81–82
objectivity, 6, 36, 38, 46, 83, 121–23, 166,
168, 181–82, 238–39
political relationship, 12, 27–29, 31–35,
37–38, 42, 44, 53, 62, 81–84, 117,
147–48, 203, 211, 217, 238–39, 252
popular, 40, 56–57, 88–89, 91, 103,
107–08, 112, 125, 152–53, 176, 208,
235
popular culture, 4, 6, 37, 51, 113
popularity, 11–12, 27, 51, 55, 58
prestige, 13–14
public, 51–55, 174
radical, 18
'reading the signs', 163–64
social, 18, 36, 38, 48–49, 172
sources, 36–37, 39, 56, 58, 116, 118–20,
131, 141–43, 146, 150, 157–64,
170–73, 176, 178–79, 229, 237,
241–42, 249–50, 251
subaltern, 6, 160–61, 172, 187, 251, 257
time, 45, 136–37, 164–66, 178
see also Aboriginal history; Australian
history; legend; life stories; memory;
myth; oral history; nation states and
history; national histories; testimony
'history wars'
role of Aboriginal people, 4
role of white Australians, 3–4
see also Australian history, controversies
and disputation; 'culture wars';
history, political relationship; new
conservatives
Hobsbawm, Eric, 13, 36, 78, 176–77
Holocaust, *see* Jewish Holocaust
Howard, John, 27, 32–35, 60, 63, 209
Hughes, Robert, 91, 98, 223
Human Rights and Equal Opportunity
Commission (Australia), 51, 53, 218
humanitarianism, 19, 39, 41–42, 56, 125–34,
139, 185, 204, 239–40, 243, 250
Huyssen, Andreas, 12, 101, 200

Ianziti, Gary, 231
identity, 12, 55, 185, *see also* Aboriginal
identity; Australia, settler national
identity; national identity
Ignatieff, Michael, 185

immigration, 1, 21, 54, 61
Inglis, Ken, 114

Jacobs, Margaret, 69, 71
Jewish Holocaust, 90, 92, 98, 100–05,
    199, 218, 221, 223–24, 227–28,
    see also Nazism
Jones, Rhys, 143
journalism and journalists, 39, 46, 53, 62,
    65–66, 78, 82, 88, 91–92, 97–98, 100,
    108, 205, 212, 215, 235–36

Keating, Paul, 27–29, 32–33
Kelly, Paul, 209
Kennedy, Brian, 76, 215
Kimball, Roger, 75, 98–99
Knightley, Phillip, 57, 88, 90–92, 98
Koch, Grace and Harold, 173
Krygier, Martin, 77–78, 129–30, 231–32

La Nauze, John, 16
Labor governments
    Hawke, 26–28
    Keating, 27–29, 32, 64
    Whitlam, 22, 26, 28
LaCapra, Dominick, 71, 77, 181–82, 195,
    200, 255–56
'land rights', 1, 19, 20–21, 26, 34, 39, 54, 132,
    138, 146–50, 185, 217–18, 249–50, 257
Lane, Bernard, 214
Langton, Marcia, 45
law, rule of, 14–15, 112, 114, 124–35, 160,
    243
legend, 46, 108, 170, 253
Legge, Kate, 98
Lemkin, Raphael, 94
Liberal-National Party governments
    Fraser, 28
    Holt, Gorton and McMahon, 26
    Howard, 2, 21, 34, 60–61, 64, 216
    Menzies, 27–28
liberalism, 20–21, 33, 116, 137
life stories, 46, 50–51, 54, 180
linguistics, 18, 44, 58
linguists, 46, 49, 173, 249
literary critics, 46
Locke, John, 138
Loos, Noel, 161
Lumby, Catharine, 64–65, 214

Mabo, 28, 31, see also native title
McCalman, Iain, 5
McGrath, Ann, 41, 173
McGuinness, P.P., 60, 75, 97
McInnes, Neil, 98

Macintyre, Stuart, 3, 5–6, 77, 199, 209–10
McKenna, Mark, 33, 52, 57, 192, 216, 257
Macleay Press, see Windschuttle, Keith,
    publisher (Macleay Press)
Maddock, Kenneth, 48
Maier, Charles, 83, 151
Malouf, David, 53–54
Manne, Robert, 3, 52, 54–55, 60, 64, 81,
    97–98, 101–02, 199, 216, 227
Mansell, Michael, 105
Markus, Andrew, 224, 243
Marxism, see Windschuttle, Keith, political
    affiliations
'massacre history', 40, 47, 56–58, 106–12,
    135, 171–72, 175–76, 211, 228, 231
massacres, 56–57, 111, 164, 205, 243
media, 2, 4, 11–12, 51–53, 61–62, 64–65,
    80–81, 152, 211
    communication and information
    technology, 12, 51, 58
memorials and memorialisation, 11, 15, 19,
    31, 104, 113–14, 172, 234
memory, 3, 113, 167, 170, 174–75, 177,
    179–80, 253
    authenticity, 50–51, 173–74
    rise, 6, 12, 50–51, 157–58, 169, 172, 251
    see also history; oral history
Miller, James, 45
Milliss, Roger, 57
missionaries, 112, 123, see also
    humanitarianism
Mitchell, Chris, 98
modernity, 11–12, 14, 19, 21, 23, 25, 32, 43,
    136–37, 139, 165–66
Morgan, Hugh, 106
Morphy, Howard and Frances, 52, 173
Morris, Jan, 91, 94
Moses, Dirk, 220
mourning, 33, 194–96, 258, see also
    memorials and memorialisation
Muecke, Stephen, 194
Mulgan, Richard, 185–86, 190, 257
multiculturalism, 22, 54
Mulvaney, D.J. (John), 18, 40–42, 52, 82, 201,
    245, 251
Murdoch, Walter, 16
Murray, Tim, 142–43, 245
museums, 4, 11, 46, 60–61, 90–91, 208–09,
    254–55
Musquito, 115–16, 233
myth, 13, 15, 19, 46–48, 55–57, 105, 107–10,
    124, 157–58, 170, 175, 177, 253

Nance, Beverley, 41, 233–34
narratives, see also historical narratives

victim, 15, 19, 30–31, 78, 201
voyaging, 22
nation states and history, 1, 6, 13–14, 124
    moral legitimacy, 13–14, 19, 25, 28, 30,
        124, 190–92
national histories
    narratives, 14–15
    pedagogical task, 13–14, 16
national identity, 1, 3, 7, 12–14, 62
National Museum of Australia, 61, 90–91,
    209, 219, 222, 254–55
national parks, 23
native police forces, 39, 43
native title, 1, 29, 32, 34, 54, 61, *see also*
    Mabo
Nazism, 20, 88–92, 95, 97–98, 100–04,
    218–19, 221, 223–24, 227–28; *see also*
    Jewish Holocaust
Neumann, Klaus, 120, 169
new conservatives, 2, 5–7, 31, 34–35, 61–65,
    67, 74–75, 87, 124, 136, 198, 209–10,
    215–16, 250, 257
    'political correctness', 62–63, 73, 81, 91
New Criterion (magazine), 61, 75
New Zealand, 14, 191
Novick, Peter, 38, 83, 101, 168, 174, 227,
    239

One Nation Party, 34
oral history, 44, 46, 58, 142, 157–58, 167,
    170–75, 179–80, 252, 254
oral tradition, 46, 56, 157–58, 170–71,
    175–76, 254

Pandey, Gyanendra, 30
Parry, Naomi, 233
Pearson, Christopher, 60–61, 209, 217
Plumb, J.H., 11
'political correctness', *see* new conservatives,
    'political correctness'
postcolonialism, 49
'postmodernism', 49, 54, 62, 66, 68, 71–72,
    74, 112, 114, 213, 237–38, 244
public intellectuals, 53–55, 60, 67, 79, 81,
    114, 124, 139, 216
    'Howard intellectuals', 60, 62–65, 72, 81,
        83–84, 91, 219
    'Keating intellectuals', 60, *see also* Manne,
        Robert

Quadrant (magazine), 32–33, 61, 75, 97, 100,
    111

race, 1, 12, 15, 33, 39, 54, 103, 128, 144, 169,
    223–24, 227, 241, 246, *see also* anti-

racism; Australia, settler national
    identity
racial discrimination, 19, 25, 28–29
racism, *see* race
Raggatt, Howard, 90–91, 219
Read, Jay, 52, 173
Read, Peter, 42, 52, 54, 173, 223
recognition, 194–95
reconciliation, 1, 26–27, 34, 53–54, 61, 184,
    194, *see also* Council for Aboriginal
    Reconciliation
Reece, R.H.W. (Bob), 39–42, 205, 223,
    233–35, 243
referendums for constitutional change, 20,
    201–02
relativism, 55, 150, 189–90, 237–38
Renan, Ernest, 13
republic, 28–29, 54, 61
'revisionists', *see* historical 'revisionists'
Reynolds, Henry, 19, 38–42, 54, 56–57, 64,
    66–67, 81–82, 87–89, 92, 94–95, 99,
    108–09, 111–12, 123, 127, 144, 148–50,
    161, 195, 199, 201, 213, 216, 220–23,
    225–26, 228, 231, 234–35, 237, 240, 246,
    249
    Fate of a Free People, 109, 111, 114,
        247–48
    Frontier, 168, 217, 241
    Indelible Stain?, An, 94–95, 222, 247–48
    Law of the Land, The, 42, 53, 217, 240–41,
        249
    Other Side of the Frontier, The, 43–44,
        113, 149, 162–63, 166–68, 218,
        251–52
    This Whispering in Our Hearts, 56, 58, 241
    Why Weren't We Told?, 167–68, 252
    With the White People, 41, 217
rights, 20–21, 116, 128, 139, 202, 246, 250,
    see also Aboriginal rights; 'land rights'
Risdon Cove, 106–10, 171–72, 211, 228–29,
    241–42
Roberts, David, 57, 171, 175–76, 229, 254–55
Robinson, George Augustus, 116, 123, 233,
    239–40
Robson, Lloyd, 108, 228, 231
Rose, Deborah Bird, 171, 173, 180, 188–89,
    255, 257
Roth, H. Ling, 142
Rowley, Charles, 37–39, 82, 119, 166, 201
Rowse, Tim, 52–53, 112, 244
Rubinstein, William D., 226
Rundell, Guy, 63
Ryan, Lyndall, 39, 92–94, 96–99, 108–12,
    161, 220–21, 223, 225, 228–31, 234–35,
    237, 246–48

Samuel, Raphael, 11
Sandall, Roger, 60, 97, 245
self-determination, 20, 26
shame, 25, 28–34, 216, 232
Shaw, A.G.L., 42, 127
Shaw, Bruce, 52, 173
Sheehan, Paul, 60–61, 96, 99, 103
Smith, Bernard, 255
Smith, Rodney, 58
South Africa, 1, 14
sovereignty, 21, 25–26, 124, 126, 138, 151,
    191
Stanner, W.E.H., 17, 19, 201
stolen generations, 1, 28, 46, 51–52, 181, 218
Stove, David, 75
Sutton, Peter, 46–47, 52–53
Sydney Line, see Windschuttle, Keith,
    philosophy

Tasmania, see Risdon Cove; Van Diemen's
    Land
terra nullius, 29, 146–48
testimony, 50–51, 55, 180–81
Thompson, E.P., 36, 65, 78
transference, 181–82
trauma, 3, 50–51, 101, 104, 121, 123, 157–58,
    177–82, 255
treaties, 1, 26, 136, 191–93
Truth and Reconciliation Commission
    (South Africa), 51
Turnbull, Clive, 92, 205

United States of America, 14, 31, 34, 60–63,
    65, 71, 74–75, 87, 136, 147, 160, 208,
    215, 217, 224, 235–36, see also African
    Americans; new conservatives

van den Berghe, Pierre, 224
Van Diemen's Land, 91–96, 105, 115–18,
    125–34, 138, 140–45, 227, 241–42,
    247–49
    representations as site of extermination,
    87, 92, 94–95
    see also Risdon Cove
van Krieken, Robert, 77–78, 129–30, 231–32
Veliz, Claudio, 214

wars, 15, 107, 113–17, 151, 168, 194–95,
    235–36

death tolls, 39, 111, 117–19, 151, 162,
    223, 229, 239, 247–48
    see also frontier conflict
Webber, Jeremy, 193, 250
West, John, 138, 140
Whitlock, Gillian, 54
Wilkomirski, Binjamin, 51, 207
Williamson, Christine, 142–43
Windschuttle, Keith, 3, 60, 64, 105, 199, 206,
    213–14
    appeal, 73–74, 209
    background, 65–66, 211–12, 235–36
    claims about academic historians in
        Aboriginal history, 66–67, 77, 81–82,
        91–92, 106–07, 112–13, 116–17, 123,
        125, 127, 148, 152, 206, 221–22, 226,
        239–40, 246–48, 254
    Fabrication of Aboriginal History, vol. 1,
        The, 2–5, 61, 68–70, 75, 77, 79–82, 87,
        90–102, 106–35, 140–53, 199–201,
        209, 211–12, 216–17, 219–23, 225–26,
        229–45, 246–52
    Fixing the News, 68, 236
    historical method and practice, 115–16,
        118–21, 129, 132–33, 141, 146, 150,
        152, 230–31, 233, 237–38, 241–42
    Killing of History, The, 66, 68–75, 77, 82,
        95, 112, 135, 244
    nationalism, 78, 93, 102, 106, 134
    philosophy, 75–76, 237–38
    political affiliations, 65–66, 75, 77–79, 82,
        210–12, 235–36
    political work, 65–66, 76, 79, 211, 231
    publications in history and
        historiography, 73, 214
    publisher (Macleay Press), 66, 80, 245
    style, 75, 77, 209–10, 212, 215
    themes in intellectual work, 67–77, 80,
        82, 95, 112, 135, 210, 237–39, 241,
        243–44
    training, 4, 65–66, 72, 76, 78, 210, 217
    White Australia Policy, The, 223–24, 241,
        246
    work experience, 65–66, 235
    writings, 65–66, 76, 122, 203, 213, 215,
        231
Winter, Jay, 50
Wolfe, Patrick, 169